OPTIMIS COLLEGIS

G. T. GRIFFITH   F. W. WALBANK

THREE HISTORIANS OF ALEXANDER THE GREAT

The so-called Vulgate authors, Diodorus, Justin and Curtius

N. G. L. HAMMOND, C.B.E., D.S.O., F.B.A.

Honorary Fellow of Clare College, Cambridge

The right of the
University of Cambridge
to print and sell
all manner of books
was granted by
Henry VIII in 1534.
The University has printed
and published continuously
since 1584.

CAMBRIDGE UNIVERSITY PRESS

CAMBRIDGE
LONDON   NEW YORK   NEW ROCHELLE
MELBOURNE   SYDNEY

Published by the Press Syndicate of the University of Cambridge
The Pitt Building, Trumpington Street, Cambridge CB2 1RP
32 East 57th Street, New York, NY 10022, USA
10 Stamford Road, Oakleigh, Melbourne 3166, Australia

First published 1983
Reprinted 1985 1986

Printed in Great Britain at the University Press, Cambridge

Library of Congress catalogue card number: 83-7630

British Library Cataloguing in Publication Data
Hammond, N. G. L.
Three historians of Alexander the Great.
1. Alexander III, *King of Macedonia*
2. Macedonia — Kings and rulers — Biography —
Criticism and interpretation
I. Title
938′.07′0924   DF234

ISBN 0 521 25451 5

CAMBRIDGE CLASSICAL STUDIES

General Editors
J. A. CROOK, E. J. KENNEY, A. M. SNODGRASS

THREE HISTORIANS OF ALEXANDER THE GREAT

Our knowledge of Alexander the Great is derived from the widely varying accounts of five authors who wrote three and more centuries after his death. The value of each account can be determined in detail only by discovering the source from which it drew, section by section, whether from a contemporary document, a memoir by a companion of Alexander, a hostile critique or a romanticising narrative. In this book the three earliest accounts are for the first time studied in depth, and it becomes apparent that each author used more than one source, and that only occasionally did any two of them or all three use the same source for an incident or a series of incidents. This evaluation enables the historian to winnow the grains of historical truth from the chaff of eulogistic, condemnatory and romantic writing. It lays a foundation for the understanding of what Alexander was and what he achieved.

This book will be valuable to ancient historians and of interest also to those studying Alexander the Great.

CONTENTS

PREFACE

This book fulfils an ambition of long standing. When I was writing my *History of Greece* in the 1950s, I was fascinated, as any historian must be who writes from the original sources, by the differences in outlook and in information of the Alexander-historians. The opportunity to pursue this interest came in the writing of my book on Alexander, published in 1980, and it was then that much of the work which underlies this book was accomplished. For one respect in which I differed from my very numerous predecessors was in drawing the reader's attention to the differences in the sources at each major event in Alexander's career. Since then I have been able to attack the main problem — the so-called Vulgate — in a manner which has not previously been attempted.

During my work on Diodorus I was greatly helped by my colleagues, Mr G. T. Griffith and Professor F. W. Walbank, who made criticisms of my draft and offered suggestions. It is a pleasure to dedicate this book to them, not least because they have collaborated so generously with me in *A History of Macedonia* II and (forthcoming) III. Professor R. K. Sinclair helped me in the same way over Diodorus, and Dr M. Hatzopoulos of the National Research Foundation in Athens encouraged me in my work on Justin and stimulated in me the idea that Satyrus' work might be relevant to Justin's account of Philip's death. Finally I am most grateful to the Editors of this series for their comments on the typescript and for their part in the publication; and to Susan Moore of the Cambridge University Press for her assistance.

The typescript was completed at the end of 1981, and a few pages were added in 1982.

Swarthmore College, Pennsylvania   N. G. L. Hammond
April 1983

ABBREVIATIONS

Atkinson	J. E. Atkinson, *A Commentary on Q. Curtius Rufus' Historiae Alexandri Magni Books 3 and 4* (Amsterdam, 1980).
Berve	H. Berve, *Das Alexanderreich auf prosopographischer Grundlage* (Munich, 1926).
Borza	E. N. Borza, 'Cleitarchus and Diodorus' account of Alexander', *Proceedings of the African Classical Associations* 11 (1968) 25ff.
Bosworth *C*	A. B. Bosworth, *A Historical Commentary of Arrian's History of Alexander I, on Books I–III* (Oxford, 1980).
Brunt	P. A. Brunt in the Loeb edition of Arrian vol. I (Harvard, 1976).
EH	*Entretiens Hardt* [*Fondation Hardt Entretiens*] 22 (1975).
FGrH	F. Jacoby, *Die Fragmente der griechischen Historiker* (Berlin, 1923–).
FHG	C. Müller, *Fragmenta Historicorum Graecorum* (Paris, 1841–70).
Fränkel	A. Fränkel, *Die Quellen d. Alexanderhistorikers* (Aalen, 1969).
Goukowsky	P. Goukowsky, in the Budé edition of Diodorus Siculus 17 (Paris, 1976).
Hamilton	J. R. Hamilton, *Plutarch, Alexander: A Commentary* (Oxford, 1969).
Hammond, *Alex.*	N. G. L. Hammond, *Alexander the Great: King, Commander and Statesman* (New Jersey, 1980; London, 1981).
Hammond and Griffith	N. G. L. Hammond and G. T. Griffith, *A History of Macedonia* II (Oxford, 1979).
Pearson	L. Pearson, *The Lost Histories of Alexander the Great* (New York, 1960).
OCD	*The Oxford Classical Dictionary*, 2nd ed. (Oxford, 1970).
Schubert	R. Schubert, *Die Quellen zur Geschichte der Diadochenzeit* (Leipzig, 1914).
Seibert	J. Seibert, *Alexander der Grosse. Erträge der Forschung*, 10 (Darmstadt, 1972).

Sinclair	R. K. Sinclair, 'Diodorus Siculus and the writing of History', *Proceedings of the African Classical Associations* 6 (1963) 38ff.
Tarn	W. W. Tarn, *Alexander the Great II: Sources and Studies* (Cambridge, 1948, reissued 1979).
Welles	C. Bradford Welles in the Loeb edition of Diodorus Siculus vol. VIII, books 16.66–95 and 17 (London, 1963).

INTRODUCTION

The need for source analysis

The basic task for the historian of Alexander (henceforth A) is to assess the value of each of the five main accounts which have survived. It is rendered formidable not only by the length and the complexity but also by the unevenness of Arrian, *Alexandri Anabasis* (henceforth Arrian), Diodorus (henceforth D.), Justin (henceforth J.), Curtius (henceforth C.) and Plutarch, *Life of Alexander* (henceforth P*A*). There is only one way to discharge this task fully, and that is to analyse each individual account and determine, as far as it is possible,[1] which earlier source it was using at any given point. In this book I attempt to do so only for D., J. and C.

The reason for selecting these three is that they have often been grouped together as 'The Vulgate', and have been set apart from the other two. In itself such a grouping is innocuous; and its own inner rationale is that at some points D., J. and C. do have some features in common. But what has been damaging to the evaluation of each has been the exploitation of this grouping. Thus they have been given the label 'The Vulgate Tradition'. The implication that a single tradition is conveyed in these three works is fallacious; for they differ frequently one from the other, and often in major matters. Worse still is the label attached by E. Schwartz and F. Jacoby, 'The Cleitarchan Vulgate'; for this indicates not only that all three derive from one source but also that that one source was Cleitarchus.[2]

The first attempt to break the spell of 'The Vulgate' was made by W. W. Tarn. Although many of his arguments were unconvincing, he seemed to me to demonstrate that 'The Vulgate Tradition' and 'The Cleitarchan Vulgate' are both myths of a simplistic kind. Two of his conclusions may be quoted. 'How two such totally different historians as D. and

C., with such different points of view and such different main portraits of A, ever got bracketed together is very hard to understand.' 'There never was any such thing as an Alexander-vulgate or Cleitarchan vulgate, exhibited by D., C. and J.'[3] But it then became incumbent on Tarn to provide his own analysis and identify the sources of each work. Here he failed lamentably. His analysis was too superficial (he analysed only one chapter of D.), and the sources he identified included two — 'The Mercenaries Source' and 'The Peripatetic Tradition' — which were not mentioned in ancient literature and have not been accepted in modern literature either.[4]

A younger generation of writers, reacting against the work of Tarn, have thrown out the good with the bad. What is worse, they have not only resumed 'The Vulgate Tradition' but have also introduced 'The Vulgate Sources', by which is meant not, as one would expect, 'the sources of the vulgate tradition' but the 'vulgate' accounts themselves. And worst of all, some writers have lost the origin of the term 'vulgate', and they have included among 'the vulgate sources' PA, the *Metz Epitome* and almost anything which is not Arrian.[5] The final step is to match the entire array against Arrian and see how he stands up to the assault, if at all. And as the name of Cleitarchus still clings to 'The Vulgate Tradition', Cleitarchus gets the benefit of the good things which do occur in D., C., J., PA and the minor works concerning A. He becomes quite a gifted writer! Recently advances have been made in the studies of two of our authors. In the Budé edition of D. 17 P. Goukowsky has summarised views which he had already published in specialist articles. In particular he refuted the idea that D. excerpted throughout from Cleitarchus. 'Ainsi,' he wrote, 'de nombreux détails inconnus des autres historiens de la "Vulgate" (ou même d'Arrien) peuvent être le fruit des lectures personnelles de Diodore et provenir soit des sources historiques utilisées dans d'autres sections de la Bibliothèque soit de traités techniques.' In his Commentary on C. 3–4 J. E. Atkinson has concluded from his study of these two books (out of nominally ten but really eight) that 'Curtius used several sources' and that one of these sources 'may have been Cleitarchus'. If either one or both of them are right, as I believe they are, then the concept of 'The Vulgate' as enunciated by Schwartz and Jacoby is mistaken — and even more so the later elaborations of it. In consequence, the term 'vulgate' is not used in this book. What I attempt is an analysis of the sources of each writer separately — D., J. and C.

The need for a detailed analysis of these three Alexander-accounts has been stated often in recent years. For instance, E. N. Borza writing of Cleitarchus and Diodorus 17 remarked that 'more is needed of the order of Hammond's study of the sixteenth book [of Diodorus]', and P. Goukowsky in considering the same topic asked for 'une analyse détaillée du livre 17'.[6] And E. Badian in *Entretiens Hardt* 22 (1975) 301 noted that C. and D. were still practically untreated, and that comments on them tended to be either limited or arbitrary; and he expressed the need for a thorough investigation of each. That is, *inter alia,* the purpose of this book.

D., J. and C. are inevitably contrasted with Arrian, from whom they differ radically. 'The generally high quality of Arrian's history', wrote P. A. Stadter in his admirable study, 'is due in no small degree to a discriminating use of sources.'[7] What is more, Arrian alone of Alexander-historians stated who his sources were and why he had chosen them: namely Ptolemy and Aristobulus, because they had campaigned with A and were the most trustworthy of all the authors whose works he read. For these reasons, as well as for its 'generally high quality', Arrian's work has generally been regarded as far superior in the main to the works of the other writers on A. Indeed it has often been used as a touchstone for testing the quality individually of D., J. and C. However, the trend of recent scholarship, especially in the writings of E. Badian and A. B. Bosworth, has been to try to reverse this verdict in regard to many issues, such as A's complicity in the murder of Philip, the course of the battle of the Granicus river, the cause of the fire at Persepolis and the cause of A's death. The weakness of this trend is that its advocates have not tackled the problem of identifying the sources used by D., J. and C. Until they have done so and have shown that those sources are more trustworthy than the known sources of Arrian, there is a danger that their judgements are unduly subjective.

Alexander's last days as an example

It will be illuminating for the reader to take now as an example the accounts of Arrian on the one hand and of D., J. and C. on the other hand which were concerned with the last days of A. For the reader will see at the outset that the differences are sharp not only between the ancient authors but also between modern scholars.

When Arrian's narrative approached the illness of A, he abbreviated and paraphrased a passage in the *King's Journal*, which he called simply αἱ βασίλειοι ἐφημερίδες (7.25.1 – 26.3). Plutarch had already done likewise in writing his *Life of Alexander* (76-77.1).[8] The similarity of the paraphrases confirms what we have no reason to doubt, that each was telling the truth and each was drawing independently on the same passage in the same *King's Journal*. At the end of his paraphrase Arrian commented as follows. 'The accounts of Ptolemy and Aristobulus', i.e. in their own works which Arrian preferred to those of other writers, 'were not far from this [account];[9] but others recorded remarks by A in conversation with his Companions', i.e. about the succession; and yet others attributed A's death not to a natural illness but to poisoning at the instigation of Antipater.

At the end of his paraphrase Plutarch discussed the allegation of poisoning, which most writers, he said, regarded as a fabrication. Plutarch helped to confirm Arrian's point about Aristobulus' account being 'not far from' that in the *King's Journal*; for at 75.6 he cited Aristobulus as saying that having a raging fever and an excessive thirst A drank wine, 'after which he became delirious and died on the thirtieth day of the month Daesius'. It was this excessive fever and delirium which prevented him from being able to speak. However, D., J. and C. all provided remarks allegedly uttered by A in conversation with his Companions (D. 17.117.3–4; J. 12.15; C. 10.5.1–6), and in particular his dying words (D. 17.117.4; C. 10.5.6 'suprema haec vox fuit regis, et paulo post exstinguitur'). J. and C. present the story of the poisoning as a matter of general belief or as a fact (J. 12.14; C. 10.10.14–17), while D. is more cautious (17.117.5 – 118.2).

Thus the accounts of the *King's Journal*, Aristobulus, Ptolemy, Plutarch and Arrian are totally incompatible with those of D., J. and C. In the former group Alexander was represented as speaking only of military and naval affairs and then being speechless for four days before he died; and he neither said nor did anything about the succession. The symptom too of a continuous high fever is incompatible with death by poisoning. According to the latter group Alexander retained his power of speech till the last and made astute remarks about the succession, and in particular he gave his signet-ring to Perdiccas; and the tradition that A was poisoned is treated as being worthy of serious consideration.

Which group is to be regarded as correct? Pearson, Samuel, Hamilton, Bosworth, Brunt and Lane Fox favour the latter group. They all maintain that the *King's Journal* was a forgery made in antiquity.[10] In addition, Badian and Bosworth, for instance, accept the statements of this group that A did give his royal signet-ring to Perdiccas, and Badian thinks that Perdiccas retained it until his own death. Bosworth accepts the poisoning as historical.[11] I am perhaps alone in regarding the first group as superior and in judging the *King's Journal* to be genuine. Let us look at the arguments. And let us bear in mind that until Pearson wrote his article in 1954 'it has been almost universally held that Arrian derived his version from Ptolemy, who had access to the original Diary [*King's Journal*]'.[12] It seems to me that Pearson's case for denying the genuineness of the *Journal* has been uncritically accepted by subsequent writers.

The King's Journal

That a *King's Journal* was kept for Philip and then for A, and that *Alexander's Journal* did record the last words and the last days of A is beyond question.[13] It was from the latter that Plutarch and Arrian believed themselves to be making their paraphrases. The fact that they had *Alexander's Journal* in front of them and were practised in assessing the genuineness or otherwise of such documents might be enough in itself to convince us that they were right.[14] Then we have the further fact that the accounts given by Aristobulus and Ptolemy (though lost to us) were judged by Arrian to be 'not far from' the account in *Alexander's Journal*. Could these two men, being contemporaries of A and close to him, have been taken in by a forgery which misrepresented the last words and the last days of A? That is to me inconceivable. On the other hand, if Aristobulus wrote from memory and if Ptolemy either used the genuine *Journal* or wrote from memory only, is it possible that the memory of each was faulty precisely in those reports which coincided by chance with the misrepresentations of the forged *Alexander's Journal* from which Plutarch and Arrian made their paraphrases? That too is really beyond belief.

It is, of course, an exciting idea that a modern scholar, operating only with paraphrased fragments, may be able to prove an ancient work to have been a forgery so ingeniously constructed that it deceived four ancient scholars (Plutarch, Arrian, Aelian, *VH* 3.23 and Athenaeus 10.434b, cited together in *FGrH* 117). But excitement is not enough; we need very strong arguments to support the idea. Hamilton listed those of Pearson's arguments which he found 'decisive', and it will be enough in this context to consider them. The first argument arises from the *Journal*'s mention of a shrine of Sarapis, the Egyptian god of healing, whom some Companions of A consulted during the night before A died. Pearson argued that the presence of such a shrine in Babylon was an anachronism, and that in consequence the *Journal* was composed only when such a shrine existed − *c*. 280 in his belief − and so was a forgery. But we have to remember that Egyptians, like Jews, may have visited and resided in Babylon in the Persian period; that A was deeply impressed by the Egyptian priests of Zeus Ammon, practised Egyptian forms of worship in Egypt, and had Egyptian seers in his entourage from 331 onwards (C. 4.10.4); and that he intended his body to be embalmed by Egyptian priests when he lay dying at Babylon. Thus it is probable rather than improbable that a shrine of Sarapis should have existed in Babylon in 323.[15] On the other hand, if a shrine of Sarapis was such a glaring anachronism as Pearson and others have supposed, would a forger have made the stupid error of introducing it into his account? Would not Peithon, Attalus, Demophon, Peucestas, Cleomenes, Menidas and/or Seleucus[16] have protested that there was no such deity in Babylon and they never went near such a shrine?

The second 'decisive' argument cited by Hamilton is that Arrian seems to mention the *King's Journal* as 'a familiar literary work'. Arrian passes no such comment. It is a matter of modern taste whether one considers such sentences as 'next day he bathed again, sacrificed the appointed sacrifices and after sacrificing continued in constant fever' to be the mark of a literary work rather than a factual diary of events and sayings.[17] Rareness of citation from it is another point; but this applies equally to a genuine *Journal* and to a forged *Journal* supposed to be genuine. We have to remember the difference between the research scholar and the ancient writer. The latter did not go back in the primary material, if he could avoid it by using a literary account, and particularly so in the case of a *Journal* which covered in diary form the thirteen years of A's exceedingly active reign and was packed with original documents. Next, it is argued that 'the other references to the *Journal* do not suggest an official document'. Here again we must keep a historical perspective. Modern scholars may not be interested in A's hunting, sleeping, drinking, illness and health, but there is no doubt that in the fourth century B.C. the royal hunts were of the greatest importance (cf. the fresco at Vergina and C. 8.1.14–16), that the royal banqueting and the heavy drinking at banquets with the consequent daytime sleeping were normal at court (cf. the palace of Vergina[18] and the affair of Cleitus), and that the last days of such a king were important to his followers.

Lastly, 'it is surprising, if Ptolemy used the *Journal*, that he failed to mention his use of so reliable a source'. This too applies to a forged *Journal* as much as to a genuine one; and again it rests on the tacit assumption that an ancient writer behaved like a modern writer who is continually citing and evaluating his sources. In any case we possess very little indeed of Ptolemy's own writings.

More general aspects of such a forgery may be considered. It had to be very different from the real *King's Journal* in order to make the undertaking worthwhile; and the undertaking was enormous, to construct bogus diaries for thirteen years of intense and documented activities — a work perhaps twice the length of Winston Churchill's *Second World War*. To fake spurious but plausible reports, letters, orders and documents was by itself a daunting task. Bosworth tried to evade this difficulty by postulating a truncated Diary, a mere fragment covering 'the last few months'. But this only creates difficulty. 'What is this fragment?' people would say when it was published, 'Where is the rest of the *Journal* if this fragment is from it?'[19]

When was the fake *Journal* produced? Pearson opted for *c*. 280 when men's memories might have become dim. But who was interested then? Surely the real *King's Journal* was already known and even written about by 280? Bosworth went to the other extreme. He had the forger write and publish between June 323 and winter 322–321. As this early date was incompatible with Pearson's chief argument, namely that the worship of Sarapis did not arise at Babylon until much later, Bosworth argued — as Bickerman had already done and I have done here — that such a worship was practised at the time of A's death in Babylon. Forger though he was, Bosworth's faker got that right. But could a forger have imposed his version on the minds of the Macedonians in the very year after A's death? Hundreds of leading Macedonians knew the true facts, their memories were green and they would surely have rejected a false version. At that time the corpse of A and his possessions were still in Babylon, and the real

Journal was there. It could have been used at once to expose the forgery.[20]

Who was the forger? Bosworth proposed Eumenes. Now Eumenes and his team of secretaries had already composed the entire *Journal* since A's accession. Did Eumenes in the twelvemonth after A's death sit down and compose a false version of A's last few months? Any secretary or anyone having access to the *Journal* could have exposed him at once as a falsifier. Pearson was more subtle. He made use of a little-known writer called Strattis of Olynthus (*FGrH* 118), who wrote three works according to the Suda. One of these works, as cited by Pearson, was 'five books about The *Journal of Alexander*', περὶ τῶν Ἀλεξάνδρου ἐφημερίδων βιβλία πέντε.[21] This title is found also in Athenaeus 10.434b, where we are told that Eumenes of Cardia and Diodotus of Erythrae wrote up *The Journal of Alexander*, ἐν ταῖς ἐφημερίσιν αὐτοῦ (i.e. Alexander). At first sight one would make two deductions: that *The Journal of Alexander* was very lengthy and that Strattis being an Olynthian wrote his commentary before *c.* 300, since he took his citizenship as an adult from a city which Philip had destroyed in 348. Not so Pearson. He supposes that the forger used 'a faked author's name for a fictitious diary' which he was publishing *c.* 280; so he chose to call himself 'Strattis of Olynthus'. This double supposition is a strain on anyone's belief. Further, why did the forger choose to call himself an Olynthian? Would not people have wondered at the time: 'Who is this Strattis, no youngster but a man of 86+, as he became a citizen at Olynthus?' It is more in accordance with the dictates of reason to believe that there was a real Strattis and that he did write five books of commentaries on the real *Journal of Alexander,* than to suppose with Pearson that an unknown man wrote five books about a (?his own) faked *Journal of Alexander* and assumed a faked name and an unlikely citizenship *c.* 280.[22]

Let us limit ourselves to a real *Journal of Alexander*. The corpse and the possessions of the deceased king were to be taken to Aegeae, but they were intercepted and removed by Ptolemy to Memphis and then to Alexandria (Paus. 1.6.3).

Among them surely was the *Journal*. Ptolemy himself used it in writing his history and he may have given favoured persons access to it; perhaps Strattis of Olynthus was one. The original or a copy of it went, one imagines, into the Library of Alexandria; and copies were available later for Plutarch, Arrian, Aelian and Athenaeus to consult. On the other hand, early writers such as Cleitarchus did not have access to the *Journal*.

If the conclusion is correct that what Arrian and Plutarch were paraphrasing was a passage in a genuine *King's Journal*, then the reader will see that Arrian and Plutarch in this instance are to be regarded as dependable and D., J. and C. as not. For the source of Arrian and Plutarch was a factual record of the day-by-day happenings in which the King was involved, made at the time and not intended for publication. He will see also that, since Ptolemy's account and Aristobulus' account were 'not far from' the version of the *King's Journal*, Ptolemy and Aristobulus were dependable authors in this instance, and that Arrian's choice of them as participants at the time and as trustworthy writers was justified. On the other hand, D., J. and C. provided items of fiction; not because they invented the items, but because they obtained them from one or more sources who were writing fiction or propaganda. The points which D., J. and C. have in common evidently came from a common source of this kind, one who wrote probably before the detailed accounts of Aristobulus and Ptolemy were published and so had a free field for invention. This source must have been a writer who was popular in the time of D., J. and C. As we shall see later, he was probably Cleitarchus, who was regarded by ancient authors as having a lively style but little or no regard for the truth. Thus the reader will have no hesitation in discarding as unhistorical the giving of the signet-ring to Perdiccas, the sayings of A about the succession and the alleged poisoning of A; and in rejecting the views of Badian and Bosworth, for instance, which were based on their belief that D., J. and C. were in this instance more dependable than Arrian.

This example provides an introduction to the methods which any historian of Alexander should employ. Whenever differences occur between the five main accounts, the historian has to consider which version has the best claim to be accepted as historical. Some writers have made their own arbitrary choice; and they have then written a life of A which is built around their own concept of what A was like and what in their opinion he would have done. But if one is concerned first to ascertain what A did and what in some cases he wrote or said, then one has to analyse the sources of the various accounts and determine as far as possible which accounts are dependable and which are not at each stage. Then it is the results of the analysis and the determination which lead to an understanding of A's actions and from them to some concept of his personality. The chapters which follow are, it is hoped, a contribution to that understanding.

CHAPTER 1

THE SOURCES OF DIODORUS SICULUS 17.1–63 AND 87–88

The method

More has been written and less has been agreed about the source or sources of D. 17 than of any other of his books. The admirable summary of work prior to 1970 which was published by J. Seibert shows a wide range of conclusions: a single source directly used by D.; a single source, indirectly used; two sources directly used; two sources indirectly used; and so on up to many sources from which titbits were put together to form a mosaic. The last of these conclusions was reached by Tarn. For after an analysis of only one of the 118 chapters he found that within ten full-stop sentences of our text D. changed from source to source no less than nine times.[1] Tarn was modelling himself on an earlier school of source-analysis, exemplified for D. 16 by Laqueur and Momigliano. In my articles on that book[2] I pointed out that this type of conclusion entails a most arduous form of composition, which seems entirely alien to common sense and to the temperament of D., which is usually regarded as lazy and careless. Tarn's next step was to look for relationships between points in that one chapter and points in the scanty fragments of the Alexander-historians. As I pointed out for book 16, such relationships are highly problematical; and Tarn's deductions for the fragments of Cleitarchus have been shrewdly criticised by Borza.

The method which I propose to use for D. 17 is the same as that which I used for D. 16. My description of it then was as follows. 'By regarding the narrative from the general angles of fullness, accuracy, military and political detail and conception of the central theme I hope to find separable groups of narrative. For each group an author of the same general qualities will be identified as a hypothetical source; fragments of the author and discrepancies in D. will then be applied to test the identification.'[3] Of course one is almost always dealing with probabilities in individual cases, but the hope is that the tissue of probabilities will become a texture of dependable quality. This seems to have happened for most of book 16, in that my conclusions there were generally accepted.[4]

I begin with a number of passages which share definite and peculiar characteristics and may therefore have been derived from one and the same source whom we name for convenience Source 1. Square brackets contain my comments.

Some passages attributable to Source 1

The passages are 8.2 – 14 (the sack of Thebes), 19.3 – 21 (Granicus to Sardis), 32.2 – 38.3 (Issus and the Persian women), 56–61 ('Arbela') and 87–88 (battle against Porus). Let us consider 8.2 – 14 simply as military narrative. The rising is introduced in sensational terms with 'many of the Greeks in revolutionary mood and many of the Greek states rushing into revolt' (8.2). [The actuality in 8.5–6 is very different.] However, the odds are stacked high against Thebes. A proceeded 'from Thrace' 'into Macedonia' (8.2 with 9.1), collected 'his whole force' (8.3 and 9.1) and descended 'suddenly' on the city (8.3). [It is however obvious that 'suddenness' and 'unexpectedness' (8.3 $\mathring{a}\phi\nu\omega$; 9.1 $\mathring{a}\nu\epsilon\lambda\pi\acute{\iota}\sigma\tau\omega\varsigma$) are incompatible with a route through Lower Macedonia for huge forces and a siege train; for news travelled quickly by sea from Lower Macedonia.] The 'whole force' was defined as being 'at that time more than 30,000 infantry and not less than 3,000 cavalry, all trained in the hazards of war, experienced in Philip's campaigns and almost undefeated in all the battles' (9.3); and with the force a siege train (9.6).

The Theban dispositions were extraordinary. Their cavalry was placed *behind* a palisade which had been constructed 'in front of the city' (11.1–2 $\pi\rho\grave{o}$ $\tau\tilde{\eta}\varsigma$ $\pi\acute{o}\lambda\epsilon\omega\varsigma$). [An excellent target for Macedonian archers, slingers and catapults, the cavalry was incapable of attacking from behind a palisade.] Their infantry, mindful of victories at Leuctra and Mantinea

(10.6 and 11.5), were lined up 'in front of the city' (11.2 πρὸ τῆς πόλεως) and faced the enemy in the open. Their walls were entrusted only to liberated slaves, refugees and resident aliens. [No way to defend a walled city in the fourth century B.C.; but the analogy is in the Heroic Age when the Trojans fought gallantly in the plain.] A divided his army obligingly into three divisions: one to attack the palisade, one to face the Theban infantry and one in reserve to bolster any Macedonians who might be defeated (11.1 ἐφεδρεύειν).

The battle between the opposing infantrymen began with trumpets blaring, war-shouts uttered simultaneously and volleys of missiles from both sides (11.3). When all missiles had been discharged, they engaged in sword-play, and a great contest began in which the Macedonian 'phalanx' had the greater weight (11.4). [In the fourth century B.C. Greek phalangites fought with the spear and the Macedonian phalangites with the pike, and neither used missiles: but the analogy is again with the Heroic Age, for which see *Iliad* 14.400 and 422.] Although the Macedonians had the advantages of superior numbers and weight, the Thebans had greater physical strength, regular athletic training and elation of spirit. Many of both sides suffered wounds on the front of their bodies (11.5 ἐναντίας λαμβάνοντες πληγάς), and there was much groaning, shouting and exhortation to remember past glories. The fight was in the balance for a long time, as each side showed superlative courage. But the Thebans, fighting in the cause of liberty, wore down and exhausted the first phalanx of Macedonians, whereupon A brought the force in reserve forward to bolster his defeat. Even so, the Thebans fought more recklessly than ever, shouting out that the Macedonians had admitted their inferiority and refusing to yield up their victory; indeed they were confident of defeating the reserve force also (12.4). [Shouts and taunts characterised the battle of champions in Heroic Age warfare, not the clash of many thousands of close-packed infantry.]

At this point A spotted an undefended postern-gate. He sent Perdiccas with some troops to capture it and to open the way into the city; others followed. The Theban cavalry and the Theban infantry abandoned their positions at once and retreated to the walls, where the jam of traffic was such that the cavalry trampled the infantry underfoot and some cavalrymen were impaled on their own weapons (12.5). The Macedonian troops who were garrisoning the Cadmea had been under attack, but now they made a sortie. This added to the confusion and the slaughter. Even so, the Thebans fought superbly inside the walls, some inviting wounds and others dragging their opponents to death even as they fainted themselves (13.2 and 4). The children and the women had taken to the altars and made supplication to the gods (11.3); now children and maidens were dragged away, shouting out the pitiable cry 'Mother!' (13.3). They and aged persons were torn from sanctuary with utter ruthlessness (13.6). No one could have failed to pity them. Yet among the Greeks the peoples of Thespiae, Plataea, Orchomenus and other states were campaigning on the side of the king, and they vented their hatred on the Thebans openly (13.5).

As a military narrative, the account is entirely fanciful and fantastic, and totally incompatible with the conditions of fourth-century warfare. Its object is sensation. To that end the impending doom of Thebes is constantly foreshadowed by the writer's comments (9.1; 9.2; 10.1 εἰς ὁμολογουμένην ἀπώλειαν; 10.6) and by no less than five portents and two oracular utterances (10.2–5). The *aristeia* is that of the Thebans in the face of huge numbers and unfair tactics. Their fight is in the cause of liberty [not in the cause of Persia, as her Greek enemies were to maintain]; and in the conflict of proclamations our sympathies are enlisted not for A's offer of pardon to any who will join the Greek League but for Thebes' call 'to free Greece from the tyrant of Greece', namely Alexander (9.5; cf. 13.1).

The eye of the writer is on the Greeks throughout: the Greek allies of Thebes (8.2; 8.5–6; 10.1), the Greeks' 'common peace' (9.5), the Greek involvement in the sack of the city (13.5–6), the convening of the Greek League Council (14.1), the Council's decree to raze the city and sell the survivors as slaves (14.3) and in general the treatment of

Greeks by Greeks (13.6 Ἕλληνες γὰρ ὑφ' Ἑλλήνων ἀνηλεῶς ἀνῃροῦντο). On the Macedonian side two leading Macedonian officers are named — Philotas and Perdiccas — probably for verisimilitude only[5] (8.7 and 12.3), and the reader's attention is focused on Alexander. He would have preferred to settle by negotiation and so free his hands for the war with Persia (9.4); but once thwarted in this matter, he decided to destroy Thebes utterly (9.4 διέγνω τὴν πόλιν ἄρδην ἀνελεῖν) and by terrorisation to deter any would-be rebels. Stung by the Theban proclamation A fell into an excess of rage; he resolved on total revenge, and set up his siege-engines in a fit of bestial fury (9.6 ἀποθηριωθεὶς τὴν ψυχήν). And so it proved: a savage vengeance was exacted (13.3 τὴν ὠμότητα τῆς τιμωρίας) and terrorisation deterred the would-be rebels (14.4 πολὺν ἐπέστησε φόβον τοῖς ἀφισταμένοις τῶν Ἑλλήνων).[6]

The military narrative for the battle of the Granicus river is equally fanciful and fantastic (17.6 – 21). It is at variance with the introductory statements that the armies were situated on either bank of the river and that the aim of the Persians was to attack the Macedonians while they (the Macedonians) were crossing the river (18.4 – 19.2). At this point D. changed from a sensible source to a sensational source. He did not trouble to make a smooth or consistent transition. An unexplained miracle enabled A to take his army across the river unopposed and draw up his army for battle before the enemy could do so (19.3). A put his cavalry in front and his infantry behind, as we are made to infer from the fact that the Persians put their cavalry in front and their infantry behind (19.5 ὄπισθεν δ' ἑστῶτες τεταγμένοι) and that there was first a cavalry battle (19.6) and only after the conclusion of the cavalry battle an infantry battle (21.5). [This complete lack of co-ordination between cavalry and infantry on the Macedonian side is totally unacceptable; for all the victories of Philip and Alexander were due to the co-ordination of the two arms.] There is no appreciation of tactics: 'chance' brought the best troops of both sides into conflict (20.1). In a later passage, 23.2, the move of A across the river is explained as due to his desire to prevent his Macedonians from running away in face of the enemy (for they would be afraid of the current of the river); and after the battle he gave a magnificent funeral to the Macedonian dead in order 'to make his soldiers more zealous in facing danger' (21.6). [The implication is that A's Macedonians were not really dependable in battle.] It is the Greek cavalry in the person of the Thessalians who fought better than any cavalry unit on either side (21.4). On the other hand the complete defeat of the Greek mercenary infantry which was in the service of Persia is never mentioned. Only two Macedonian officers — Parmenio and Cleitus the Black — figure in the narrative. On the other hand nine leading Persians receive their mention in despatches, and some numbers and geographical origins are given for Persian cavalry units (19.4). The *aristeia* is that of A: he was hit no less than six times, but his armour saved him and he fought on in exaltation of spirit (21.2). 'It seemed that he in particular was responsible for the entire victory' (21.4). His epic valour won the applause of those Persian and Macedonian cavalrymen who were near the scene of action (20.5 αἱ μὲν πλησίον τάξεις παρ' ἀμφοτέροις . . . ἀνεβόησαν). [The account is sensational, being related not to the exigencies of tactics and topography but to the painting of an epic scene.] The Thessalian cavalry and the Persian commanders receive high praise, and the victory of Macedon is explained by the actions of 'Chance' and the personal valour of A.[7]

The movements of Darius and A before the battle of Issus (32.2 – 33.1) are described with a lack of topographical precision which makes them almost unintelligible.[8] But at the end of the movements A has captured Issus town. He then advanced $5\frac{1}{2}$ kilometres to engage Darius, who does not expect A to venture on a set battle 'in the plain' (32.3; 32.4; 33.1-2). [There is no river Pinarus in this battle, although it is the main topographical feature in the other accounts; our source just dispensed with it.] The battle develops as at the Granicus. The cavalry of each side is in front and the infantry behind, the Macedonian infantry being 'in reserve' (33.1 fin.); the showers of missiles are so thick that their force is broken by collisions in mid-air (33.3); trumpets blaring and massive shouting by half a million barbarians in unison make the mountainside ring (33.4). A, being eager to win the battle by his own effort (33.5 τὸ δι' αὐτοῦ περιποιήσασθαι τὴν νίκην), looked about for Darius. The battle between the rival cavalry forces swayed to and fro; blows never failed to find so vast a target, and the wounded had their wounds on their fronts (33.7 τραύμασιν ἐναντίοις).

This time the *aristeia* is accorded to Oxathres and his Persian peers, who are inspired by love of glory (34.2–5). Both sides fought most passionately (34.4 ἐκθυμότατα). Then Darius' horses panicked. Darius seized the reins himself, but when another four-horse chariot was brought for him to mount he himself panicked; and the Persians, sensing his panic, set off in headlong flight. Cavalrymen collided with one another in rough and narrow places and trampled one another underfoot, and many were killed without any enemy action, as men became impaled on one another's sabres. The cavalry's line of flight led 'to allied cities'. [This is vague and unintelligible.] Then the Macedonian phalanx and the Persian infantry engaged in battle but not for long; for the flight of the Persian cavalry was but the preliminary to the flight of the Persian infantry. The entire area was soon heaped high with corpses (34.9). [The writer's recipe for battle is much as at the Granicus; the Persian defeat is due to the panic of Darius, and no particular credit is given to the Macedonians.]

Night descended on the scene. The Persians escaped 'easily'. The Macedonians, abandoning the pursuit, engaged in an orgy of looting (35–36). Gold, silver and vestments were found in abundance, but what interests the writer is the women not only of the royal house but also of the King's kinsmen and friends. They had come riding in gilded chariots with masses of gold, silver and jewellery. They suffered the worst imaginable that night. Some were clad only in a tunic-nightdress (μονοχιτῶνες; cf. E. *Hecuba* 933 of the girl μονόπεπλος at night during the sack of Troy); they were stripped even of that by the victors, who struck them with the butt-ends of their spears and laid hands upon their nakedness — a bit of luck for the troops (35.7 ταῖς τῆς τύχης δωρεαῖς; cf. 36.3)! The change of fortune for the royal women was particularly poignant. Some decent Macedonians were moved to tears at the sight; for they saw these women, unaware of the fate of Darius, watching the looting of the royal quarters and the unseemly acts of the armed looters. When the women of the nobles fell at the feet of the royal women and implored their help, the royal women themselves asked for help (36.4). Meanwhile a bath, dinner and magnificent illuminations were being prepared in the royal quarters of Darius for A, so that he might regard that night as the omen for total rule over Asia (36.5). The losses are then given: on an epic scale for the barbarians at more than 100,000 infantry and 10,000 cavalry, and for the Macedonians up to 300 infantry and about 150 cavalry. 'The battle at Issus in Cilicia had such a conclusion.'

[In this narrative the writer has used again the same techniques as he had employed at the Granicus. Cavalry fight first, infantry fight second and A is eager to win victory all by himself. The effects are added as in the description of the fighting at Thebes: the din, the missiles, the battle swaying to and fro with all wounds on men's fronts, and the poignancy of the women being treated ruthlessly by the victors. Imagination runs riot and creates highly sensational images.][9]

The aftermath of the campaign, as it affected the royal figures, is given in 37 and 38. Darius rode hard and escaped. A returned to his own camp about midnight, took the bath prepared for him (36.5 in Darius' tent) and was dining there when he heard the wailing of the royal women. He sent Leonnatus to tell them that Darius had not been killed. Thus A's reaction was like that of the decent Macedonians of 36.1. Next day A and Hephaestion visited the women (37.5 – 38). The description is highly charged with emotion. A calls Sisygambis 'Mother', kisses her grandson and piles even greater honours on the women than they had had before. They weep uncontrollably, but now for joy (38.3). The sending of Leonnatus was historical; for Ptolemy and Aristobulus *inter alios* recorded it (Arr. 2.12.3–6). But it is uncertain whether the visit by A and Hephaestion was historical, since Arrian

19

mentioned it only as a λόγος. The sensational style of these chapters is certainly appropriate to Cleitarchus. It seems probable, then, that D. used Cleitarchus for the whole account of Issus down to 38.3, and he then appended his own opinion of A's behaviour (38.4–7).

A dramatic start to the next military narrative, that describing the battle of 'Arbela' (56–61), is provided by the anxiety which kept A awake until the approach of the dawn watch. Thereafter he slept deeply and he was aroused only by his friends. He explained to them that his anxiety had been dispelled by Darius' concentration of his forces in one place. [In fact A had known that the day before, when he was 'close to the Persians', 55.6. The idea that this concentration favoured A is repeated from Issus, 33.1.] The same recipe for battle: A's cavalry in front, his phalanx of infantry behind (56.4 τῆς τῶν πεζῶν φάλαγγος τὰς τῶν ἱππέων εἴλας προτάξας; cf. ὄπισθεν at 57.2). In this case names are provided for the Macedonian phalanx units and their commanders. The Macedonian cavalry receive little description (57.1); the Greek allied cavalry considerably more; and the Thessalian cavalry are 'far superior in courage and in horsemanship to any other cavalry' (57.3–4; as at the Granicus, 21.4). Being heavily outnumbered A added angled wings to his line. [It is not clear whether D. is referring to A's cavalry line or the line of infantry behind the cavalry.] Then he told his men how to deal with the Persian scythed chariots. He led his formation forward at an inclined angle in relation to the enemy line (57.6 fin. λοξὴν τὴν τάξιν ποιούμενος). He led on the [advanced] right; for he had resolved to decide the whole issue by his own effort (δι' ἑαυτοῦ, as at the Granicus 21.4 and at Issus 33.5). [Here too there is no understanding of A's co-ordination of cavalry and infantry in the front line and of the purpose of the oblique advance to his right.]

Simultaneously Darius led his army forward. Trumpets blared, men shouted. The scythed chariots charged; and to add to the effect the massed cavalry squadrons of Mazaeus charged also (58.3). [As the scythed chariots were sent against the infantry, it is not clear what the Persian cavalry squadrons were supposed to be doing; for they could not charge into a phalanx line of infantry.] The chariots filled the Macedonians with much consternation and fear; but by obeying A's instructions they made the horses bolt and cause more harm to the Persians. Some chariots were successful. They inflicted terrible forms of deaths: shield-holding arms were lopped, necks were scythed right through, and heads rolled with eyes still open and a fixed expression; others were totally disembowelled. Next, as the armies closed, there were clouds of arrows, sling-bullets and javelins, and in the hand-to-hand fighting the cavalry engaged first and the Persian cavalry gained two victories: the first where Darius on his left wing had 10,000 Kinsmen, 1,000 Apple-Bearers, Mardians, Cossaeans, Indians and his personal guards and wore the Macedonians down (59.4); and the second at the Macedonian camp where the Cadusians and Scythians set the prisoners free, except for the Queen Mother Sisygambis. She distrusted this vagary of 'Chance', τύχη, and stayed, out of gratitude to A. The *aristeia* is awarded to Mazaeus (59.5–8, 60.5–6, and 61).

Two Persian victories brought A into action. Eager to correct defeat by his own effort (60.1 δι' ἐαυτοῦ) A with his Royal Squadron and the rest of the most distinguished cavalry charged at Darius himself. While Darius hurled javelins from his chariot, A hurled a javelin at Darius, missed him and chanced (κατατυχών) to hit and lay low the charioteer.[10] Those near the King uttered a shout; those farther off thought the King had fallen and began a general flight which was joined by others, until Darius himself was exposed on his other flank and he too fled. [As at Issus, 34.7, the Persians failed through their own misunderstanding, panic and headlong flight, and not through any superiority of Macedonian generalship or fighting power.] Alexander lost sight of Darius in the clouds of dust, but he heard the groans of falling men, the clatter of cavalrymen and the continuous cracking of whips. [The din apparently enabled him to pursue Darius; for he did so (see 60.7)].

On the left the brilliance of the Thessalian cavalry saved the day, but the Macedonian cavalry suffered so severely

21

that Parmenio sent mounted messengers to A for help; but in vain, since A was far off with the pursuit.[11] It was only the courage of the Thessalians and the skill of Parmenio which drove the Persian cavalrymen back; then too the flight of those with Darius discouraged them most of all (60.8). However, Mazaeus saved his entire force by taking through the clouds of dust the opposite route to that which the Macedonians expected, and so he ended up behind them (61). [This seems to be impossible, because the as yet unengaged Macedonian infantry were in an unbroken line behind the cavalry.] All the barbarians were now in flight and the area near the plain was soon filled with the corpses of 90,000 dead. The Macedonians lost up to 500, and very many were wounded, among them Hephaestion, Perdiccas, Coenus, Menidas and other leaders. 'The battle by Arbela had such a conclusion.'

[As at the Granicus and Issus there is a complete failure to understand the Macedonian tactics and A's brilliance in devising them. The scales of battle were tipped by a mischance, when it was supposed that Darius and not just his charioteer had fallen. The Macedonian infantry are never in action except when charged by the scythed chariots. The wounds caused by stampeding horsemen at Thebes and at Issus are paralleled here by those inflicted by the scythes of the chariots. The usual accompaniment of blaring trumpets, war cries, and shouts in action is here improved by the addition of groans, clatter, clouds of dust and cracking of whips. The description is as puerile as its predecessors. Once more the Thessalians are the best of all.]

Lastly, the military narrative of 'the battle against Porus' (for D. does not mention in 87.3 – 88 the river Hydaspes after which the battle was usually named). A decided to attack Porus because he heard that 'Embisarus' [Abisares] was about to join Porus and was some 400 stades (74 km) away. Porus put a force of cavalry on each wing of his line, his elephants at intervals along and in front of the infantry line, and some 'hoplites' in the spaces between the elephants (87.4). A arranged his forces 'in a formation appropriate to that of Porus'. As battle was joined, Porus' chariots were almost all destroyed by A's cavalry. Then the elephants went into action, trampling the Macedonians underfoot, lifting some in their trunks and bashing them against the ground, and impaling others on their tusks. Yet the Macedonians fought back. The battle hung in the balance. Then wounded elephants in their agony went berserk and trampled on their own men. Next we have the *aristeia* of Porus, a giant hurling javelins with the force of a catapult but being himself so vast a target that his enemies could not miss with their missiles (88.4–6 as at Issus, 33.7). So Porus slipped swooning from his elephant. As the rumour spread that he was dead, the remaining masses of Indians fled.

[In this military narrative there is the same ignorance of topography and tactics which we have noted in the descriptions of the other battles. It is an impressionistic account with the emphasis on the elephants and the horrible wounds analogous to those inflicted by scythed chariots at Arbela, and with an epic *aristeia* for the giant Porus.]

In the next chapter, at 89.6, D. was using a different source. For he wrote of 'the place where A himself crossed the river' and meant not the Indus which he had mentioned in his narrative at 86.4 but the Hydaspes which he had omitted altogether.

Now that we have considered these five specimens of military narrative, we may summarise their salient characteristics. First is a flagrant disregard of historical truth. Siege and battle are treated not in terms of contemporary weaponry, tactics, strategy and topography but as episodes of epic warfare in the Heroic Age of Homer with missiles, champions, duels, taunts, cheers and *aristeiai*. Second is a baroque sensationalism. Woundings and killings are bizarre and bloody; there are highly coloured scenes of rapine and brutality; and the pathos of women, children and old people in captured city or camp is poignantly described. Third, heroism in action receives its meed of praise whether in the case of Greeks or Persians or Alexander himself. Fourth is an ingenuous, almost puerile bias in favour of the Greeks and especially the

Thessalians; a sympathy for the Persians; and an antipathy towards the Macedonians, whose achievements are depreciated. Alexander, apart from his heroism in action, is belittled. His successes are due to luck and to errors of the Persians (12.3; 18.2–3; 32.3; 34.7; 55.2; 60.2–3). He is the enemy of liberty, a man of bestial rage and low cunning, and an example of the 'tyrant'.

We may contrast these military narratives with two others. In the account of the battle of Chaeronea, ascribed to Diyllus as source, there are no sensational episodes or bizarre wounds, but a clear definition of spheres of command on both sides and a coherent strategy on the Macedonian side with the first breach of the Greek phalanx-line by the Macedonian left, then the extending breach and the flight of the Greek right, and finally the forceful advance of Philip with the picked men on the Macedonian right (16.86). The account of the battle of Gabiene (19.40–43), in which, as A. M. Devine remarked to me, there were incidents similar to those in the battle of Arbela, gives a clear statement of dispositions and a careful timing of the phases of the action. The plain was salty and therefore uncultivated so that dust was raised by the masses of cavalry; and Antigonus took advantage of the dust-clouds to pass a cavalry force outside the enemy wing and capture the enemy camp unseen. Meanwhile (ἅμα δὲ τούτοις πραττομένοις) Antigonus' elephants and cavalry were gaining the upper hand on their right wing, and Eumenes accordingly took his cavalry out of the battle there and transferred it to the cavalry on his right wing under Philip, who had abstained in accordance with prior orders from engaging. As Eumenes moved his cavalry his infantry went into the attack with devastating success and so on. Once again we see a clear sequence. There is none of the confusion and ambiguity which reigned in D.'s account of the battle of Arbela.

A fully developed and consistent attitude towards Persia runs through the accounts of the battles of the Granicus, Issus and Arbela. The high spirit and the prowess of the Persians and especially of Oxathres and Mazaeus are praised, and many more names are provided for Persian officers than for Macedonians. Distinctions are made between satraps and generals, between members and relatives of the royal family (20.2; 21.3; 34.2; and 36.2) and between the Kinsmen and other élite troops (20.2; 21.2; 35.3; and 59.2–5). The purposes and the plans of the Persian commanders and of Darius himself are described quite fully (18.2–4; 19.2; 32.3; 51.1). There is an unusual knowledge of Persian customs and laws: special chairs were provided at the royal court for envoys from Thebes (14.2; cf. Hdt. 8.67.2), the King was forbidden by law from taking the reins of the chariot horses (34.6), and the ladies of the court in accordance with a traditional custom rode in gilded cars and were completely veiled from the sight of men (33.3–5).

Another characteristic of this source is a love of round numbers, usually highly inflated, as follows. Philip's trained army of 30,000 infantry, 3,000 cavalry (9.3); 30,000 prisoners at Thebes (14.1); 100,000 Persian infantry, 10,000 cavalry at the Granicus (19.4–5); losses there on the Persian side 10,000 infantry, 2,000 cavalry, 20,000 captured (21.6); 400,000 Persian infantry, 100,000 cavalry at Issus (31.2 and 33.4); losses there 100,000 Persian infantry, 10,000 cavalry and on the Macedonian side 300 infantry and 150 cavalry (36.6); 800,000 Persian infantry, 200,000 cavalry at Arbela (53.3); losses there 90,000 Persians, 500 Macedonians (61.3); Indian forces of Porus 50,000 infantry, 3,000 cavalry, 1,000 chariots and 130 elephants (87.2); losses there 12,000 Indians killed, 9,000 captured, 80 elephants taken alive, 700 Macedonian infantry and 280 cavalry (89.2–3).

The identification of Source 1

We can exclude all authors who were concerned with actual events and not with imagined military actions, such as Callisthenes, Ptolemy and Aristobulus; all authors who put the Macedonian point of view, such as Callisthenes, Ptolemy and Marsyas of Pella; and all authors who were interested in topography and positions, such as Callisthenes and Polycleitus of Larissa. On the positive side the author has to have the characteristics of Source I and to have been a writer who was well known towards the end of the Roman Republic, so that he would appeal to Diodorus. The field in fact is narrowed down to Cleitarchus, whose *Histories of Alexander* was a popular work in the late Republic and was known to Diodorus (2.7.3). His rhetorical gifts which showed themselves in sensational writing were balanced by his disregard of the truth, as Cicero remarked (*FGrH* 137 T 7 and F 34). Quintilian put the matter in a nutshell: 'Clitarchi probatur ingenium, fides infamatur' (T 6). Those who disliked his work found him superficial, pretentious and childish (T 9).[12] Cleitarchus came from a Greek city in Asia Minor, probably Colophon, and his father Deinon had written a famous work on Persian customs; thus we see where Source 1 obtained his special knowledge of and interest in Persian affairs.

The most important of Cleitarchus' fragments[13] from our point of view is F 1. It is contained in a passage in Athenaeus (4.148d–f), which may be corrupt (see Jacoby II B 485f.) but preserves intact the citation relating to Diodorus. 'In the first book of his *Histories of Alexander* Cleitarchus says in discoursing about the Thebans that after the razing of the city by Alexander the entire wealth (πλοῦτος) of the Thebans was found to amount to four hundred and forty talents.' If there were no other passage available to us which dealt with the fate of the Thebans, we should be at a loss to understand exactly what Cleitarchus intended; indeed we might suppose, as Goukowsky remarks, that the sum was 'l'évaluation des objets précieux trouvés dans la ville'. But we see from D. how it is to be understood. D. describes four stages. (1) Rapine as resistance was being overcome within the walls (13.6). (2) The final reckoning of the fighting and rapine: over 6,000 dead, over 30,000 souls taken prisoner, and 'an incredible amount of valuables' (14.1 ἄπιστον πλῆθος χρημάτων). (3) After the decision of the Council of the Greek League the razing of the city's buildings (14.3–4). (4) The sale of the prisoners as spoil (i.e. as slaves) yielding four hundred and forty talents (14.4). Thus when stages 1 to 3 were completed, the wealthy city of Thebes was reduced to its ultimate poverty, the sum realisable on the slave market for the survivors, 440 talents.[14] Thus the fragment of Cleitarchus in Athenaeus makes sense as the last piece of a description derived by D. from Cleitarchus. We can with confidence identify the source for 17.8.2 – 17.14 as Cleitarchus, and notice that D. was here using Cleitarchus directly and accurately.

Another citation from Cleitarchus about the wearing of the tiara by the Persians and by their kings (F 5) is an example of his knowledge and his exposition of Persian customs. He may have had the information from his father, Deinon (*FGrH* 690 F 25). Then F 25, the killing of 80,000 in the kingdom of Sambus, shows his fondness for huge round numbers. Next, F 8 has some relevance to D.'s placing of A at Issus before A received news of Darius' proximity (32.4 – 33.1). In that fragment Cicero mentioned that he had often heard from Caelius about Alexander's defeat of Darius as described by Cleitarchus, the location of the defeat being 'near Issus' (*Ad fam.* 2.10.3 apud Issum quo in loco . . . superatum). In another letter of this time Cicero mentioned the camp which A had had 'near Issus' in facing Darius (*Ad Att.* 5.20.3 'contra Darium habuerat apud Issum'). The likelihood is that Cicero was writing from knowledge of Cleitarchus' account as retailed so often by Caelius. If that is so, Cleitarchus had described A as camping at or near Issus on the night before the battle. Two accounts mention or imply that A camped there then. *Fragmentum Sabbaiticum* (*FGrH* 151) F 1, 3–4 has A encamped at Issus and Darius come up to attack him there; this passage is discussed below, p. 48. D. has A capture Issus on the day before he heard Darius was some four miles away and the battle was joined (32.4 – 33.1). We conclude, then, that D. was drawing on Cleitarchus for the campaign of Issus.

It is of course satisfying from an academic point of view to put a name to Source 1. But what matters far more to a historian is the identifying and the characterising of passages ascribable to Source1; for these passages of their own nature are of little or no value as historical evidence, whether Source 1 is named or remains anonymous.

Source 2 in some early chapters (2.1 – 8.1 and 15–16)

The first chapter is the Proem. It is so vacuous in content and so pompous in style that it should be regarded as an unadulterated composition by D. himself.[15] It expresses in an ingenuous manner a total admiration for A's 'intelligence, courage, glory', his heroic ancestry and his achievements; and its sentiments are resumed in the first person, i.e. by D., at 38.6–7, where the *aretai* of A are to be praised by posterity, and at 117.5, where his achievements are said never to have been surpassed up to the time of D. himself. This view of A, however, is not imposed by D. in his narrative (e.g. in the narrative of the capture and sack of Thebes); it is the views of his sources which appear there.

In the Proem to book 16 D. had proposed to include within the book the events of Philip's reign of twenty-four years (16.1.3 and 95.1, being in terms of D.'s archon years 360/359 to 336/5). Again in the Proem to book 17 he made the same proposal about the events of A's reign, with a back-reference to the principle he had followed for book 16 (17.1.1); and he estimated the reign of A at twelve years and seven months (17.1.4 and 117.5, being in archon years 336/5 to 324/3). However, D. did not do what he had proposed. For he included in book 17 some events which ante-dated the death of Philip by some years; indeed they occurred in the years *c.* 340 to 336 B.C. This departure from his proposed course was presumably due to his use of his sources.

The narrative starts at 2.1. 'On succeeding to the throne A first thought that the murderers of his father deserved a condign punishment, and then after taking all possible care for the burial of his parent he arranged affairs in his sphere of rule far better than anyone had expected.' D. is in a hurry. He does not tell us who 'the murderers' were and how they were punished, or what form of funeral was accorded to Philip. The source which he is abbreviating no doubt did contain that information, and it was evidently the source which he had used for the account of the assassination in book 16. That account was very detailed and it ended abruptly in D.'s version at 16.94.9 with the murderer being killed by — among others — Attalus, the brother-in-law of Philip. The source will not have stopped at that point; rather it will have gone on to describe the arrest of suspects, the conviction of others as 'the murderers' (i.e. privy to the plot), the demand for their execution by the King as prosecutor (hence D's word ἠξίωσε at 2.1), and the splendid funeral of Philip.[16] D. reduced this to a brevity which is obscure.

The success of A in establishing his authority was so unexpected because A was 'utterly young' (2.2 νέος παντελῶς) and a 'stripling' (νεανίσκος). This idea recurs as the leitmotif at 3.6, 4.5, 7.1 and 7.2, and it is given as a reason for others 'scorning', i.e. underestimating, A (2.2, 4.5, 7.1 καταφρονούμενος). This concept of a boy-king at the age of twenty was natural in a Greek city-state where political responsibilities began only at the age of thirty, and Demosthenes was not the only Athenian to scoff at A as a lad and a Margites (Plut. *Dem.* 23 παῖδα καὶ Μαργίτην); but the truth in Macedonia was that the three predecessors of A had come to the throne in their early twenties, and A himself had already had wide experience as regent for Philip, founder of a city, a commander at Chaeronea, participant in Philip's Danubian campaign and envoy to Athens. No Macedonian writer would have stressed his utter youth and on that ground have underestimated his capacity. The source D. is using has to be a Greek writer.

The success of A in the early period is attributed to his humane attitude and his persuasive oratory (2.2 οἰκείοις λόγοις ... χρηματίσας φιλανθρώπως ... παρεκάλεσε; 3.6 πειθοῖ διὰ τῆς ὁμιλίας προσηγάγετο; 4.1 λόγοις φιλανθρώποις ... ἔπεισε; 4.2 ἔπεισεν; 4.3 φιλανθρώπως ὁμιλήσας ἔπεισεν; 4.9 φιλανθρώπως ἀποκρίσεις δούς ... λόγοις ἐπιεικέσι χρησάμενος ἔπεισε). As neither of these qualities was mentioned among the laudable qualities of A in the Proem, we may conclude that D. derived this picture from his source. And as this favourable attitude is incompatible with the view of A as he is represented in the campaign and capture of Thebes (8.2 – 14), the source here is not Source 1. We may then number this source as Source 2.

The arrangement of events in chapters 2 to 16, all placed under the archon year 335/4 in D.'s chronological system, is somewhat unexpected.

The King's actions in Macedonia come first, in 2.2 – 6, but most space is given to A's reasonable suspicions (εὐλόγως) of the Attalus who had figured in the account leading up to the killing of Philip and then of his assassin (16.93.5, 93.8–9, 95.4), and to A's sending of Hecataeus to arrest or, failing that, to kill Attalus in Asia (16.91.2, mentioning the posting of Attalus and Parmenio to Asia by Philip, is resumed at 17.2.4).[17] Hecataeus set out probably in the winter of 336/335.

D. then turns to A's actions in Greece where trouble was brewing (3–4). He begins with Athens as the centre of intrigue with Attalus and with other Greek states against A. However, A succeeded in winning the positions which his father had held and in particular in being elected *strategos autocrator* by the Greeks and obtaining their collaboration in the war against Persia (4.9), probably late in 336.

At chapter 5 D. resumes the episode of Attalus and Hecataeus with a brief indication of Attalus' collusion with Athens and his subsequent change of front. But he changed in vain. Early in 335 Hecataeus killed him 'in accordance with A's instructions' (5.2, being unable presumably to arrest him). This episode evidently came from the source which lay behind 3.2, 5.1 and the narrative in 16.91.2 to 95.4.

D. now makes a chronological leap backwards to 340 or so. He describes at 5.3 the death of Artaxerxes Ochus (dated in *POxy* 1, no. 12, col. II to 341/0), and he takes Persian affairs down to some time *before* the assassination of Philip, i.e. to before summer 336. Towards the end of that period Darius was on the throne. Darius planned to divert the coming war 'into Macedonia', but he gave up the idea on the accession of A, since he scorned 'the youth of Alexander' (7.1). Later Darius realised his mistake. He then raised large forces and appointed the best commanders. Of them Memnon of Rhodes was outstanding in courage and generalship, and his operations against the Macedonian commanders in

Asia — Parmenio and Callas — are described down to 7.10 in the winter of 335/4, shortly before A's arrival in Asia (which occurred in May/June 334). This factual and detailed account[18] is unlike anything derived from Source 1.

At chapter 8 D. turns to the Balkan peoples. He had already mentioned at 3.5 the unrest and disaffection among 'no few of the tribes inland of Macedonia', and he had foreshadowed their subjugation by force (3.6 τοὺς δὲ βίᾳ χειρωσάμενος ὑπηκόους ἐποιήσατο). This subjugation is described very briefly: he campaigned first in Thrace, then in Paeonia and Illyris and territories adjacent to them, and in these campaigns 'subjugated all the neighbouring barbarians' (χειρωσάμενος ὑπηκόους ... ἐποιήσατο). D. turns at 8.2 to the campaign against Thebes. This he describes from Source 1, as we have argued. An indication that D. has changed from his present source to Source 1 may be seen in the fact that A is described at 9.1 as having come from Thrace and not from Illyris where he was in 8.1.[19]

After the sack of Thebes we read in chapter 15 a full account of developments at Athens with the names of many orators and with reports from speeches in the Athenian Assembly (as in 4.8). While the account is favourable to Athens, it also shows A to be humane in his attitude to the city (15.5). In chapter 16 A returns to Macedonia, where he holds a debate with his army commanders and his leading friends about the crossing to Asia. The advice of Antipater and Parmenio, that he should beget an heir first, was rejected by the King; for he was 'energetic and opposed to any deferment of action' (16.2 δραστικὸς ὢν καὶ πρὸς πᾶσαν πράξεως ἀναβολὴν ἀλλοτρίως διακείμενος). A's energy and quickness to act had already been mentioned at 4.5 and 7.2 (ἡ διὰ τῶν πράξεων ἐνέργεια and ἡ ὀξύτης). On this occasion A's eloquence prevailed (as earlier with the Macedonians at 2.2 and with the Greeks at 4.9). There follow sacrifices, festivals (one to the Muses lasting nine days) and banquets. Thus while our source writes throughout these early chapters from the Greek and in particular from the Athenian point of view he has also

31

considerable knowledge of Macedonian procedures and festivals.

The identification of Source 2

The unusual order of events in chapters 2 to 16 and in particular the inclusion of Persian affairs of 340/339 to 335/4 in book 17 demand an explanation. If we confine ourselves to book 17 alone, as Tarn and others have done, no explanation is forthcoming. We need rather to consider book 16 and book 17 together.

My conclusions in *CQ* 31 and 32 were that D. used the following sources for the latter part of book 16 (omitting the section on Sicilian affairs). For Persian affairs 356/5 – 341/0 (in D.'s chronology) Ephorus; for Greek affairs other than the Sacred War in the period 356/5 – 341/0 Diyllus, *Syntaxis* I; for Greek affairs 340/339 – 336/5 Diyllus, *Syntaxis* II, which went down to the death of Philip in 336/5 (D. 16.76.5).[20] A peculiar feature of book 16 was that D. gave no account of Persian affairs for 340/339 – 336/5. It was odd that D. broke off his narrative of Philip's death with the death of the assassin Pausanias (16.94.4); for it would seem probable that Diyllus included the inquiry into Philip's death and his funeral in *Syntaxis* II.

In book 17 D. starts with a very much abbreviated account of the punishment of 'the murderers' and of the funeral of Philip. We may infer that D. was still using Diyllus, *Syntaxis* II. In the ensuing narrative there is the follow-up of Attalus' conspiracy with Athens against Philip and of the killing of Attalus at 5.2; this came presumably from Diyllus, *Syntaxis* III. Then in chapters 5.3 to 7.10 D. fills the gap he had left in book 16 by giving an account of Persian affairs 340/339 – 336/5 (ending at 7.1) and he continues with Persian–Macedonian affairs 335/4 (ending at 7.10). Where did he find a convenient account of that particular period? The answer is supplied by book 16. The fact that D. included there such specific details about the work of Diyllus establishes the strong presumption, if not the certainty, that D. was using

Diyllus, *Syntaxis* I (D. 16.14.5) and Diyllus, *Syntaxis* II (D. 16.76.6), the former covering 'Greek and barbarian affairs'. Thus 'the barbarian affairs' of Diyllus, *Syntaxis* II which D. had omitted in 16 were available for D. to use in 17 for the years 340/339 – 336/5 inclusive. He obtained the required join for Persian affairs of 335/334 by continuing with Diyllus, *Syntaxis* III. Thus the use of Diyllus by D. in the latter part of 16 and the early part of 17 provides a satisfactory explanation for the unusual order of events in D's narrative.[21]

There are features in common between the late chapters of 16 and the early chapters of 17 which support the theory that D. was using the same source for both. The idea that A was 'utterly young' appeared first in 16 at 86.1 ἀντίπαιδα τὴν ἡλικίαν, and it runs through the early chapters of 17. Also at 86.1 there appears the antithesis 'the quick energy' of A, τὴν ὀξύτητα τῆς ἐνεργείας, and this recurs in 17 at 4.5, 7.2 and 16.2. The fascinated interest in the setting of the assassination of Philip and in the ramifications of the plot are common to 16 and 17. Attalus is a prominent figure in both books: posted to Asia at 91.2, a confidant of the younger Pausanias at 93.5, his maltreatment of the older Pausanias at 93.7, his connection with the King through Cleopatra at 93.8–9, and his part in the killing of Pausanias at 94.4; then suspected by A at 2.3, his influence with the troops in Asia at 2.4, the plan to arrest or dispose of him at 2.5, the secret negotiations of Athenians with him at 3.2, his letter to A at 5.1, and his death at 5.2. The relationship between Macedon and the Greek League is one of 'alliance' and Philip himself is elected *strategos autocrator* at 16.89.2–3; so too at 17.4.9 the Greeks agree to join in the campaign, συστρατεύειν (cf. συμμαχίδες at 22.5) and elect A as *strategos autocrator*.[22] And there are in 17 many references to Philip, the subject of 16: at 2.1, 2.2, 2.3, 3.1, 3.3, 3.4, 4.1 πατροπαράδοτον, 5.1, 5.3, 6.2 and 7.1; and these suggest that the source used in these chapters had written fully also about Philip.

Diyllus, an Athenian, was 'very probably' a son of the writer of Athenian local history called Phanodemus, son of

Diyllus.[23] Born, then, in the decade 350–340,[24] he lived well into the third century, and he wrote a general history of Greek, Persian, Macedonian and Sicilian affairs from 356/5 to an unknown date in 26 books, of which the ninth described an event of 316/15. Plutarch regarded him as a historian 'not neglected' (*FGrH* 73 F 3). Diyllus' interest in Athenian affairs and especially in Athenian politicians was apparent in 16.84–85 quoting Demosthenes' words, 87 quoting a phrase of Demades, 88 quoting from a speech by Lycurgus; and in 17.3 with secret communications between Athens and Attalus, 4.6 quoting Aeschines' taunting of Demosthenes, 5.1 mentioning a letter from Demosthenes to Attalus, 8.5 Demosthenes sending arms to Theban insurgents and persuading the people to back Thebes, 15 reporting a debate in the Assembly at which Demosthenes, Lycurgus, Phocion 'the Good', and Demades figured and Phocion's *bons mots* were uttered.

Only three certain fragments survive. The first shows Diyllus' interest in the state funeral accorded by Cassander to Philip III, Eurydice and Cynna at Aegeae, and the gladiatorial combats then of four Macedonian soldiers. We can see that he would be interested in the funeral accorded to Philip II by Alexander (17.2.1) and in the festivals and feasts held by A in Macedonia (17.16). The second concerns a homosexual affair of Demosthenes with a young lad; it reminds one of the homosexual intrigues over Pausanias in 16.93.3–7. The third reports the Athenians' 'gift' of ten talents to Herodotus; and an interest in the granting of money for services rendered or expected appeared in 16.55.2 and 4 and 17.4.8, 8.5 and 15.3. It reports also the proposer of the decree in the Athenian Assembly; and an interest in decrees[25] is apparent at 16.85.1 and at 17.4.6, 8.6 and 15.3–4. A characteristic common to Diyllus and some other writers according to Plutarch was a delving into the memoirs of kings and generals (T 4). We find examples of this interest in anecdotes in 16.87 and 92.3–4, and in 17.2.2 and 16.1–3 which reports a discussion between A, Antipater and Parmenio in a council of military commanders and the Friends.

The case, then, for identifying Source 2 as Diyllus is very strong in regard to 17.2.1 to 8.1, and 15 to 16. The intermediate sections 8.2 to 14, describing the affair of Thebes, came from Source 1, namely Cleitarchus, as we have seen. They are entirely different in character and outlook.

Here too we must emphasise that the naming of Source 2 is less important for the historian than the defining and the characterising of passages ascribed to Source 2. These passages command much respect. For Source 2 is very remarkable in the fact that he used primary sources − for instance, speeches by Attic orators, decrees by the Athenian people, a decision by the Amphictyonic League Council (17.4.2) and a decision by the Greek League Council (17.4.9) − and this establishes a probability that his facts and his figures are correct. The concern with primary sources makes it likely that Source 2 preferred eyewitness accounts − for instance, in his description of the assassination of Philip in 16.92–94 and in the numbering of Alexander's forces where he evidently followed Ptolemy's account (see later).

The attribution of the other chapters

17.1–3. The acts of A on crossing to Asia are recounted in a factual and unrhetorical manner which is unsuitable for Cleitarchus. When these acts are mentioned in Arrian (1.11.7, A in his armour being first to land on Asiatic soil, and 1.12.1, A honouring the tomb of Achilles and others), they are introduced by the qualifying word λέγουσι, 'they say', which means that they were not so reported by Ptolemy and Aristobulus (Arr. Pref. 3). D., then, did not derive these acts from Ptolemy or Aristobulus, whether at first hand or at second hand. The review of the army 'that was accompanying him' was carried out on Asiatic soil. It was no doubt intentionally analogous to Xerxes' review of his army after its passage from Asia to Europe at Doriscus.

17.3–5. The numbers of troops are then given. The beginning − 'they were found', (i.e. to be at the review) − and the conclusion − 'those who crossed with A to Asia were so many in number' — leave us in no doubt that Macedonian and other troops previously posted to and still in Asia were not included. This is equally true of numbers given by Callisthenes (*FGrH* 124 F 35, 'A made the crossing to Asia with . . .') and by Arrian (1.11.3, 'on the way to the Hellespont with A'). Other numbers, and also money and supplies available for so many days, i.e. from the day of the crossing, were given to Plutarch (*De Alex. fort.* 1.3; cf. *Alex.* 15.2), citing Anaximenes, Aristobulus, Ptolemy and Duris. These numbers clearly do not include troops and supplies already in Asia.[26]

One might have expected that all writers would have given the same figures. But this is not so. Plutarch (*Alex.* 15.1) noted that the figures varied — the highest being 43,000 infantry and 4,000 cavalry, and the lowest being 30,000 infantry and 5,000 cavalry — and then in another passage (*De Alex. fort.* 1.3) he gave a higher figure still, 43,000 infantry and 5,500 cavalry, recorded by Anaximenes (= *FGrH* 72 F 29). The explanation is presumably that A did not reveal either the total number or the detailed numbers of his troops at the time, for the very good reason that he did not wish the Persians to know how few (relatively) they were. Later, perhaps by a year or two, Callisthenes as the official historian of the expedition published the numbers A did wish the Persians to receive, namely (as we shall see) an exaggerated number of infantry — the arm the Persians most feared (e.g. Arr. 1.12.9 and C. 3.11.1) — and a reduced number of cavalry, of whose strength the Persians had a shrewd idea from the battle at the Granicus river; 40,000 infantry and 4,500 cavalry. For whatever reason, Callisthenes' numbers were not believed by Greek and Macedonian writers. Anaximenes gave higher numbers; as a native of Lampsacus on the Hellespont he may have trusted some local estimates. Aristobulus and Ptolemy gave lower numbers, for infantry each 30,000 but for cavalry 4,000 and 5,000 respectively (*FGrH* 139 F 4 and 138 F 4).

Now Arrian used Aristobulus and Ptolemy as his sources; so, as Arr. 1.11.3 gave 'not much above 30,000 infantry and over 5,000 cavalry', it follows that Arrian took these numbers from Ptolemy. What is more, Arrian said that the infantry total included light troops and archers; and this implies that Ptolemy had given the numbers of these groups separately and, if so, no doubt those of other groups.

The unique feature of D.'s figures is that he gives the figures for groups, and among them are the light troops (Odrysae, Triballoi, Illyrioi, and Agrianes) and the archers. D.'s ultimate source, then, is probably Ptolemy. This probability becomes a certainty when we compare Ptolemy's 'not much above 30,000 infantry and over 5,000 cavalry' in Arrian with the true total of D.'s detailed figures for infantry, 32,000[27] and the true total of detailed figures for the cavalry, 5,100. It is true that D. made a fool of himself by giving a total for the cavalry at 4,500 which disagreed with his own detailed figures for the cavalry; this was probably due to his omitting the figure for Greek cavalry (excluding the Thessalians), 600.

D. certainly did not use Ptolemy directly at 17.1–2 or here. The immediate source was probably Diyllus, to whom the factual style is appropriate; and Diyllus as an Athenian would have been interested in the detailed numbers of the Greek units, who were differentiated as 'allies', mercenaries, Thessalians and non-Thessalian Greeks. We have already noted that Diyllus represented the relationship between Macedon and the Greeks as an alliance. If the source is Diyllus, he preserved from Ptolemy the number of troops under Antipater in Macedonia (17.5).

If we may digress, it is worth remarking that Ptolemy could have obtained his detailed figures of units at the time of the crossing only from a record made at that time but not published until Ptolemy himself published it. Callisthenes, Anaximenes, and Aristobulus gave wrong totals because they did not have access to that record. As I have maintained elsewhere,[28] that record was in the *King's Journal* which passed into the possession of Ptolemy. This Journal was not available even to Aristobulus. For Ptolemy himself wrote in the third century and probably published in 285–283 B.C.,[29] when the works of Callisthenes, Anaximenes and Aristobulus had already appeared, and for that matter the work of Cleitarchus, as we shall argue later.

17.6–7 – 18.1. The interest in portents and omens and their correct interpretation are compatible with Diyllus being the source, because the same interest appeared in 16.91.2–3 and 92.2–4, where Diyllus was the source in our opinion. The taking of Athena's shield was a commonplace in the tradition.

18.2 – 19.2. The account of a debate in the council of Persian commanders is like the account of the debate in the council of Macedonian commanders at 16.1–2 which we have ascribed to Diyllus as source. The idea of 'transporting the war into Europe' by attacking Macedonia itself had already been broached at 7.1 and Memnon had received high praise at 7.2 in the section on Persian affairs which we have attributed to Diyllus as source. The mention of the advance into Phrygia at 18.4 prepares us for fulfilment of the omen at 17.6. At 19.2 the present source, Diyllus, is dropped, and at 19.3 Cleitarchus is followed for the battle of the Granicus river, the change of source being betrayed by the inconsistency of 19.2 with 19.3 (see p. 16 above).

22–8. The description of the siege of Miletus is unrhetorical, factual and concise, and it is marked by A's humane treatment of the Greek population of Miletus (22.5, φιλανθρώπως). The disbanding of the fleet is mentioned concisely, and it is noted that among the ships which A kept were the 'allied' ships of Athens, an epithet reminding us of the alliance between Macedon and the Greek League. This is all characteristic of Diyllus.

Next comes a digression, introduced by the expression 'some say', which indicates a move to another source or sources.[30] Whereas the narrative had ascribed the disbanding of the fleet to its ineffectiveness and expense, the digression at 23.1–3 attributes to A the childish idea that the Macedonians would be left without a means of escape by sea and so fight more desperately, and cites two analogies, one from the battle of the Granicus, drawn from Cleitarchus as we have seen (pp. 16ff. above), and the other from Agathocles' burning of his ships in 310/9. This digression, then, is derived from Cleitarchus. The next two sections, 23.4–5, come probably from Cleitarchus; for it is typical of his psychological interpretation that Memnon's calculations are entirely selfish.

The end of the narrative at 22.5, mentioning the retention of ships to transport the siege train, is resumed at 24.1 with A conveying the siege train by sea to Halicarnassus. Thus at 24.1 D. returns to Diyllus, and we find that A is winning over the Carians by his humaneness (24.1 ταῖς φιλανθρωπίαις) and ensuring their loyalty (εὔνοια) a refrain which began at 2.2. He treated the Greek cities liberally; for the aim with which he had undertaken the war against Persia was 'the liberation of the Greeks', and this had been stated in Philip's case at 16.91.2, a passage which we have attributed to Diyllus as source.

The siege of Halicarnassus (24.4 – 27.6) is a purple patch. Sorties and battles outside the walls (24.6) are conducted with trumpets blaring, troops shouting their applause at deeds of heroism (25.1; cf. 26.5), frontal wounds for all (25.4 τραύμασιν ἐναντίοις) and an *aristeia* for Ephialtes, an Athenian of superlative strength and valour (26.6). The Macedonians fought courageously (24.6) but many were killed on one occasion or another (24.6; 25.5 twice; 26.6; 26.7).[31] The defenders were superb in their deeds of prowess. The climax came during a battle outside the walls which raged from dawn (26.3) to nightfall (27.4).[32] The Persians were on the verge of victory (27.2 fin.). A was nonplussed (26.7 εἰς πολλὴν ἀμηχανίαν ἐνέπιπτεν). Then came a paradoxical change (παραδόξως). The oldest among the Macedonians — veterans of Philip's time, victorious in many battles, exempt now from combat duty — plunged into action and saved the day, taunting the young shirkers for their cowardice and holding up the enemy with their own locked shields (27.2). Fortunes were now reversed. The Macedonians charged into the city on the heels of the fleeing Persians as night fell; but A had the trumpeter sound the retreat. That very night the Persian commanders got the bulk of their troops away by sea, without A realising it until dawn broke. They had left

39

their best men to hold the acropolis. A razed the city to the ground.

These excitements are quite unlike the sober description of the siege of Miletus, but they find their parallels in the description of the siege of Thebes. There are also palpable fictions, as at Thebes. When Ephialtes sortied at the head of a deep column of picked men, A responded with a three-tiered formation: himself out in front of the first group, 'the champions' (τοὺς προμάχους), then 'in reserve' the picked men (τοὺς ἐπιλέκτους), and then, next to them, those who were outstanding in deeds of valour. This is epic stuff, whereas the Macedonians operated prosaically in phalanx brigades.[33] The old veterans and the young shirkers is a salutary theme. But we must remember that Philip's veterans fought on until the end of the campaigns in India, and we may be sure that in this the first year in Asia he had not brought non-combatant veterans with him. Chapters 24.3 fin. – 27.6 are inspired by a narrative of Cleitarchus.

D. added a short passage of his own composition which forms the rest of chapter 27. It is inaccurate and misleading. But he is eager to narrate a paradoxical reversal of fortune which involved a suicide pact among a people called the Marmareis (28). This affair too he drew evidently from Cleitarchus.[34] A was 'enraged' in the course of it (28.2 παροξυνθείς).

29–32.2. D. returned evidently to Diyllus for a factual and well-informed account of Memnon's naval offensive in the Aegean and the rising hopes of those of the Greeks who chose 'the cause of Persia';[35] also many of the Greeks were persuaded by bribes to take the Persian side. Two earlier examples of bribery (at 4.8 and 15.3) were in passages ascribed to Diyllus as source. The death of Memnon ruined the cause of Darius, for Darius had intended to transfer the war entirely from Asia to Europe — an idea mentioned at 7.1 and 18.2, passages ascribed to Diyllus as source.

In the latter part of 30.1 the scene changes to the court of Darius and we are given a clearly fictitious account of a discussion in the council of Darius' Friends. The Athenian

Charidemus[36] angled cleverly for the command of the Persian forces, but when the Friends outwitted him he lost his temper and offended Darius, who 'in accordance with Persian custom' seized the belt of Charidemus, which meant immediate execution. Once Charidemus was dead, Darius repented; but he could not make what was done undone by his royal authority (compare 101.6). No other general was competent; so Darius himself was compelled to take the field. He mustered 400,000 infantry and 100,000 cavalry at Babylon — they reappear as the roar of 500,000 throats at the battle of Issus. Thus D. used Cleitarchus as his source for 30.1 (the latter part) to the end of 31.2.

D. turns back in time to the fears of A when Memnon planned to operate against Macedonia, i.e. in fulfilment of Darius' plan mentioned at 30.1. Thus he is resuming Diyllus. Next comes A's illness. When Philip the doctor offered to treat him with a dangerous but quick-working drug, A accepted because he had heard that Darius was on the march from Babylon; and recovering unexpectedly he promoted the doctor to the rank of 'most loyal friend' (31.6). This less dramatic version was probably taken from Diyllus. Other versions said that A was warned against the doctor in a letter from Parmenio (Arr. 2.4.9, citing it as a 'story', i.e. not from Ptolemy and Aristobulus) and that he was warned in a letter from Olympias (Seneca, *De ira* 2.23). It so happens that D. goes on to mention a letter from Olympias to A at 32.1, which gave him 'other good advice as well as grounds for safeguarding himself from Alexander Lyncestes' ($\tau \acute{a} \ \tau \epsilon \ \acute{a} \lambda \lambda a \ \tau \widehat{\omega} \nu \ \chi \rho \eta \sigma \acute{\iota} \mu \omega \nu \ \kappa a \grave{\iota} \ \delta \iota \acute{o} \tau \iota \ \kappa \tau \lambda.$). This letter can hardly be any other than that mentioned by Seneca; and then 'the other good advice' was a warning against the doctor.[37] It seems probable that D., having adopted the version of Diyllus, found in another source this letter of Olympias; and that he did not repeat the bit about the doctor but he gave the warning about Alexander Lyncestes. Who was the other source? It was almost certainly Cleitarchus, because he was popular in the time of Seneca.

Thus the letter of Olympias and the arrest of Alexander Lyncestes are most likely based on Cleitarchus' narrative. And the succeeding chapters, which describe the campaign of Issus, have already been attributed on other grounds to Cleitarchus (32.2 – 38.3).

Chapter 39 covers Darius' actions from the defeat at Issus in 333 to the eve of battle at Gaugamela in 331. D.'s own reflections on how men should respond to good fortune (38.6) may have inspired him to introduce that idea into Darius' letter to A (39.1). The general impression is that D. wrote this chapter after a reading of Cleitarchus but in an extremely concise manner. For the unbroken spirit of Darius, the low cunning of A in forging a letter, and Darius' levy of troops being twice that at Issus and so reaching 1,000,000 men are all characteristic of Cleitarchus.

40.2 – 47. The account of the siege of Tyre has some features in common with the account of the siege of Thebes. A is angry (40.3; 9.6), the Tyrians over-confident (40.3; 10.2), taunts are made (41.1; 9.5) and portents proliferate (41.5–8; 10.2–5). The idea that action was taken in order to give Darius time for his preparations (40.3) will recur at 65.5, a passage ascribed to Cleitarchus as source. There are similarities with the battle-scenes which were attributed to Cleitarchus. Missiles never miss their mark, the target being so large (42.2, 44.4, as in the account of battles at 33.7 and 88.6); or missiles are intercepted in mid-air (43.1, 45.3 by catherine wheels; cf. 33.3). Attention is given to horrific wounds (44.1–4, 45.6). The Tyrians defended so well that A twice thought of abandoning the siege; indeed on the second occasion only one of his Friends supported his decision to persist. A could not bear to be 'despised' (40.4; cf. 9.4) or to lose 'glory' (45.7). Tyre fell through the *aristeia* of A fighting from a gangway (probably unhistorical, as Arrian mentioned the heroism of Admetus and not of A at 2.23.4 and 2.24.4). The description as a whole[38] is highly coloured and sensational; but it is not apparent why and how Tyre fell. We may confidently see in chapters 40–46 the influence of Cleitarchus as source.

The story of 'Ballonymus' (properly Abdalonymus) is introduced at chapter 47 as an example of a sudden reversal of fortune, a *peripeteia*, a theme dear to Cleitarchus. The story may well be inspired by a Persian folk-tale such as Cleitarchus' father, Deinon, might have retailed. Its setting was probably transferred from Sidon to Tyre by D. himself.

48–52. In chapter 48.1–2 D. gives a plain and factual account of Agis furthering the cause not of liberty (as Cleitarchus had put it in the case of Thebes) but of Persia, which he compelled many states in Crete to adopt (cf. 29.3, a passage attributed to Diyllus as source). The account in 48.2–6 of the commanders of mercenaries who had escaped from Issus is appropriate to Diyllus and not to Cleitarchus, who had not mentioned Greek mercenaries in Persian service in A's battles (at least as retailed by D.). The mention of the Greek League's compliment to A and the citation of the decree which no doubt gave the number of envoys in 48.6–7 indicate the attention of Diyllus to Greek affairs and decrees; and the statement in 48.7 that Gaza was garrisoned by Persians is an implicit contrast to garrisoning by Greek mercenaries. The factual and detailed narrative continues to the treaty of friendship and alliance with Cyrene at 49.3. These sections seem all to be based on Diyllus.

The description of A's visit to the oracle of Ammon in 49.3 to 51 is very remarkable for its fullness. The scale is inappropriate to Diyllus who was covering a period of sixty or seventy years, but is appropriate to Cleitarchus, whose subject was Alexander. Since Cleitarchus lived in later life at Alexandria in Egypt, he had the opportunity either to visit the shrine himself or to learn about the shrine and its methods of divination; moreover, he would have the desire to write fully since the visit was sensational. D.'s details are not the same as those in Callisthenes F 14 (*FGrH* 124). A's force runs out of water through consuming what it had brought, whereas in C. the force goes astray in a dust-storm. Four days later the way was lost through the huge expanses of sand but the guides were shown the line of the track by crows croaking on their right, whereas in C. the crows belonged to the first occasion, led the way themselves and rounded up the strayers at night by their cries.[39] For D. the shower of rain and the omen of the crows croaking on the right are signs of divine aid for A. The report by D. of the question and the responses is certainly fictitious.[40] It is only of interest in showing what D.'s source wished to establish, i.e. that A was son of the god, was destined to rule the world, had punished all the murderers of Philip, and would be invincible (ἀνίκητος). There is general agreement among scholars that the source of D. here is Cleitarchus.[41]

D. is unusual in putting the foundation of Alexandria not before but after the visit to Siwa, and this was probably due to his following Cleitarchus; for Cleitarchus, living at Alexandria, may have adopted the local dating, in April.[42] The description of the city, no doubt drawn from Cleitarchus, leads D. to make one of his rare interjections (52.4–6).

53–5. The preparations of Darius in 53.1–3 include the Cleitarchan figure of a million men, as at 39.4 (a passage ascribed to Cleitarchus as source), and the typically Cleitarchan puerility of Darius' anxiety at his forces speaking many diverse languages (as Persia's forces had done for two centuries). The lengthy description of the scythed chariots is also appropriate to Cleitarchus, since he made much of them in his narrative of the battle of Gaugamela as reflected in D.'s account.[43]

There is considerable confusion over the movements of Darius in Mesopotamia, as there had been over his movements in Cilicia before the battle of Issus. This may be due in part to compression by D., but there are indications that the confusion was there in the source. The idea that Darius chose to fight in 'the plains round Nineveh' echoes his choice of 'the plain' in Cilicia (32.3). Arbela, where Darius is said to have camped and kept his troops under continuous training (53.4 and 55.1), is represented in the narrative as being the scene of the battle. That this was an error committed by 'the generality of writers' (Arr. 6.11.4 ὁ πᾶς λόγος) was noted by Arrian and by Plutarch (*Alex.* 31.6); 'the generality' included Callisthenes (*FGrH* 124 F 14a) and probably Cleitarchus, as well as Diodorus.[44]

D. inserts into the period of training at Arbela two events, the sending of a mission by Darius to A and the death of Darius' wife, which are associated together in other accounts (*PA* 29.7 – 30.1). The insertion was certainly placed here, on the eve of the decisive battle, in order to produce a sensational effect; and it has on that account been attributed to Cleitarchus.[45] The negotiations seem to confirm that attribution. At 54.1 D. mentions the earlier mission, described at 39.1, and it is followed by the summoning of the council of Friends, as at 39.2, which we have attributed to Cleitarchus as source. No one dared to speak on so enormous an issue except Parmenio − a hint perhaps at the tyrannical nature of A, as at Thebes (9.5) − and he was neatly snubbed. A's reply to Darius emphasised world-rule, as forecast in Cleitarchus' account of the visit to Siwa at 51.3.

In chapter 55 Mazaeus made two miscalculations: he failed to guard the crossing of the Tigris because he thought the river to be impassable, and his burning of the land did not stop the advance of the Macedonians, as he had expected. So too Darius miscalculated before the battle of Issus (32.3). The vivid account of the crossing of the fast-flowing Tigris was derived surely from some of the participants, and Cleitarchus is a likely writer to have questioned them and retailed their reminiscences.

Cleitarchus, then, was most probably the source used by Diodorus in 53–55.

62–63. Affairs in Europe were treated last in 48.1-2, when Agis 'compelled most states in Crete to adopt the cause of Persia', a section which we attributed to Diyllus as source. Now Agis and some Greek states rose in the cause of freedom, but their collaboration with and dependence on the help of Persia, especially in money to hire mercenaries, are stated. The account is factual, objective and knowledgeable, and there are no signs of partiality. The attitude of Athens is explained on the ground that she had been especially honoured by Alexander, and the action of 'the Greeks in alliance' (τῶν συμμαχούντων Ἑλλήνων, i.e. as allies of Macedon against Persia, as mentioned earlier in passages we attributed to Diyllus as source) is neither condemned nor condoned. The figures of combatants and losses are not highly inflated. Certainly the source here is not Cleitarchus, whose partiality for Thebes was so clear in 8.2 – 14; on the other hand its characteristics fit Diyllus of Athens.

The account of the war is concluded in the normal way with the lists of casualties at 63.3. Then, although at 63.2 'Agis fell fighting', at 63.4 he appears again: 'Something peculiar happened in regard to Agis' death.' He fell with many wounds on his front (πολλοῖς τραύμασιν ἐναντίοις), dismissed those who were carrying him out of the battle, and then in a kneeling position drove back his enemies, killed some of them and was killed himself by a javelin. This is surely something outside the account on which 63.1–3 was based. It was presumably in D.'s other source, Cleitarchus.

The personal contribution of Diodorus

In my study of book 16 I concluded that 'as a medium of transmission D. lends neither historical causation nor political colour to the source whom he employs'. These words apply equally well to the first half of book 17. Thus D. has not imposed a standard political interpretation on A's dealings with the Greek states and the actions respectively of Thebes and Agis; rather the particular political slants of the sources are clear and unimpaired. Similarly, although D. gave his personal view of A in the Proem, he lets A appear in whatever form he found in each source. What D. did add in 16 was 'a number of link-phrases, a reference or two to contemporary times, an occasional cross-reference, a number of refrain-passages to lend some colour of unity and an Epilogue'. In the first half of 17 we find the first three (e.g. 5.1, 52.6 and 54.1 respectively), but there are no refrain passages. The Epilogue as a free composition by D. in 16 is balanced by three pieces in the first part of 17: the vacuous Proem with undiluted adoration of A; the praise of A's decency to the

Persian royal family (38.4–7); and the praise of A's foundation, Alexandria in Egypt (52.4–7).

It should be noted that D. does not attempt to conceal his additions. Rather he proclaims them by using the first person; presumably he was proud of them. For those who suppose that he sometimes tried to conceal his additions, it is sobering and instructive to compare the text of D. with the text of Polybius, where D. was drawing upon Polybius as his source. As R. Drews expressed it,[46] 'in checking D. against Polybius we see that in some cases he has appropriated intact the philosophical observations of Polybius and in other cases has improved on them' (the improvement being a more positive statement). This seems to be true also of the first half of 17; for D. simply 'appropriated' Source 1's view of A as a tyrant of bad temper and Source 2's view of A as a man of decency, despite the fact that in his own Proem he had praised A for different qualities.

Of course D. put his own veneer of style on all that he appropriated and he had his own favourite clichés.[47] This is most apparent in descriptions of battles and sieges whether in book 16 or the first half of 17: the battle is stern ($\kappa\alpha\rho\tau\epsilon\rho\grave{\alpha}$ $\mu\acute{\alpha}\chi\eta$), evenly poised ($\iota\sigma\acute{o}\rho\rho\sigma\pi\sigma\varsigma$) and deeds of heroism abound ($\grave{\alpha}\nu\delta\rho\alpha\gamma\alpha\vartheta\acute{\iota}\alpha\iota$).[48] Whether the fighting is at Chaeronea or Arbela, there are piles of corpses (16.86.4 $\pi\sigma\lambda\lambda\tilde{\omega}\nu$ $\sigma\omega\rho\epsilon\upsilon\sigma\mu\acute{\epsilon}\nu\omega\nu$ $\nu\epsilon\kappa\rho\tilde{\omega}\nu$ and 17.61.2 $\grave{o}$ ... $\tau\acute{o}\pi\sigma\varsigma$ $\nu\epsilon\kappa\rho\tilde{\omega}\nu$ $\grave{\epsilon}\pi\lambda\eta\rho\acute{\omega}\vartheta\eta$). In sieges and in any fighting in a confined space there are relays of fighters in attack and in defence. This was a commonplace of war from the fighting at Thermopylae onwards (Hdt. 7.211.1–2 $\grave{\epsilon}\nu$ $\sigma\tau\epsilon\iota\nu\sigma\pi\acute{o}\rho\omega$, 212.2 $\grave{\epsilon}\nu$ $\mu\acute{\epsilon}\rho\epsilon\iota$ $\acute{\epsilon}\kappa\alpha\sigma\tau\sigma\iota$), and each author had his favourite expression, e.g. $\grave{\epsilon}\nu$ $\mu\acute{\epsilon}\rho\epsilon\iota$, $\grave{\alpha}\pi\grave{o}$ $\mu\acute{\epsilon}\rho\sigma\upsilon\varsigma$ and $\grave{\epsilon}\kappa$ $\delta\iota\alpha\delta\sigma\chi\tilde{\eta}\varsigma$. D. favoured the last, not only in book 17 but in many books, e.g. in 13.55.5 and 56.4.[49] Another commonplace of war is the part played by Chance, $\tau\acute{\upsilon}\chi\eta$, both in producing the unexpected, $\tau\grave{o}$ $\pi\alpha\rho\acute{\alpha}\delta\sigma\xi\sigma\nu$, and in sudden reversals of fortune, $\pi\epsilon\rho\iota\pi\acute{\epsilon}\tau\epsilon\iota\alpha\iota$. References to these vagaries of Chance occur throughout D.'s work (e.g. of women in a captured city at 13.58.2, and of the unexpected at Aegospotami at 13.106.5); it figures prominently in speeches at Syracuse (13.22.5, 23.3, 24.6, 27.6), in a judgement of Philip (16.1.6) and in D.'s reflections on A (17.38.5).[50]

That these clichés and reflections were the common coin of Greek historians is obvious enough. That they occurred in particular in the works of Diyllus and Cleitarchus is likely to be true but cannot be demonstrated from the surviving fragments of their works. However, we have fragments of two Hellenistic histories of Alexander which reveal the influence of Cleitarchus and the attitudes of the Hellenistic period; and we see from them that D. was often repeating the traditional viewpoints and the clichés of that period. Thus in *POxy* 1798 (*FGrH* 148) A is distraught before battle (F 44, Col. II ἐν ἀγωνίαι — as in D. 17.56.1–3 πάσης ἀγωνίας); and he is nonplussed in *Fragmentum Sabbaiticum* (*FGrH* 151) F 1,7 ἐν ἀπορίαι — as in D. 17.26.7 and 42.6. He decides in anger to kill the Tyrians in *FGrH* 151 F 1,7 ὀργιζόμενος . . . διέγνω — as in D. 17.9.6 the Thebans. 'The unexpected' and 'Chance' play their part in *FGrH* 151 F 1,2 τὸ παράδοξον and τῆι τύχηι. Although descriptions of battles are reduced to a sentence or two in *FGrH* 148, space is found for the plain being full of corpses at F 44, Col. III τὸ πεδίον πλῆρες ἦν νεκρῶν.

Although these two Hellenistic historians were writing much shorter accounts than D., yet the fragments warn us against supposing that D. frequently invented some points and misunderstood others. Thus D. is alone among the main Alexander-historians in defining Darius' offer to A as the territories west of the Halys river and 20,000 talents (17.39.1 and 17.54.1); but the offer is so defined in *FGrH* 151 F 1,5.[51] He is also alone among them in making A capture Issus and be there on the evening before the battle (17.32.4 – 33.1); but both A and Darius encamp and engage there in *FGrH* 151 F 1,4. In the battle of Issus D. did not mention the Greek mercenaries (we attributed the omission to the prejudice of his source); *FGrH* 151 F 1 does not mention mercenaries at all, but *FGrH* 148 F 44 Col. III and Col. IV mentions their position and their losses in the battle of Issus. D. had the cavalry fight the cavalry and then the infantry fight the infantry at Granicus and at Issus; so it is in *FGrH* 148 F 44 Col. III at Issus. After the battle of Issus D. had the Macedonians loot the luxurious wealth of the Persian king's headquarters (17.35.1-2); so too *FGrH* 148 F 44 Col. III πληρεῖς δ᾽ ἦσαν ποικίλης γάζης. D. described the scythed chariots and the bizarre wounds they inflicted at the battle of Gaugamela; so too in *FGrH* 151 F 1,12 with severed arms still holding their shields, as in D. The huge numbers for the Persian armies in D. are even exceeded by *FGrH* 148 F 44 for Issus and equalled by *FGrH* 151 F 1,12 for Gaugamela. Geographical confusion is not peculiar to D.; *FGrH* 148 F 45 confuses the Tigris with the Euphrates. D. gave a sensational account of the visit to Siwa and especially of the oracle's responses; *FGrH* 151 F 1,10 is even more explicit about the responses, affirming that A is the son not of Philip but of Zeus Ammon himself, and that, lad though he is, A is undefeatable, μειράκιον, ἀνίκητον εἶ.[52] D. was unusual in dating the foundation of Alexandria in Egypt after the visit to Siwa; *FGrH* 151 F 1,11 does likewise.

When we consider that D. had available to him not only the sources used by these two Hellenistic historians (probably of the second century B.C.) but also the works of these two themselves, we can see that D. did not choose too unwisely and that he was accurate on the whole in reproducing the sources he chose to reproduce. His language and his clichés were through his own taste and inclination those of the Hellenistic period. They are like a plastic cover and do not distort the dimensions of the sources from which he drew his material.

Summary of attributions

In passing from book 16 to book 17 D. laid aside the text he had been excerpting, Diyllus, *Syntaxis* II, and composed out of his own head an Epilogue to 16 and a Proem to 17, expressing unstinted praise of Philip and of A in what can only be called a simple-minded manner. The reason for this

49

exceptional effort by D. was that he was embarking on the centre-piece of his entire history, the career of A until his death (1.4.6); for it was in this book, which proved so long that it was divided into two parts, that D. was to give the supreme example of kingship and the greatest achievement of human history which placed A on the level of 'the heroes and the demi-gods of old' (17.1.4; cf. 17.117.5).

D. then returned to his task. This was not to create for himself an image of A — he was no creative author[53] — but to make excerpts from existing texts, excerpts which would speak for themselves of A, albeit with differing voices. There were a great many texts available, including those known to us as *POxy* 179 and *Fragmentum Sabbaiticum*. He chose Diyllus, *Syntaxis* II and *Syntaxis* III, probably for three main reasons: the scale of the work (the section on Alexander being only part of the history of a longer period from 356 to perhaps *c.* 280), the fullness of detail and the picture of A, D.'s hero. There was also a practical reason; in writing 16 he had failed to include an excerpt from Diyllus' section on Persian affairs 340–336 B.C., and in 17 he was able to make that omission good, in such a way that 16 and 17 fitted together. But he found one defect in Diyllus. The accounts of sieges and battles were relatively brief (not as brief as those of *POxy* 1798 and *Fragmentum Sabbaiticum*), and they lacked sensational effects. D. turned to the most popular writer of the day on A, Cleitarchus, who excelled in sensationalism. He excerpted from Cleitarchus his accounts of operations at Thebes, the Granicus river, Halicarnassus, Marmara, Issus, Tyre and Gaugamela. For the narrative, apart from these purple patches, he excerpted from the comparatively staid Diyllus, and it was these excerpts which conveyed a picture of A more to D.'s taste. But D. yielded to the temptation to include a few more sensational excerpts from Cleitarchus: some Persian affairs (a speciality of Cleitarchus), a letter from Olympias, the visit to Siwa, the description of Alexandria (Cleitarchus' home by adoption), and the heroism of Agis.

There is one passage which I have not treated: 7.4–7, a digression about Mt Ida in the Troad. It is so wildly irrelevant that it can hardly have come from Diyllus.[54] Otherwise the chart gives the suggested sources for the first half of 17, excepting the chronographic headings.[55] It is intended for convenience of reference.

1	Proem	D.		
2.1	Funeral of Philip		Diyllus, *Syntaxis* II	
2.2 – 5.2	Actions of A		Diyllus, *Syntaxis* III	
5.3 – 6	Asia 340–336		Diyllus, *Syntaxis* II	
7.1–3	Asia 336–335		Diyllus, *Syntaxis* III	
7.4–7		Unallocated		
8.1	Balkans		Diyllus, *Syntaxis* III	
8.2 – 14	Thebes			Cleitarchus
15	Athens		Diyllus	
16	Macedonia		Diyllus	
17–19.2	Entry into Asia		Diyllus	
19.3 – 21.6	Granicus			Cleitarchus
21.7	Sardis	D. (summary)		
22	Miletus		Diyllus	
23.1–3	Digression			Cleitarchus
23.4–5	Memnon			Cleitarchus
24.1–3	Carians		Diyllus	
24.4 – 27.6	Halicarnassus			Cleitarchus
27.7	Towards Cilicia	D. (summary)		
28	Marmara			Cleitarchus
29–30.1	Aegean		Diyllus	
30.1 – 31.1	Darius			Cleitarchus
31.3–6	Memnon; A ill		Diyllus	
32.1–2	Olympias			Cleitarchus
32.3 – 38.2	Issus			Cleitarchus
38.4–7	Reflections on A	D.		
39	Darius	D. (summary based on Cleitarchus)		
40.1–2	Issus–Phoenicia	D. (summary based on Diyllus)		
40.3 – 47	Tyre			Cleitarchus
48–49.3	Agis etc.		Diyllus	
49.3 – 51	Siwa			Cleitarchus
52.1–3	Alexandria			Cleitarchus
52.4–7	Alexandria, etc.	D.		
53–55	Mesopotamia			Cleitarchus
56–61	Gaugamela			Cleitarchus
62–63.3	Agis' war		Diyllus	
63.4	Agis' heroism			Cleitarchus
.....				
87–88	Porus battle			Cleitarchus

THE SOURCES OF DIODORUS SICULUS
17.64–86 AND 17.89–118

Consideration of 17.64–86

In chapter 1 it was argued that D.'s account of the battle against Porus (87–88) was drawn from Cleitarchus. Let us then start by considering the immediately preceding chapters.

83.9 – 86. The similarity between 83.9 and Livy 8.24.14–15 seems not to have been noted by source-critics of the histories of Alexander. In each case we read a horror story of mutilation. At 83.9 the relatives of Darius inflicted on Bessus, the pretender, 'every form of outrage and torture, cut his body up bit by bit and catapulted the dismembered parts'. At that grim point the text breaks off. In the passage of Livy Alexander, the Molossian king, was already dead when his body was washed up by the Acheron river into the hands of the enemy, the Lucanians. 'There a foul mutilation was enacted. They cut through the body at the waist, sent part to Consentia and kept part themselves for their own sport. It was pelted from a distance with javelins and rocks . . .' We have met such horrors in passages of Diodorus describing ghastly wounds and mutilations which we have ascribed to Cleitarchus as source. The entire narrative of Livy in chapter 24 came apparently from a Greek source, as W. Weissenborn maintained (3rd ed. p. 226 'die griech. Quelle, welcher L. hier zu folgen scheint'), and the popular writer of such sensational stuff who was widely read in Livy's day was Cleitarchus. There is then good reason to regard Cleitarchus as the source behind 83.9 and Livy 8.24.14–15.[1]

There follows a lacuna in the text of D., and then the narrative recommences with the Queen Cleophis admiring A's greatness of spirit — an admiration which may have led to a love-affair in the source (see C. 8.10.35–36 and J. 12.7) — and with the sensational account of A's trickery and the desperate fight by the Indian mercenaries and their women, a fight in which every sort of death and wounding occurred (παντοῖαι διαθέσεις θανάτων καὶ τραυμάτων), missiles did not miss their mark, women clung to the shields of the fighting Macedonians and impeded their movements. The pathos and the setting for the scene are typically Cleitarchan. The mercenaries had no idea of what was coming (84.1), and A planned the trap with hatred for them (84.2); the narrative consists of imagined pictures rather than of participants' memories of actual events, as at Thebes (13.2–4) and after Issus (35.1–7). The purpose is to show the brutality of the Macedonians and the treachery of A 'shouting in a great voice' (84.2) − for all the world to know! Details are added for verisimilitude rather than for accuracy, such as the mercenaries' camp being 80 stades away (it was near the town in *Epit. Metz* 43 and 'by the Macedonians' in Arr. 4.27.3).

The storming of Aornis in 85 has special features. A's eagerness to rival the god Heracles is made somewhat ridiculous by the remark that what stopped Heracles was (not the strength of the place but) huge earthquakes and heavenly signs, sent by Zeus (not mentioned in Arrian's account, in which the sense is that Heracles tried to storm the rock and failed, 4.28.1). The measurements of the rock are given for verisimilitude (they differ from those in Arrian, which are factual); and 'the utterly poor old man with two sons who lived in a cave' and who was duly enriched for his services (85.4–6 and 86.1), the attacks in relays for seven days and seven nights (there are no assaults after the completion of the mound in Arr. 4.29.2), and the trick of removing a group of guards (85.7; contrast Arr. 4.30.2–3) all have the air of fiction (compare the poor old man made king of Tyre at 47.3–5, a passage attributed to Cleitarchus as source). We have here another example of D. using Cleitarchus.

In 86 the colourful narrative of the Indian king being decapitated and of the head being presented to A, and the 'paradoxical reversal of fortune' in the mock battle-array of 'Mophis', re-named Taxiles, bear the signs of Cleitarchus. For we may compare τὴν ἰδιότητα τῆς περιπετείας at 27 fin.

and τὸ τῆς περιπετείας παράδοξον at 46 fin., both being passages ascribed to Cleitarchus as source.

There follows the battle against Porus. At 87.3 a number of stades is given for verisimilitude, and then comes an imaginary picture of the battle which ended in the usual manner with losses, funerals and sacrifices at 89.3. D. then turned from Cleitarchus to another source. For whereas no river at all had been mentioned in the narrative of the battle drawn from Cleitarchus, D. (89.6) tells of a city founded 'across the river at the place where he himself crossed'.

64–83. Since we attributed to Cleitarchus the mistaken view that the battle was fought by Arbela and so near the camp of Darius, it is apparent that D. was continuing to use Cleitarchus in saying that the stench of the dead on the battlefield caused A to leave after taking the loot of Arbela (64.3).[2] The mention of billets (τὰς ἐπισταθμίας) may be Cleitarchus, as A in fact kept his troops in camp. At the beginning of this chapter Darius is represented as aiming to gain time and so prepare a new army (64.1 χρόνον ἱκανὸν εἰς παρασκευὴν δυνάμεως). This interpretation of Darius' plans by Cleitarchus occurs again at 65.5, which is an important passage for us. There the satrap willingly surrendered Susa to A, and D. continues as follows: 'As some have written, Darius had so ordered those trusted by him, his aim being that he might gain time by flight for the preparation of the war, while Alexander would be kept busy by remarkable distractions, capture of the most glorious cities and great treasuries.' We conclude, then, that D. cited Cleitarchus here for this childish view and that D.'s source just before it was other than Cleitarchus. Again at 73.2 Darius is represented as intending to raise forces from Bactria and the upper satrapies and as already having with him 30,000 Persians and a number of Greek mercenaries when A's speed outmanoeuvred him. This again is from Cleitarchus, and the figure 30,000 is certainly incorrect.[3]

Let us now turn to consider the source other than Cleitarchus. The narrative from 64.5 to 65.5 has a very different character from 83.9 – 89.3, which we have been considering and have attributed to Cleitarchus as source. This narrative is remarkably detailed, giving Macedonian names with city ethnics for instance, detailed financial figures, bounties, reinforcements, days of marching in the form 'on the sixth day' (ἑκταῖος), and changes in army organisation which were designed to encourage loyalty (εὐνοίᾳ πρὸς τὸν ἡγούμενον). The same love of detail appears in 66.1–2 with financial figures, and the huge sums are attributed to the Persian kings' desire to insure against the unexpected vagaries of Chance (πρὸς τὰ παράλογα τῆς τύχης ἀπολιπόντες αὑτοῖς καταφυγάς).

The story which follows illustrates just these vagaries of Chance and is drawn then from the same source. When A sits on the royal throne, a page put 'the table of Darius' under A's feet; thereupon a eunuch wept at 'the change of fortune' (τῇ μεταβολῇ τῆς τύχης). A thought he had done 'something presumptuous and very unlike his decency towards the captive women' (τῆς ἐπιεικείας; this recalls 38.3 and D.'s own comment at 38.6). He was about to have the table of Darius removed when Philotas said 'it is not a matter of presumption but the omen sent by a good deity'. A accepted his words as an omen (i.e. of subjugating Darius) and had the table stay where it was. This story shows A in an admirable light as modest, tactful and pious.[4] It is certainly not from Cleitarchus.[5]

This story is very much in line with some passages which we have ascribed to Diyllus in the first chapter, namely 16.2, 17.6–7 and 37.5 – 38.3, in which A was shown as responsive to omens, pious, gentle and treating the captive women with decency. As the story is introduced to illustrate a point in the preceding narrative, I attribute the passage from 64.5 to 67.1 (this last section continuing with the captive women) to Diyllus as source.

At 67.2 D. gives the first of several descriptions which concern areas east of the Euphrates. In the first part of the book there was only one such description, that of the country around Siwa in 49–50, which we argued came from Cleitarchus. The probability that this description also came from

55

Cleitarchus is heightened by the confusion about the river's name and its connection with Babylonia.[6] Two actions follow in 67.4 – 68. In the first the capture of the pass not by A but by a detachment and the guiding by a native Uxian are so different from what is narrated in Arr. 3.17 that it must be largely fictional in the Cleitarchan manner. The second action, at the 'Susian Rocks', is highly coloured and probably exaggerated (with waggon-sized rocks, no missing of a target and very heavy losses); A does not ask to recover his dead, because he does not want to admit his defeat and prefers to act dishonourably in leaving his dead unburied (68.4).[7] But a Lycian shepherd comes to the rescue, leads A over the snow and enables A to rout the enemy; he kills most of the entourage of Ariobarzanes. This too has the air of Cleitarchus.[8]

In 69.2–9 the episode of the mutilated Greeks is one which would interest any Greek writer (Ptolemy and Aristobulus, writing from the Macedonian viewpoint, did not mention it apparently). We see from D. that his source had a long account with speeches made to A, by A, between the leaders of the mutilated Greeks, and again to A and by A. The scale of that account and the emotional nature of the narrative in D. are especially appropriate to Cleitarchus, whom Pearson 239, for instance, regarded as the source.

Persepolis provides a purple patch which certainly came from Cleitarchus. The sack of the city first with the massacre of all males and the looting of luxurious materials with such greed and ferocity that the Macedonians fought with one another, even killed one another, cut priceless pieces in two and even sheared off one another's hands as they were stretched out to seize the loot! And the women of course were part of the loot. A went to the citadel and found there 120,000 talents in precious metals which he arranged to remove to other places; for 'in his hatred of the native people [compare 70.1 'his worst enemy'] he was eager to destroy Persepolis[9] utterly' (71.3) — as in the case of Thebes at 9.4, a passage due to Cleitarchus as source.

At this point D. interrupts his narrative to give a description of the citadel, the royal tombs on the Royal Hill[10] and the treasuries. The description must have been composed after the construction of 'the tombs' (71.7), i.e. of Artaxerxes II ob. 358 B.C. and Artaxerxes III ob. 338 B.C. and before the destruction wrought by A in 330 B.C., and the probable author is Deinon, whose work was used by his son Cleitarchus.

A carries out his eager desire in 72, but the initiative is given to the Athenian courtesan Thaïs. When A and his Friends were mad with drink at their banquet in celebration of victory, one of the women there, who was called Thaïs, said that A's finest achievement would be for him to burn the palace and for a woman's hands to destroy in a moment of time the notorious splendours of Persia. The party becomes 'a victory-komos in honour of Dionysus'. 'The entire district around the palace was soon a mass of flames', and the Acropolis of Athens was avenged by a woman of Athens. The style is entirely that of Cleitarchus, and the survival of a fragment of Cleitarchus which makes Thaïs responsible (*FGrH* 137 F 11) leaves no doubt that D. was drawing here upon the narrative of Cleitarchus.[11] The impression in D.'s narrative, that the whole city of Persepolis was destroyed in accordance with A's intentions (71.3), was no doubt deliberately conveyed to his readers by Cleitarchus. In fact the palace area only was burnt (so Arr. 3.18.11); for the city continued to be the capital (19.22.1).[12]

In 73.1, on a campaign through Persis, A acted with a mixture of force (βία) and clemency (ἐπιείκεια). D. used ἐπιείκεια here as a variant for πειθοῖ (19.2), 'by fair dealing', and not in the sense of 'decency' as in his treatment of the captive women. As we noted (p. 54 above), the plan of Darius to raise forces from the upper satrapies and the reported number here of troops with Darius, i.e. more than 30,000, came from Cleitarchus. When A caught up with Darius, he had just been killed (73.3 ἄρτι). This too is presumably from Cleitarchus. D. then enters a note of a version in another source (or sources), ὡς ἔνιοι γεγράφασιν, in which Darius was still alive, A sympathised with him and undertook to avenge him. This version is known to us in the *Alexander*

Romance of Pseudo-Callisthenes. D. obtained it from there or from an intermediate source.

In 73.5 the narrative of affairs in Europe is resumed from where it had left off at 63.3, a passage ascribed to Diyllus as source. The style of the narrative is as in 62.1 – 63.3, and the correct description of the procedures followed by Sparta, Antipater and the Council of the Greek League (τὸ κοινὸν τῶν Ἑλλήνων συνέδριον), is appropriate to Diyllus. It so happens that a fragment of Cleitarchus (*FGrH* 137 F 4) also gives the number 50 for the hostages provided by Sparta; but this number is likely to have occurred in other historians and in particular in Diyllus, who is punctilious in mentioning numbers. This passage then I attribute to Diyllus as source.

In 74.1–2 Bessus is treated with sympathy. He is a fighter for 'freedom' and 'autonomy' in raising his army; so too the Greeks had fought for 'freedom' at 62.1 and 3, a passage ascribed to Diyllus. In 74.3–6 we read of A's oratory in winning the obedience of his Macedonians (compare 2.3 and 3.6), details of the bounties and gifts, the Greek troops described as allies, and details of the sums captured and paid out. Thus the indications are that the source is Diyllus. In the narrative the bounties paid to the Macedonians occur before the army reaches Hecatompylus; this error is due probably to D. rather than to the source.

We should expect the description of Hyrcania, like that of the country round Siwa and that of the Pasitigris basin (67.2–3), to come from Cleitarchus. This expectation is supported by the Cleitarchus fragment (*FGrH* 137 F 14) which mentions the τενθρηδών. This becomes ἀνθρηδών in D. 75.7. Cleitarchus himself may well have used accounts by Polycleitus and Onesicritus.[13]

In 76.1–4 the narrative is very compressed. The reputation of A for clemency (ἐπιείκεια) and its effect in bringing in the last Greek mercenaries may be echoes of Diyllus rather than of Cleitarchus, who seems to have kept silent about Greek mercenaries; but there is not enough detail on which to reach a conclusion. In 76.5–8 the story of Bucephalas is not from Ptolemy and Aristobulus, since Arrian placed it in the land of the Uxii, but it could have come from any other Alexander-historian.

In 77 the story of Thalestris, the Amazon queen, bedding with A for thirteen days is due to Cleitarchus; for Plutarch named him first of those who told this story, and none of the others is likely to have been used directly by D.[14] Next comes A's adoption of Persian dress and Persian customs with the detail that the girls of the harem taken over by A from Darius numbered 'the days of the year'. It is generally agreed that D.'s source here is Cleitarchus. His father, Deinon (*FHG* F 1,7), described the girls as 'outstandingly beautiful' and 360 in number (the Persian year having 360 days). It is typical of Cleitarchus to picture the 360 girls parading past A's bed each evening for him to make his nightly choice, and to attribute to A a sparing use of the girls not because he was continent or impotent or whatever but because he was afraid of offending the Macedonians (77.7).

In 78 the narrative is too concise for any conclusion to be reached about the source. In 79–80 the conspiracy which led to the deaths of Philotas, Parmenio and others is told with more justification of A and certainly with less condemnation of A than in other narratives. In 79.1 the outcome is foreshadowed as being 'foreign to A's personal goodness'. Whereas the narrative does not prejudge Philotas and attributes his silence to either complicity or laziness (79.3), the instigator of the plot (Dimnus) is made to tell all to A *before* committing suicide;[15] and the implication of telling all is that A knew from that moment that Philotas was an accomplice. When Philotas denied the charge of complicity and pleaded laziness as the cause of his silence, A did not produce his own knowledge but followed the correct legal procedure of referring the matter to the Macedonians for trial (τὴν κρίσιν . . . τοῖς Μακεδόσιν ἐπέτρεψεν). Sentence of death was passed by the Macedonians on Philotas and on those under accusation, Parmenio being among them. Philotas was tortured and confessed his complicity; he was then executed 'in accordance with the custom of the Macedonians'. Thus the responsibility for the decisions and for the execution of Philotas is placed firmly on the assembly of the Macedonians in accordance with Macedonian customary law. And the guilt of Philotas is not in question. Dimnus had told all to A; the assembly found Philotas guilty; and Philotas under torture confessed his guilt.

At 80.2 Alexander Lyncestes is brought to trial by the Macedonians (εἰς τὴν κρίσιν τῶν Μακεδόνων παραχθείς) after a three years' delay which was due to his 'relationship with Antipater'.[16] Finding no words to make his defence he was executed. No comment is passed by D. Next comes the execution of Parmenio, again without comment (Parmenio had already been condemned to death by the assembly of the Macedonians);[17] and the execution leads on to the formation as a separate unit of 'the Disorderlies' (ἀτάκτων τάγμα), so that the rest of the Macedonians should not be corrupted. The whole passage 79–80 was not based on Cleitarchus who would have taken a sinister view of A's actions; on the other hand, it fits well with the general attitude of Diyllus towards A.

In 81 the explanation of the name Euergetae for the Ariaspi from the actions of Cyrus the Great may have come from Deinon via Cleitarchus in the first place, but it may have been repeated by other writers. The narrative of the rest of the chapter is concise and yet has detail; so it is more likely to have come from Diyllus than from Cleitarchus. The description in 82 of the country and houses of the Paropanisadae is like the descriptions which we assigned earlier to Cleitarchus as source; and it is certainly too long to have come from the work of Diyllus, which covered a long span of time. It is colourful and interesting in the style of Cleitarchus, and it has also a typical exaggeration, if not misconception, in placing their land 'under the bears themselves', i.e. under the North Pole (A was to penetrate much farther to the north). The Macedonians are given credit for toughness and daring in overcoming the difficulties of the terrain (82.6), and there is reference to looting in the Cleitarchan manner (82.8). Chapter 82, then, was based on Cleitarchus.[18]

In 83 the confusion of Mt Paropanisus and Mt Caucasus and the placing of the cave of Prometheus among the Paropanisadae were probably commonplaces in the histories of Alexander, since they derived ultimately from reports of men with A (so Eratosthenes supposed, according to Arr. 5.3.2–3). Again Cleitarchus is more likely to have included the story than Diyllus. The two cities which A is said to have founded (83.1 and 2) were mentioned long afterwards by Theophylactus Simmocata, whereas all other writers mentioned only one city; and as Goukowsky has pointed out,[19] the author whom Theophylactus is likely to have read is Cleitarchus. The graphic picture of Satibarzanes taking the helmet off his head with his hands and revealing his identity before the single combat (83.5) looks like Cleitarchus. The account of Bessus in 83.7–8 is not as in Arrian. Bessus and Bagodaras fell out while drinking at a banquet, Bessus was enraged, intended to kill Bagodaras and was then restrained by his friends; so Bagodaras fled to A and became a go-between, whereupon the leading commanders arrested Bessus and brought him to A. In Arrian's account there is nothing of the drinking and Bagodaras, and the first contact is made by men sent from Spitamenes and Dataphernes (3.29.6); and it was not the commanders but Ptolemy who brought Bessus to A. Now Arrian says he gave his account from Ptolemy, but that Aristobulus had a different story, namely that it was Spitamenes, Dataphernes and their staff who brought Bessus to Ptolemy and handed him over to A (3.30.5). Next, in 83.9, comes the chopping up into little pieces of Bessus and the slinging of the pieces, which we discussed at the start of this part and assigned to Cleitarchus as source. Now the Bessus–Bagodaras story (so similar to the Alexander–Cleitus story except in the sequel) has the same uniqueness as the chopping up of Bessus; both were evidently invented by Cleitarchus, or by his informants.

For the lacuna which now intervenes in D.'s text we have a synopsis of contents which mentions that in quelling the revolt by the Sogdians A killed more than 120,000 of them. This recurs in Theophylactus Simmocata, who says that A burnt that number (καταφλέξας). The huge number is typical of Cleitarchus (as in *FGrH* 137 F 25), and Goukowsky has observed that the author whom Theophylactus is likely to have read is Cleitarchus; moreover, death by burning seems to have had a special appeal for Cleitarchus, along with other grisly forms of woundings and deaths (e.g. at Marmara in 28.4–5).

Consideration of 17.89–104

We move on to 89.4–6. As we noted in the first part of chapter 1, D.'s account of the battle against Porus had no mention of a river, but at 89.6 D. mentioned the crossing of 'the river'. We inferred from this that D. used one source for the battle, namely Cleitarchus, and another source for what followed in 89.4–6. That source noted the building of a fleet and the intention of A: 'on reaching the end of Indike and on subjugating all the natives to sail down the river into Ocean.'[20] The fleet and the intention are resumed at 95.3 and 96.1. Next comes the mention of the two cities which A founded; they are resumed at 95.5. Thus we shall attribute to the same source 89.4–6 and 95.3 – 96.1. On our analysis so far this source is likely to be Diyllus.

In 90.1–3 a peculiarity (ἴδιόν τι) is introduced, which makes a break in the narrative. It is a description of flora and fauna, resembling those we ascribed earlier to Cleitarchus, and in this case we have evidence in two fragments of Cleitarchus (*FGrH* 137 F 18 and F 19) that D. was using him. It is probable that Cleitarchus had drawn some of his information from Onesicritus.[21] The description of huge trees and of poisonous snakes in 90.5–7 comes evidently from Cleitarchus. The section in between, 90.4, refers back to the start of the battle against Porus; for the king Embisarus[22] who was 400 stades away when A decided to attack Porus (87.2–3) is now resumed as 'the king who had come too late to fulfil his alliance with Porus'. In each passage the source is Cleitarchus.

There follow further descriptions which are likely to be derived also from Cleitarchus: the practice of suttee among the Cathaei, and its origin in a wife once poisoning her husband (91.3), the rule of beauty among the people of Sopeithes (91.4–7),[23] and the dogs and the lion (92).[24] In the course of 91 mention is made of A's anger at the duplicity of the bad Porus (91.2 παροξυνθείς) and of A's policy of clemency in returning his kingdom to Sopeithes (91.7 τὴν τοῦ κρατοῦντος ἐπιείκειαν); it seems that both words are well established in D.'s vocabulary at this stage of the book, and that their use here may be due to D. rather than be reproduced from a source. The mission of Hephaestion, mentioned in connection with A's anger at 91.2, is resumed at 93.1, evidently from the same source, and the combined forces advance to the river Hyphasis. The eagerness of A to continue his advance despite the report of a great desert and huge forces beyond it in the Ganges basin is attributed to his desire for honour (φιλοτιμία), a commonplace in Alexander-historians, and also to an oracular response from Delphi naming him 'invincible', ἀνίκητος, and to the promise of world-rule made to him by Ammon (93.4). Here again is the trace of Cleitarchus; for he was the source of the promise of Ammon at 51.2 and also of the first mention of A's being 'invincible' at 51.3. It seems likely that Cleitarchus gilded the lily by having an oracle from Delphi to the same effect.[25]

The graphic description of the army's exhaustion when it reached the Hyphasis — horses' hooves worn down, weapons red with rust, men in rags and tatters, monsoon rains with thunderings and lightnings, licence to loot granted by A and bounties of corn and cash to the men's wives and children — is entirely typical of an imaginative picture by Cleitarchus. The statement that A harangued his troops in assembly and failed to persuade them is almost certainly unhistorical and due to Cleitarchus' imagining; for in Arrian's account, deriving from Ptolemy and Aristobulus, no such assembly was held, and it was only the commanders who were addressed by A (Arr. 5.25.2 and 5.28.1,2 and 4).[26] This chapter, then, is derived from Cleitarchus. And so are sections 1–2 of the next chapter, 95, with its childish development of the theme of the twelve altars (in Arr. 5.29.1) into an elaborate encampment with giant beds and enlarged mangers and dedication of the twelve altars to the twelve gods of the Greek pantheon, which is probably unhistorical.[27]

In 95.3 and 5 and in 96.1 we have resumptions of passages in 89.4–6 which were drawn from Diyllus (see p. 62 above). The careful details of the reinforcements and supplies in 95.4 are typical of Diyllus.[28] So too the details of the fleet in 95.5. The naming of the two cities of 89.6 now, on A's return from the Hyphasis, is probably correct; for one was named after A's horse Bucephalas, which had died 'not immediately after the battle against Porus but later' (PA 61.1).

At 96.2 the Sibi are said to be descendants of those with Heracles who had 'failed in the siege' of Aornis (τῆς μὲν πολιορκίας ἀποτυχόντων). The implication is that Heracles and his men had failed because they found the rock to be impregnable, and this too is the implication of Arrian's words at 4.28.1 (οὐδὲ Ἡρακλεῖ τῷ Διὸς ἀλωτὸν γενέσθαι τὴν πέτραν). But at 85.2 D. had said that Heracles gave up his desire to besiege the rock because of earthquakes and signs in the sky from Zeus; in other words Heracles never attempted the siege and this is not a case of A exceeding Heracles in physical achievement. It is clear, then, that D. used a different source at 96.2 from that which he had used at 85.2: that is, Diyllus at 96.2 and Cleitarchus at 85.2, as we have argued on p. 53 above.

Chapter 97 begins with a different geography for the rivers from that which D. had had hitherto. At 96.2 A reached the confluence of the Acesines and the Hydaspes before campaigning against the Sibi and the Agalasseis. Now, after these campaigns, A reaches the junction of three rivers — Acesines, Hydaspes and Indus. This is nonsensical. D., it seems, has changed his source, from Diyllus to Cleitarchus. Thus D. drew from Cleitarchus the sensational accounts which follow: the terrific rapids, the sinking of two warships, others driven ashore (all much exaggerated as compared with Arr. 6.5.3–4), the near-drowning of A in his 'contest with the river like Achilles' (not in Arrian) and his Friends swimming alongside.

In 98–99.4 there are many features typical of Cleitarchus: very high numbers, incorrect geography,[29] the wounding of A being foretold (not in Arrian), the rebuking of the seer by A and A's disregard of his advice (inconsistent with A's piety and respect for seers), A's ambition to take the city with himself in the lead (see p. 21 above on 60.1), the preliminary *aristeia* of A (not in Arr. 6.9.1), the conversion of A's mistaken impression (Arr. 6.9.3) into a fact (98.5), the tree in the citadel helping A (not in Arrian), the description of A as alone (compare Arr. 6.9.3–4 and 6.10.1), the many blows on A (only one according to Ptolemy in Arr. 6.11.7), the fight put up by the wounded, kneeling A, the challenging of the Indians by A, Peucestas being on a different ladder (compare Arr. 6.9.3) and the city 'full of corpses'. Such a rhetorical hotting-up of the episode is typical of Cleitarchus. He had a further reason for making so much of it: he attributed the saving of A's life to Ptolemy (*FGrH* 137 F 24 = C. 9.5.21; compare Arr. 6.11.8 who leaves the writer(?)s anonymous). However, Ptolemy himself wrote that he had not been present (Arr. loc. cit.). This lie by Cleitarchus no doubt became notorious and in consequence D. suppressed the name of Ptolemy in his account.[30] D. wrote that Peucestas was 'first' to hold his shield over A, and after Peucestas several others saved A (99.4); one of the 'others' in Cleitarchus' account was Ptolemy.

In 99.5 a report that A had died of his wound, i.e. in 326/5, led to a 'revolt from the Macedonians' by the Greeks settled in Bactria and Sogdia, who had for long been discontented. A revolt at that time but of a different origin and nature and involving settlers 'round Bactra and the borders of Scythia' (i.e. Sogdia) was described by Curtius 9.7.1–11. In 99.6 the rebels 'collected together to the number of 3,000, suffered much on their journey home and were subsequently massacred by the Macedonians after the death of Alexander', i.e. in or after winter 323/2. In Curtius 9.7.11 one leader and some rebels reached their homeland; but there is no mention of a massacre. In fact it is practically certain that D. is in error; for a gap of three years between the rising and the massacre is nonsensical, and the massacring of 3,000 men once home in Greece and scattered to their cities is incredible. The best explanation is that D. himself has added the massacre here as a throwback from his next book, 18.7.1, where a massacre did occur not in Greece but in 'the upper satrapies of Asia';[31] in fact D. has made a hash of it. Next, since the long account in 18.7 says that the Greeks did not revolt until A was dead, the source of 18.7 cannot have been the source of 17.99.5. Thus I should be inclined to attribute 99.5 to Cleitarchus and 99.6 to D., and it is usual to regard Hieronymus as the source of 18.7.

In 100–101 the story of Coragus and Dioxippus is told at such length that it can hardly have come from Diyllus' general history of a period covering some seventy years. Rather, it is from Cleitarchus, whose anti-Macedonian feelings appear in D.'s narrative: the Macedonians drink too much (100.1–2; 101.3–4), they and their king gang up against the Greek (100.4; A's annoyance at 101.1), the Macedonians' trick of hiding a gold tankard beneath Dioxippus' pillow and the suicide of Dioxippus to avoid a disgrace which had been engineered by the Macedonians. Moral comments of a childish nature are added: 'Chance' did not let Dioxippus boast of his victory for long (101.2), he was a fool to engage in single combat and much more of a fool to end his life (101.4), he was an example of much brawn and little brain (101.5), A did not use Dioxippus when he had him, and he missed him when he had gone — a reflection similar to that made on the death of Charidemus at 30.6, a passage ascribed to Cleitarchus as source; and A appreciated his valour when it was too late (101.6). These comments originated with Cleitarchus and were readily adopted by D. Cleitarchan too is the epic *theomachia*, with the combatants representing Ares and Heracles.

In 102 the advance of A is recorded with a brevity which is due to D. himself. Since the number of 'barbarians' in the kingdom of Sambus who were killed by A, namely 'over

80,000', at 102.6 is the same as that given by Cleitarchus (*FGrH* 137 F 25), there is a strong presumption that D. is using Cleitarchus. This is strengthened by the very high numbers of troops (102.2), the description of the cities as 'democratic' with a council of Elders (102.2-3), the alarm at the strange and paradoxical appearance of the fleet and the 'great gifts and heroic honours' paid to A; for there is an element of sensationalism even in this abbreviated version by D. In 103 the wounding of not a few Macedonians with poisoned arrows leads to a description of the making of the poison and its effect on those who were poisoned, a description which is more appropriate to the long work of Cleitarchus than to the general history of Diyllus. The dream of A, (borrowed perhaps from the famous dream of Pericles and, if so, fictitious), the curing of Ptolemy 'which some attributed to divine providence' (103.7) and the high praise of Ptolemy 'loved by all for his valour and his exceedingly great service to all men' — these are to be attributed to Cleitarchus whose patron Ptolemy was.[32] They may have been pure invention; for Arrian, using Ptolemy and Aristobulus as his sources, did not report the affair, which one would have expected Ptolemy to have recorded, if it had happened.

At 104.1 on sailing out into Ocean A supposed that he had 'ended' the expedition he had undertaken (ὑπέλαβεν τετελευτηκέναι τὴν προκεχειρισμένην στρατείαν). However, at 95.1 in a passage attributed tentatively to Cleitarchus A was made to fix at the Hyphasis 'the limits' of the expedition (κρίνας . . . τοὺς ὅρους θέσθαι τῆς στρατείας).[33] We should then regard the source of 104.1 as someone other than Cleitarchus. The account of the sacrifices on the two islands is correct, in that Arrian made A sacrifice there; and the casting of many large gold cups into the sea is paralleled by Arrian having A cast into the sea a golden *phiale* and golden bowls (6.19.4-5). The building of altars to Tethys and Ocean was no doubt intended to mark the end of the expedition (for Ocean was at the eastern end of Asia in A's belief), and there is an analogy for these deities in the sacrifices to Thetis,

Nereus, the Nereids and Poseidon before the battle of Issus in *POxy* 1798 (*FGrH* 148) F 1,44, Col. II. The comparison of the constitutions of Pattala and Sparta with their two kings, two royal houses, military command by two kings and the supremacy of the Gerusia is both precise and brief in the manner of Diyllus, who may have obtained the information from Onesicritus (*FGrH* 134 F 24, seeing analogies between the kingdom of Musicanus and Sparta). It is probable that Diyllus is the source behind 104.1–2.

Consideration of 17.104–118

The account in 104.4–7 of the campaigning in the region between Pattala and Oreitis has some peculiar features: a confused geography, the narration at length of one incident only, and much emphasis on looting and killing. Thus the region is 'a large territory', and within it apparently are the Abritae (i.e. Arabitae) and the Gedrosians; and beyond it 'a great area of waterless country and no small desert' before one reaches the frontier of Oreitis. In reality the region is not so large and the only people in it, the Arabitae, were not won over (as D. asserts) but fled into the desert according to Arr. 6.21.3–4. The incident which D. describes was a tripartite attack on the Oreitae; and the three forces, commanded by Ptolemy, Leonnatus and A, took enormous booty and killed 'many tens of thousands'. It is not clear where this incident fits into Arrian's acount, if it fits at all. But if it is identified with Arr. 6.21.4 fin.,[34] its result was that 'those who resisted were cut down by the cavalrymen and many were taken alive'. The result of the operation in D. is the destruction of 'the tribes' (? of the Oreitae), the terrorisation of the neighbouring peoples and their submission to A. In Arrian there is no such result; indeed in his account the Oreitae and the Gedrosians mustered in defence of a defile elsewhere (6.22.1), and after some negotiation they were granted immunity from harm by A.

Without any doubt Arrian, using Ptolemy and Aristobulus as his sources, gives the correct account of A's movements and the results. The source of D. is incorrect, and in addition he has magnified the importance of the tripartite attack (if it occurred at all) far beyond its historical value. There are some pointers to Cleitarchus as the source of D. here: the confused geography, the emphasis on looting by the troops, and the huge figure for enemy casualties. Further, if Cleitarchus is the source, we may see an explanation for the blowing-up of this incident in the mention of Ptolemy as the first-named commander; perhaps Cleitarchus had his patron win special distinction and praise. It seems, then, most likely that Cleitarchus is the source behind 104.4–7.

The strange funerary customs of the Oreitae in 105.1–2 and the primitive ways of the Gedrosian maritime people in 105.3–5 receive the type of description which we have already ascribed to Cleitarchus as source. In the second description there are points which recur in a fragment of Cleitarchus (*FGrH* 137 F 27, their only food being fish which they tear with their nails and bake in the sun). Arrian's account, based on Nearchus, mentions the same points as Cleitarchus does (*Ind.* 29.9 and 12), and it is possible that Onesicritus did likewise. What rules out Nearchus and Onesicritus as sources of 105.3–5 is that they knew that A did not visit these people; and they would not have told their contemporaries that he had done so. It was Cleitarchus, then, who brought A to meet these fish-eaters; and D. has preserved Cleitarchus' inaccuracy in saying that the 'scales' of whales were used as roof-tiles.

After passing through the territory of the fish-eaters (allegedly) A's army entered the desert (105.6) where there were none 'of life's necessities'; and 'when many were being destroyed by the lack [i.e. of local food and water] the army of the Macedonians was despondent and A fell into no ordinary grief and anxiety'. However, A arranged for supplies to be brought from neighbouring areas. 'At first A lost many of the soldiers through the unrelieved lack [of supplies], and after that when he was himself on the march some of the Oreitae attacked those who were posted with Leonnatus, killed many and escaped to their own territory' (105.8).

'Having crossed the desert with difficulty' (μόγις), A found plentiful supplies and held a seven-day revel with his army dressed for the part in honour of Dionysus, he himself indulging in drunkenness and potations as he went along (106.1 μέθῃ καὶ πότοις χρώμενος κατὰ τὴν ὁδοιπορίαν).

In this account the crossing of the Gedrosian desert cost 'many' lives. In terms of the language D. uses it was comparable to the attack of the Oreitae on the forces of Leonnatus. It is not portrayed by D. as the disaster which it was to become in the accounts of Strabo 722 and PA 66. The attack by the Oreitae is not mentioned elsewhere. On the other hand, Arrian says that Leonnatus was crowned with a golden crown by A for his victory 'over the Oreitae and the neighbouring barbarians' (Arr. 7.5.5, quelling a rebellion, and Ind. 42.9), a victory in which Leonnatus lost fifteen cavalry and a few infantry and the enemy lost 6,000 killed (Ind. 23.5). The source of D. may have been describing the effect of the rebellion before Leonnatus quelled it; but, if so, he certainly exaggerated the losses of Leonnatus' troops and in making the Oreitae escape to their own land he concealed the Oreitae's subsequent defeat. As regards the seven-day revel Arrian remarked that it was not recorded at all by Ptolemy and Aristobulus or 'by any other author that one might consider to be a reliable witness' (6.28.2). He regarded it as a fabrication. The source of D., then, was in Arrian's opinion untrustworthy in this matter, and he might well have been Cleitarchus. There are two points in favour of Cleitarchus: the earlier Dionysiac 'komos' at Persepolis (72) and the drunkenness[35] then were derived, as we have seen, from Cleitarchus; and a penchant for seven days appeared in 85.6, a passage ascribed to Cleitarchus as source. Thus the probability is high that 105.6 – 106.1 were inspired by Cleitarchus.

The misconduct of many satraps and generals and the punishment of them (106.2–3) are a topic which D. might have obtained from any source. The sensational arrival of Nearchus and his meeting with the King in the theatre during a dramatic festival, the report then and there of

Nearchus' experiences, the thunderous applause by the Macedonians and the indescribable joy spreading through the whole theatre — these have all the panache of Cleitarchus. The meeting is placed at 'a coastal town called Salmous' and the fleet sailed up to it.[36] The description by Nearchus of his meeting with A, as retold by Arrian, is entirely different in every respect (Arr. 6.28.5 and *Ind.* 33.2 – 35). Our source in D. was romancing, and he even put the meeting on the coast for dramatic effect. Part of the (alleged) report in the theatre at Salmous was about the tides and the whales (106.6–7), and the effect of the tides was much exaggerated. It is all very appropriate to Cleitarchus.

At 104.3 A's orders to Nearchus had been 'to sail along the whole coast through Ocean and after observing everything to meet A at the mouth of the Euphrates'. This use of 'Ocean' to represent the sea which in Greek belief surrounded the floating land-mass of Europe, Asia and Libya is not found in Arrian who speaks of 'the sea off India' or 'the great sea'. The first part of the orders was fulfilled when Nearchus (allegedly) reached Salmous not far from the mouth of the Persian Gulf;[37] their arrival is that of the mission 'sent to sail along the coast through Ocean' (106.4). Now at 107.1 A ordered the commanders of the fleet 'to put in towards the mouth of the Euphrates ' (ἐπὶ τὸν Εὐφράτην καταπλεῦσαι), i.e. to fulfil the second part of the orders issued at 104.3. It seems, then, that 104.3, 106.4 and 107.1 should be attributed to the same source, namely Cleitarchus.

In the same section, 107.1, the story of the 'paradoxical' death of Calanus is introduced. It was no doubt a commonplace topic in the Alexander-historians, being related by Nearchus (*FGrH* 133 F 4 = Arr. 7.3.6), Onesicritus (*FGrH* 134 F 17 and F 18) and Chares of Mitylene (*FGrH* 125 F 19a). Here it is told briefly and the best clue to the source is in the final comment: 'of the bystanders some judged him mad, others vainglorious in his endurance, and yet others admired his courage and contempt for death'. It seems typical of Cleitarchus to report the worst interpretation first.

In 107.6 to 108.3 events at Susa are related in an objective manner and with precise detail, for instance, of the recruiting, training and equipment of the 30,000 very young Persians and their performance in a display of weapon-training and drill. Interest in such training was shown at 2.3 in a passage attributed to Diyllus. A chose this force 'of one consistent age group' in order to form a counterpart (ἀντίταγμα) to the Macedonian phalanx. As such counterparts were created in the Hellenistic period, this interpretation would suit Diyllus particularly well.[38] D. mentions too the frequent outcries against A in the assemblies, and it is in passages attributed to Diyllus that assemblies are most frequently mentioned (2.2 and 74.3; and as conducting a trial 80.1–2).[39] The account of Harpalus in 108.4–8 is Athens-centred. He brought two courtesans from Athens,[40] and he benefited the demos of Athens as 'an insurance against the unexpected vagaries of Chance' — this idea having already occurred at 66.1–2, a passage attributed to Diyllus as source. On A's return from the East Harpalus becomes a suppliant of the demos, and distributes to orators speaking in his defence large sums, which led after his death to the condemnation at Athens of Demosthenes and other orators. This concern with Athens, orators and bribery is typical of Diyllus of Athens, as we have seen. I conclude that 107.6 and 108 were drawn from Diyllus.

In 109 the narrative is very concise but informative and detailed. Thus we hear the exceptions to the Exiles Decree, 'except temple-robbers and murderers',[41] the number of veterans (10,000 as in Arr. 7.12.1), and the sum of the soldiers' debts (short of 10,000 talents). The numbers are not inflated: if anything, the sum of the debts may be understated because Arrian cites 20,000 talents as an amount not recorded by Ptolemy and Aristobulus but a λεγόμενον (7.5.3). The mutiny[42] occurs at an 'assembly' (ἐκκλησίαν, characteristic of Diyllus, as we noted just above); the incidents resemble those in Arrian (7.8.3; 7.11.3–5, the tears) and so come from a dependable source; and the conclusion that the Macedonians only with difficulty (μόγις) persuaded

A to become reconciled is one which favours A in that it overestimates the strength of A's position. Thus the likely source is Diyllus.

The same style of narrative continues in 110.1-3 with detailed and not exaggerated figures,[43] and we find the same interest in A's Persian troops and in the purpose of his army-reorganisation as in 108, a chapter which we attributed to Diyllus as source. Details of marches follow, with the number of days (compatible with but not exclusive to Diyllus) down to 110.7. The note of the bilingual descendants of the Boeotians deported by Xerxes shows the interest in Greeks living within the Persian empire which we saw in the cases of the multilated Greeks at 69 and the descendants of Heracles in India in 96.2, both passages being attributed to Diyllus as source. During the resting of the army by Ecbatana A gave dramatic performances and 'continuous drinking parties for his Friends', at which Hephaestion engaged in 'untimely[44] drunkenness', fell ill and died (110.8). This account resembles that of Arrian who mentioned the drinking parties and Hephaestion falling ill in successive sentences (7.14.1), and it is different from that of Plutarch (*Alex.* 72.2) in which, for instance, Hephaestion was under medical treatment before he drank so deeply.[45] This passage, then, comes rather from Diyllus (leaving Cleitarchus to be the source of Plutarch's much more sensational account).

In 111.1-4 the antecedents to what was to become the Lamian War are described. The war itself broke out after A's death and its course is described in book 18, where the antecedents are resumed as in 111.1-4 but at greater length — with one exception, the probably mistaken mention of 'Persian satraps', i.e. of Darius' satraps, reaching Taenarum in the Peloponnese at 111.2. Two alternatives face us. Either D. used a source who wrote annalistically and therefore mentioned the antecedents in their chronological place and resumed them in the year of the war's outbreak; or D. himself made his own extract of the antecedents from a source who described the antecedents and the outbreak of war together after A's death. In either case the author cannot be

Cleitarchus since he ended his history with A's death. If our analysis has been correct so far for book 17, the source is Diyllus, and it will follow that the source at 18.9 is also Diyllus, as has been supposed on different grounds by Schubert 243f. The mistake at 111.2 may be due to Diodorus himself remembering what he had written (and read in his source) at 48. The campaign of A against the Cossaei (111.4–6) is told in the brief and factual style of Diyllus with a mention of the days and important cities founded.[46]

In 112, as A advances towards Babylon, the foreknowledge of A's impending death is conveyed to the reader, just as that of Philip's was at 16.91.3, a passage derived from Diyllus. For the Chaldaeans 'knew the future end of the king in Babylon' (γνόντες τὴν μέλλουσαν γίνεσθαι τοῦ βασιλέως τελευτὴν ἐν Βαβυλῶνι), as the Pythian priestess knew Philip would be killed at the festival like a bull for sacrifice. Philip did not understand the meaning of the oracle; A did and obeyed the Chaldaeans' instructions, until some Greek philosophers and others dissuaded him. Then he entered Babylon and the troops were welcomed 'as before' (i.e. at 64.4).[47] In 113 embassies arrive 'from almost all the inhabited world' (i.e. from Asia, Libya and Europe). Among them are the Carthaginians and the Galatae (probably from countries west of Italy)[48] but not the Romans, whom Cleitarchus did include (*FGrH* 137 F 31).[49] A gave precedence to the sacred envoys, beginning with the Eleans (i.e. from Zeus of Olympia), and he sent them away with fair answers as far as possible. D. concerns himself only with Greek shrines (including that of Ammon at Siwa as such), and gives a favourable view of A's piety and fair dealing; these suggest Diyllus as the source.

In 114 a saying of A about Craterus and Hephaestion is cited, and A's words to Sisygambis are cited for the second time (previously, at 37.6, in a passage attributed to Diyllus as source). The mention of Olympias at 114.3, as at 108.7, is appropriate to an author who wrote also of events which happened after the death of A. The reports of sayings and the citation of a letter at 114.3 are typical of Diyllus, as we have seen at 16 and 37, for instance; they are examples of his concern with the memoirs of kings and generals (*FGrH* 73 T 4). A's order to quench the sacred fire throughout Asia in mourning for Hephaestion, as was customary for the death of a king of Persia, is taken by the masses to be an omen of A's impending death. D. adds that many other 'paradoxical' signs occurred, but he proposes to relate them after what we should call a digression on the funerary arrangements for Hephaestion.

The lengthy description of the monumental grave of Hephaestion is comparable to the even longer description of the funerary car of A in 18.26, and it is most probable that D. obtained both from the same source. If so, the source was not Cleitarchus; for the description of A's car is attached not to his death but to events two years later. It could be Diyllus, but we may doubt whether he would have included two very long descriptions (D.'s being abbreviations of the originals) in his own general history. The probable source is Ephippus, *On the End of Alexander and Hephaestion* (*FGrH* 126).

Other factors in favour of Ephippus are the attention to the extravagant gifts by A's associates[50] at D. 115.1 and 5 (as in Ephippus F 5) and the sensational exaggerations which occur in D.'s account. Thus the total cost of the funeral of Hephaestion, 'they say', exceeded 12,000 talents (115.5); but Arrian gave 10,000 as the standard version (so P*A* 72.5), 'but some said even more'.[51] At 115.6 D. says that A ordered worship of Hephaestion as a $\vartheta\epsilon\grave{o}\varsigma\ \pi\rho\acute{o}\epsilon\delta\rho o\varsigma$ (usually emended to $\pi\acute{a}\rho\epsilon\delta\rho o\varsigma$);[52] but Arrian said that most writers reported that A ordered worship of Hephaestion 'as a hero' (7.14.7). At 115.6 D. has a 'chance' oracle from Ammon[53] that Hephaestion was to be worshipped as a god. This too is different from the normal account of a majority of authors, that Ammon was asked but refused permission for Hephaestion to be worshipped as a god (Arr. 7.14.7). Thus it appears that D. did not give the account of even the minority of writers but of an extreme case. This is appropriate to Ephippus who wrote with hyperbole and venom, to judge from his fragments. We conclude, then, that the digression in 115 was inspired by Ephippus.

At 116.1 come the signs promised at 114.5. They arrive when A seemed to be at the height of his power and divine blessing (δοκοῦντος ἰσχύειν τότε πλεῖστον καὶ μάλιστ᾽ εὐδαιμονεῖν). 'Fate' too was at work (probably D.'s own contribution, as at 16.1.5).[54] The first sign, an Oriental prisoner slipping his bonds miraculously and putting on A's clothes and diadem, had an obvious interpretation. The seers advised A to execute the prisoner in order to direct the bad omen onto the prisoner's head (116.4), and A sacrificed his clothing to the evil-averting deities. But A was alarmed, feeling he had been ill advised to disregard the warning of the Chaldaeans (this refers back to 112.5, a passage ascribed to Diyllus as source). A second omen follows. The diadem falls from his head into a lake and is recovered by one of his oarsmen who put it on his own head as he swam back to the boat. This happened at the end of three nights and three days (a mystic number), during which A had lost his way. A consulted the seers (116.7), who told him to sacrifice to the gods. Instead, A went to hold a 'komos' (a party in honour of Dionysus) with Medius the Thessalian (117.1).

The first story is similar to but not identical with a story told by Aristobulus which Arrian reported (7.24.1–3 = FGrH 139 F 58); for D. adds a plausible occasion (A anointing himself), A stripped of his clothes, the prisoner's fetters loosening of their own accord (αὐτομάτως), the prisoner putting on A's clothes, the execution of the prisoner, the sacrifice of the clothing, and the reference back to the Chaldaeans.[55] The second story is related also by Arrian as a λόγος, i.e. not verified by Ptolemy and Aristobulus (7.22.2–5). According to Arrian the event occurred in a lake near the tombs of the Assyrian kings and the diadem floating off settled on a reed near a tomb, this being an omen in itself; it is some of the flotilla and not A who lost the way in the lake; the diadem is knocked off by a wind, not by branches overhead; and the fate of the sailor is added. The story was told by many historians (7.22.4). D.'s version had some minor variations from that reported by Arrian. From whom did D. obtain his versions? Both Diyllus and Cleitarchus reported omens and oracles, as we have seen at 16.91–92 (Diyllus) and 17.10 (Cleitarchus). But the particular additions in D.'s two stories smack rather of Cleitarchus, since they add to the sensational effect: A stripped, fetters loosened miraculously, the prisoner dressing up in A's clothes, the execution of the prisoner and the sacrifice of the clothes; and A losing his way for three days and nights (compare three months at 10.4), A despairing of his life, and the unexpected salvation of himself and his diadem (which ironically may have raised A's hopes in the unabbreviated version).

In 116.7 – 117.1 A is represented as failing to carry out 'the magnificent sacrifices recommended by the seers'. But in Arrian's account, deriving from Ptolemy and Aristobulus, A made 'the customary sacrifices and also some recommended by the seers' (7.24.4 ἐκ μαντείας). Here Arrian is likely to be correct, since A was punctilious in religious matters and on this occasion had himself consulted the seers, and D. is likely to be incorrect. The purpose of D.'s source was no doubt to suggest that A's neglect brought divine retribution upon him for his impiety; and this suggests that Cleitarchus rather than Diyllus was D.'s source at this point.

A's death is attributed to his capping 'much unmixed wine' with a huge beaker in honour of Heracles' death. On swallowing the lot, 'as if he had been struck a hard blow', he cried aloud, groaned and was led away by the arm (117.1–2). After much pain A despaired of life, took off his ring and gave it to Perdiccas; but he had enough breath to make two remarks (117.4, both *obiter dicta* in fact). This account is not true; for the correct version was preserved in the *Ephemerides*[56] from which Arr. 7.25f. and PA 76 gave their narratives. Plutarch indeed refers to the version which we read in D. as untrue (75.5). He writes,

The fever did not come upon him after he had quaffed a 'bowl of Heracles', nor after he had been seized with a sudden pain in the back, as though smitten with a spear; these particulars certain writers [τινες] felt obliged to give, and so, as it were, invented in tragic fashion a moving finale for a great action. But Aristobulus says that he had a

raging fever, and that when he got very thirsty he drank wine, whereupon he became delirious, and died on the thirtieth day of the month
Daesius.   (Transl. B. Perrin)

The most likely candidate for the invention of this sensational finale is certainly Cleitarchus; indeed his name has
been cited without question as the author of the account.[57]
But he was not alone: Ephippus of Olynthus (*FGrH* 126 F 3)
and Nicobule (*FGrH* 127 F 1 and F 2) also attributed A's
death to excessive drinking, and they have their followers in
modern times.

So died A, says D. and adds his own meed of praise
(117.5). But he cannot resist appending another version,
that of poison, engineered by Antipater in his hatred of
Olympias.[58] According to D. 118.2 this story was not
published by historians until after the death of Cassander,
which was in 287 B.C. (so too C. 10.10.18–19).[59] The most
likely author writing after that date is Hieronymus of Cardia,
who is generally regarded as D.'s chief source in books 18
and 19, and it is in 19.11.8 that we find the clearest indication that Antipater's sons were held responsible for A's
death. Thus it seems that D. described the death of A as due
to drinking and went straight on to the death of Sisygambis
in his original draft; but then he added from perhaps Hieronymus the other version, putting it between the death of A and
that of Sisygambis. In the original draft the order was logical;
for A's achievements had exceeded those of all kings of the
past and of all men down to the time of D. (117.5), and one
of these achievements was in D.'s opinion A's treatment of
Sisygambis and the other captive women (38.4). It was thus
sensible to conclude the narrative of the book as follows.
'Sisygambis, the mother of Darius, mourned deeply for
the end of A and for her own desolation. Being close to the
limit of her life she abstained from food and on the fifth
day she died, yielding up her life in pain but not without
glory.' Perhaps it was Diyllus, having described the decency
(ἡ ἐπιείκεια) of A towards the Persian women, who chose
to end his book on Alexander's life with these or similar
words.[60]

Summary of attributions

As in chapter 1, I append a list of the suggested sources for convenience of reference:

64.1–4	To Babylon			Cleitarchus	
64.5 – 67.1	To Susa		Diyllus		
67.2 – 69.1	To Araxes			Cleitarchus	
69.2–9	Mutilated Greeks			Cleitarchus	
70–73.3	Persepolis			Cleitarchus	
73.4	Darius alive	D. (from ? Ps.-Callisthenes)			
73.5–6	Sparta		Diyllus		
74	Allies dismissed		Diyllus		
75	Hyrcania			Cleitarchus	
76	Bucephalas	Unallocated			
77	Amazon; harem			Cleitarchus	
78	Drangiane	Unallocated			
79–80	Philotas plot		Diyllus		
81	Ariaspi		Diyllus		
82	Paropanisadae			Cleitarchus	
83	Erigyius; Bessus			Cleitarchus	
lacuna	Sogdians			Cleitarchus	
84	Massaga			Cleitarchus	
85	Aornis			Cleitarchus	
86	Taxiles			Cleitarchus	
87–89.3	Porus			Cleitarchus	
89.4–6	Fleet and cities		Diyllus		
90–95.2	To Hyphasis			Cleitarchus	
95.3 – 96	To Agalasseis		Diyllus		
97–99.5	Malli			Cleitarchus	
99.6	The 3,000 Greeks	D.			
100–101	Dioxippus			Cleitarchus	
102–103	To Harmatelia			Cleitarchus	
104.1–2	Pattala		Diyllus		
104.3 – 105.2	Orcitis			Cleitarchus	
105.3–5	Fish-eaters			Cleitarchus	
105.6 – 106.1	Gedrosia			Cleitarchus	
106.2–7	Carmania			Cleitarchus	
107.1–5	Calanus			Cleitarchus	
107.6 – 108	Susa; Harpalus		Diyllus		
109–110	To Ecbatana		Diyllus		
111	To Cossaei		Diyllus		
111.2	Persian satraps	D.			
112–113	Babylon		Diyllus		
114	Hephaestion's death		Diyllus		
115	Funeral of Hephaestion				Ephippus
116	Omens			Cleitarchus	
117.1–4	A's death			Cleitarchus	
117.5	Note	D.			
118.1–2	Poison	D. (from ? Hieronymus)			
118.3	Sisygambis		Diyllus		
118.4	Finis	D.			

Some general conclusions

The general conclusion of chapters 1 and 2 is that D. used Diyllus (as in the latter part of book 16) throughout book 17 for the backbone of the narrative but not for the great occasions in A's career. For these he preferred to draw on Cleitarchus: for spectacular sieges (Thebes, Halicarnassus, Tyre, Massaga, Aornis and the city of the Malli), set battles

(Granicus, Issus, Arbela, Porus), daring deeds (Marmara, Agis' death, Erigyius, Dioxippus, Calanus), and colourful happenings (visit to Siwa, Alexandria in Egypt, Persepolis, the Amazon's visit, mutiny at the Hyphasis, the rapids of the Indian rivers, the 'komos' in Carmania, the meeting of Nearchus and A in the theatre, the death of A etc.). D. drew also on Cleitarchus for the description of outlandish places, customs and fauna. He made no effort to correlate the viewpoints of Diyllus and Cleitarchus but left their very different attitudes to life and to A side by side. He used Diyllus more in the first part than in the second part of the book.

D. contributed very little of his own: a simple-minded proem, praise of A for his treatment of the Persian women, praise of Alexandria, two variant versions (73.4 and 118.1–2) culled from elsewhere, minor additions (e.g. 7.4–7) or cross-references, some errors and a sequel (118.4). He did, of course, add a stylistic veneer but in sympathy with his sources. Thus the factual, detailed narrative of Diyllus remained largely unvarnished in D.'s version; but a rhetorical passage in Diyllus, for instance 69.2–9, seems to be reproduced with many of Diyllus' prose rhythms and with some of D.'s own clichés.[61] On the other hand, the richer rhetorical style of Cleitarchus was more to D.'s own taste. Cleitarchus' descriptions were reproduced probably with little alteration (e.g. 82.2–5, the land of the Paropanisadae); but when it was a matter of set battles and thrilling events D. was carried away and deployed his own rhetorical gambits. Even so, the veneer of D.'s own style and vocabulary in these passages does not hide the style and the animus of the original.

That this should be so is not surprising if we bear in mind one clear example where we have both D.'s original source and D.'s version. After the discovery of the *Hellenica Oxyrhynchia* attributed to 'P', I. A. F. Bruce wrote as follows. 'Diodorus, most notably, reproduces much of the substance of P's history by reason of his recourse to Ephorus as a source; in all the passages of Diodorus which are parallel to the extant fragments of P there can be no doubt that the narrative of the former derives ultimately from that of the latter.' This is apparent, for instance, if we compare *Hell. Oxy.* 6.4–6 and D. 14.80.2–4 for the battle of Sardis. The nature and the substance of P have both survived the abbreviations and mistakes made first by Ephorus as intermediary and then by Diodorus.[62] Again, we have instances where D. was using an extant source directly. Thus when we compare D. 31.10.1–2 and 31.12 with Polybius 29.21.1-9 and 29.22, we see that D. adhered closely to his source and tended, if anything, merely to exaggerate the views of the source.[63]

The close study of this book has raised one's opinion of Diyllus. In book 16 the conciseness and the accuracy of the account of the Social War (7.3; 21–22) were overshadowed by some rhetorical passages, which were based on the Attic orators (54–55 and 84), and by the graphic description of Philip's end (91–94). But in book 17 it is the conciseness and the accuracy of the narrative which predominate, together with a remarkable care for detail extending even to medical supplies; and only an occasional passage in which Diyllus gave rein to his form of rhetorical embellishment is included by D. Indeed it is the parts of book 17 which derive from Diyllus that are of historical value. On a different plane from that of accurate recording Diyllus was interested in the reasons for A's success. As he saw them, much was due to A's ability to win the loyalty of the Macedonians by his generosity, oratory and firmness. He appreciated the purposes of A's organisation and training of his troops, both European and Asiatic, and the importance of leadership and discipline. He portrayed A as generous towards the mutilated Greeks; emotional and moved to tears; deeply religious and respectful of seers, whether Greek or Oriental;[64] and constitutionally correct in his dealings with the Macedonians, with his Greek allies and with the Council of the Greek League.

To what date did Diyllus carry his general history? It began with the profanation of Delphi in 357/6 (*FGrH* 73 T 1), reached an event of 316/5 in the ninth book (F 1) and consisted of twenty-six books in all (T 1 and T 3). Even if we postulate more crowded years in the later books, we can hardly put the events of the last book any earlier than the later 280s. That sort of closing date is suggested by D.'s mention of Diyllus ending and of Psaon starting after him in a fragment of book 21, a book which spanned the period *c.* 301–281. We may assume, then, that he was still writing in the 270s (as Schubert suggested; see n. 24 to chapter 1). He was thus in a position to have read the works of all the Alexander-historians, including the most recent, the work of Ptolemy. Indeed we have seen that D.'s figures for A's army at the crossing into Asia were derived through Diyllus from Ptolemy's work. And that he did read the memoirs of Aristobulus and Ptolemy is to be expected also from Plutarch's statement that Diyllus was one of those historians who 'set out the achievements of generals and kings and immersed himself in their memoirs' (T 4). Because he was so well read, Diyllus was able to include an impressive amount of detail in his narrative (e.g. if we compare 64.5 – 66.2 with Arr. 3.16.3–11), and as far as we can judge from the passages in D. which we have ascribed to Diyllus as source, Diyllus did not make any use of the work of Cleitarchus.

The descriptions of outlandish places and customs which derive from Cleitarchus are of value because they came ultimately from participants in the campaigns. But even here one has to beware of exaggerations introduced by Cleitarchus, e.g. of the size of whalebones or the behaviour of monkeys. In narrative passages derived from Cleitarchus there are so many examples of inaccuracy, exaggeration and fiction that one has to look at everything with a critical eye. Details are added for verisimilitude, numbers are wildly exaggerated, and episodes are freely invented. This is not to deny that there *may* be much that is correct in the descriptions, for instance, of the siege of Tyre, where Cleitarchus could have met and talked with reliable eyewitnesses; but all too often his descriptions of the sacking of cities, the pillaging of the countryside, the crises of battle, the massacre or enslaving of huge numbers have the air of rhetorical pieces. It is no accident that Cicero, Strabo (e.g. 505), Curtius (e.g. 9.5.21), Quintilian, Plutarch and Arrian distrusted him as a liar or, as we might say, regarded him as a writer of historical fiction; and their opinions, since they knew his work at first hand and *in toto*, are certainly to be accepted by us who lack those advantages. Cleitarchus' attitude to A is the antithesis of that of Diyllus. He regards A as afraid of his Macedonians, treacherous and dishonourable in war, vicious in his rages, implacable in his hatreds, and ruthless in achievement, and favoured by the gods to become the invincible conqueror of the inhabited world, a destiny which A failed to fulfil through his excessive drunkenness. This baroque characterisation has failed to carry conviction with most modern scholars.

If our analysis is correct, some light is shed on the sequence of the Alexander-historians. Whenever Ptolemy wrote his book, he must have commanded the respect of his contemporaries both as a king in whom lying would be dishonourable (so Arrian in his preface, and no doubt others) and as a high-ranking participant in the campaigns — and particularly in Alexandria in Egypt, where Cleitarchus lived, enjoying the King's favour. Now Curtius wrote that Cleitarchus described Ptolemy as present at the city of the Malli (9.5.21), and that this showed Cleitarchus' lack of concern for the truth ('securitas'). And Arrian in giving a list of inaccuracies included this instance without naming Cleitarchus (6.7.8). The record was put straight by Ptolemy who denied in his history that he had been present at all (*FGrH* 138 F 26). To suppose that Ptolemy wrote first, emphasising he had been elsewhere at the time, and that Cleitarchus, writing later, went out of his way to declare that Ptolemy had been there and had saved A's life seems to be very far-fetched; yet some scholars have thought this to be actually probable.[65] However, now that we can compare Cleitarchus' account as abbreviated by D. with Ptolemy's (and ? Aristobulus') account as abbreviated by Arrian, we see that there were many trivial differences (see p. 65), which, if Cleitarchus had been writing after Ptolemy, it would have been absurd for him to introduce. Again, at 83.7–9 we have the counterpart; for Ptolemy wrote of his own part in capturing Bessus (138 F 14), but D.'s version drawn from Cleitarchus, 83.7–9, not only does not mention Ptolemy at all but even attributes the coup to Bagodaras and other Persians. Here too Cleitarchus must have written before Ptolemy did. So too in describing the end of Bessus at 83.9 (as compared with Arr. 3.30.3–5).

The relationship between Cleitarchus and Aristobulus emerges from the same incident. Cleitarchus did not mention Ptolemy at all in this affair (83.7–9); it was Bagodaras and his colleagues who arrested Bessus and brought him to A (συλλαβόντες τὸν Βῆσσον ἀπήγαγον πρὸς τὸν Ἀλέξανδρον). Aristobulus, however, said that the (Persian) entourage of Spitamenes and Dataphernes 'brought Bessus to Ptolemy' and handed him over to A (FGrH 134 F 24 = Arr. 3.30.5). Thus Cleitarchus wrote before Aristobulus did; otherwise he would have picked up Aristobulus' mention of Ptolemy and given Ptolemy a puff. Then too the differences between Cleitarchus' version of the lost diadem at 116.2–4 and Aristobulus' version of the same affair (FGrH 134 F 58 = Arr. 7.24.1–3) are best explained if Cleitarchus published first; for if Cleitarchus had had before him the account by Aristobulus, who was a participant and a confidant of A, he would not have chosen to write so different an account. So also the account of A's death by Cleitarchus was surely composed before that of Aristobulus, who mentioned the raging fever and then the wine which made A delirious (FGrH 134 F 59 = PA 75.6), and before that of Ptolemy, who (I believe) cited the relevant part of the King's Journal.[66]

The conclusion that Cleitarchus published before Aristobulus and Ptolemy is certainly compatible with the evidence concerning the latter writers. 'Aristobulus is said to have lived into his nineties; and he began to write his history when he was in his eighty-fifth year, as he himself states at the beginning of his work' (FGrH 139 T 3). On Jacoby's calculation of his probable date of birth Aristobulus cannot have begun to write before 291.[67] The case of Ptolemy is more complicated, but it is generally agreed that he wrote in the last years of his life, which ended in 283/282.[68] When Cleitarchus started to write, perhaps soon after the death of A, the only published work about A was the official history of Callisthenes for the years 334 to c. 330, and it was disliked and distrusted in Greek circles for its adulation of A. The records and the memories of various participants in A's campaigns — surveyors, court officials, and officers such as Onesicritus and Nearchus — were mostly published before *c*. 310 and provided a rich variety of anecdotes, episodes, facts and fancies, and attitudes towards A. None of them, it seems, was a complete history of Alexander's achievements. This was the opportunity of Cleitarchus. He wrote 'a full-length work in at least twelve books',[69] making use of hearsay evidence from participants and of published works, and he provided not for the Macedonians but for the Greeks a sensational, romantic and not too sympathetic account of Alexander's conquests, conduct and personality.[70] It was only later, and perhaps in reaction to his work, that Aristobulus and Ptolemy[71] gave accounts which they claimed to be nearer to the truth.

Any historian who studies this book of Diodorus has to separate the grain from the chaff. As we have seen, the passages ascribed to Diyllus as source rest on the best evidence available down to and including Ptolemy's account. On the other hand, most of the passages deriving from Cleitarchus are partly or entirely fictional, and we should dismiss as imaginary such items as the dawn crossing of the Granicus river,[72] the priest's string of answers to A at Siwa, the initiative of Thaïs at Persepolis, the revel in Carmania, the meeting of Nearchus and A in the theatre and the destruction of A through drink.

CHAPTER 3

THE SOURCES OF JUSTIN'S ACCOUNT OF
ALEXANDER (9.5.8 – 13.1)

Introduction

Consideration of Justin's sources is complicated by the fact that J. was epitomising the very long work of Pompeius Trogus, *Historiae Philippicae* in forty-four books, which began with the first empire, that of Assyria, and ended with events in the principate of Augustus. As an epitomiser, J. was both ruthless and careless, omitting much and muddling names, as we can see from a comparison of Trogus, *Prologues* with J.'s text. Yet what he has preserved in his epitome does contain the essence of Trogus' narrative, and it does include attitudes and inconsistencies which may be due to Trogus' sources. J.'s account is of particular importance in that it is independent, as we shall see, of the only earlier extant account, that of D. 17, and some topics either appear for the first time (for us) in J. or are more fully treated than in D. 17. Some of these, for instance the allegations that Olympias instigated the assassination of Philip and that Alexander was poisoned, have been treated recently in articles which, in general, have not evaluated the ultimate sources (for example, by E. Badian in *Phoenix* 17 (1963) 244ff. and by A. B. Bosworth in *CQ* n.s. 21 (1971) 112ff.). These topics in particular cannot be properly considered without a study of J.'s source or sources.

While there have been some studies of the sources of J. in a general way, there has been none worthy of the name for the books on A. For the few pages which Tarn devoted to J. 11–12 are really of no significance. He reckoned the sources 'hardly worth considering at all except on one point' (p. 122), this being a portrait of A at 11.11.12, which he attributed to 'the teaching of the Stoics' (p. 123 cf. p. 126). He concluded as follows. 'To talk of sources for this mass of rubbish would be idle; it is merely somebody — perhaps not always

Trogus himself — writing with the flowing pen of the popular historiographer' (p. 124). Yet to identify a bad source is just as important as to identify a good source.

In the course of this chapter I shall refer to chapters 1 and 2 on the sources of D. 17, and I shall do so for convenience in the form e.g. D. 17.15 (Diyllus), by which I mean that I have argued there for the source of that passage being probably Diyllus.[1] On the other hand, I do not usually refer to the later narratives of Curtius, Plutarch and Arrian, which Trogus cannot have used and Justin appears not to have used.

There are four parts to this chapter. J. 9.5.8 – 10; J. 11; J. 12–13.1; and general conclusions.

Consideration of Justin 9.5.8 – 10

In 9.6 J. deals with the assassination of Philip. He starts with the marriage of Philip's daughter and Alexander the Molossian, sets the scene, gives the motives of Pausanias and ends with him obtaining his revenge ('ultionemque . . . exegit'). The account is self-standing and complete. So too is the account in D. 16.93.3 – 94, with which it has many facts in common. Yet the two accounts certainly come from different sources. J. has the bodyguards present and the two Alexanders present, but D. has the bodyguards present and the two Alexanders sent ahead. J. puts the assassination in 'the narrow place', i.e. the *parodos* (so too Trogus, *Prologue* IX. 9) but D. puts it in the *orchestra*. J. makes the assassin Pausanias an 'adulescens' and has him raped 'in primis pubertatis annis', but D. has him a Bodyguard and Friend of Philip and thus a mature and top-ranking officer. J. has him raped by Attalus himself and by Attalus's guests, but D. left the raping to Attalus' grooms. Thus J. and D. followed different sources. So J. (Trogus) used a source other than Diyllus on my interpretation.

In 9.7 J. introduces an addition which is not in narrative form but is introduced by 'creditum est', 'it has been believed' (not 'credebatur', 'it was believed at the time'; cf. 'creduntur'[2] in 9.7.8). By using this expression J. is warning the reader that he himself does not vouch for this supposition as being true in fact. 'It has been believed', he writes, 'that he [Pausanias] had been also incited by Olympias, A's mother, and that A himself had manifestly been ['extitisse'] not unaware of the plan to kill his father.' As J. develops the supposition, it becomes firmer: at 9.7.8 *both* ['utrique'] are believed to have impelled Pausanias', and at 9.7.14 it is the 'crime *committed* by her', i.e. Olympias. On the other hand D. had no mention at all of Olympias and A being involved. However, Plutarch has, in P*A* 10.4; for having described Pausanias' motives as due to his outrageous suffering and his failure to obtain redress, Plutarch says that most of the blame attached to Olympias, since she had given him additional encouragement when he was angry, and had incited him, and that 'a degree of accusation touched A'; for 'he is said' etc. This last expression, λέγεται, shows that Plutarch, like J. (Trogus), did not vouch for the truth of this story.

Why did J. and Plutarch have such reservations? Presumably because the sources in general did not involve Olympias and A in the affair, and because the source which did so was regarded by them with considerable suspicion.

J. supplies motives for the involvement of Olympias and A. She had been angered by Philip's divorce of her ('repudium') and by his preference for his new bride Cleopatra; and A had feared (the possibility of) a brother born to his step-mother (i.e. Cleopatra) being recognised as legitimate and so becoming a rival successor to the throne.[3] 'In their anger over these matters both are believed to have incited Pausanias, discontented as he was by Philip's failure to inflict punishment for the act of rape, to commit so great a crime' (9.7.8).

The essence of the story which J. gives is that the *fons et origo* of Philip's end was Olympias, enraged by divorce and by Philip's preference for Cleopatra. Now only one Hellenistic author is known to have taken this view, Satyrus, who having mentioned the marriage, continued as follows. 'By bringing her [Cleopatra] in alongside Olympias Philip confounded the whole course of his life' (ἅπαντα τὸν βίον τὸν ἑαυτοῦ συνέχεεν FHG III F 5). And it was no doubt with this in mind that Athenaeus who preserved this fragment of Satyrus at 13.557 went on to say at 13.560c that 'even whole houses were overthrown because of married women', and to give as his first instance (meaning Olympias) 'the house of Philip, father of Alexander, because of his marriage to Cleopatra'. Satyrus, then, started this story. As he wrote at a later date than the accepted Alexander-historians and was at variance with them, J. and Plutarch had their own doubts to express, although they could not resist repeating what they suspected was boudoir fiction.

Satyrus is the source used not only for 9.7.1–8 but also for 9.7.9–14, which are tied at 9, 12, 13 and 14 to the story of 1–8. The details in J. are fantastic.[4] 'In the course of the wedding banquet A quarrelled first with Attalus and then with his father, so much so that Philip drew his sword, chased A and was only with difficulty dissuaded from killing his son by the appeals of his Friends.' That Satyrus described a quarrel between Attalus and A is clear from Athenaeus' summary of what Satyrus had written at length.[5] 'Immediately at the very wedding ceremony Attalus said "Now at any rate kings will be begotten who are not bastards but legitimate", and at these words A threw the goblet in his hands at Attalus, and Attalus hurled his tankard at A' (Athenaeus 13.557e). Then at 9.7.10–11 J. attributes to Olympias actions which cannot be historical: her organisation (? from Epirus) of horses for the assassin, her running (? from Epirus) to the funeral of Philip, her crowning of the assassin's corpse with a golden crown on the night of her arrival (? from Epirus), her cremation of the corpse some days later, and her institution of an annual sacrifice by the people in honour of the assassin. Next, she killed Cleopatra's baby girl on her lap and compelled Cleopatra, the cause of Philip having divorced her, to hang herself – thus crowning her revenge which she had begun by killing Philip ('per parricidium').[6] Finally she consecrated the assassin's weapon, a sword, under her own childish name 'Myrtale' to Apollo.[7]

My conclusion is that J. 9.7 and Athenaeus 13.557 were both abbreviating an account by Satyrus, which was much longer. J. chose to mention both quarrels and described the second quarrel; Athenaeus preferred to describe the first quarrel and omitted the second quarrel. If we want both, we turn to Plutarch, who has preserved more of Satyrus in PA 9.3-5. According to Plutarch, Philip's marriages and loves caused disorders in the household and excited the bitter rage of Olympias, and Olympias spurred A on against his father. When Philip fell in love (ἐρασθείς as in Athenaeus) and married Cleopatra, the most open quarrel arose through Attalus, the girl's uncle (the same relationship in Athenaeus). For Attalus asked the Macedonians in their drinking at the wedding (ἐν αὐτοῖς τοῖς γάμοις in Athenaeus, 'in convivio' in J.) to pray for a legitimate heir to the throne from this marriage, whereupon A said 'What of me, you rascal! Do you take me for a bastard?' He then threw his goblet at Attalus (so in J., abbreviated in Athenaeus). Philip drew his sword, rushed at A (so in J.), tripped and fell, whereupon A taunted him.[8] Olympias and A then fled to Epirus, and A went on to Illyria (so too in Athenaeus 557e and J. 9.7.5).

It is at once apparent that the source of 9.6 was different from the source of 9.7 (Satyrus), because the account in 6 was complete in itself and 'the belief' in 7 was a separate matter. We can add some details which confirm this difference of source. At 9.5.9 Olympias was divorced 'on suspicion of having committed adultery'; at 9.7.12 it was Cleopatra who 'drove her out of her marriage with Philip'. At 9.5.9 Cleopatra is the sister of Attalus; in Plutarch and in Athenaeus, drawing on Satyrus, she is the niece of Attalus. Incidentally, the source at 9.7.12 is different from that of 11.2.3; for in the former passage and also in Athenaeus, citing Satyrus, the child of Cleopatra is a girl, and in the latter passage and in Pausanias 8.7.5 it is a boy.[9]

At 9.8.1 J. used yet again a different source. For whereas Satyrus, as cited verbatim by Athenaeus (13.557b), gave Philip a reign of 22 years, J. gave him a reign of 25 years. Moreover, J.'s description of the mother of Arrhidaeus as 'a Larissaean dancing-girl'[10] cannot come from Satyrus (as abbreviated by Athenaeus), since Philip was said by him to have married two Thessalian women 'in order to win the allegiance of the nation of Thessaloi', i.e. women of the leading families of the Thessaloi. Again, J. mentions 'many other sons of Philip'; but Satyrus, as abbreviated by Athenaeus, mentioned no other sons than Arrhidaeus and Alexander but did mention four daughters by name.

A surprising feature throughout J. (Trogus) is the emphasis on the Aeacidae. The Macedonian kings, being Temenidae (Hdt. 8.137.1 and 138.2; Thuc. 2.99.3), claimed descent from Zeus through Heracles and Temenus, and both Philip and A emphasised the importance of Heracles in their ancestry (cf. D. 17.1.5 and P*A* 2.1). A was proud also of being on his mother's side an Aeacides; for whatever her origins on the distaff side she was counted an Aeacid, as later was Beroë (J. 17.3.19), and A regarded Achilles 'the swift-footed Aeacides' as his direct ancestor. In J. 11.4.5, when a Theban implores A to spare the city, he does so on the ground that the Aeacid family – not the Temenid family – traced its origin to Heracles who had been born at Thebes.[11] When A first enters Thessaly in J. 11.3.1, he is made to stress first Philip's services and then descent from the Aeacidae as being common to the Thessaloi and himself; and here the link supplied by Heracles (as mentioned in D. 17.4.1, being from Diyllus) as ancestor to both the Thessalian Aleuadae and the Macedonian kings was disregarded. Then when A lay dying, he is said at J. 12.15.1 to have remarked that he accepted the destiny of his house since most of the Aeacidae had died before reaching the age of thirty – the reference here, as in the case of Thessaly, being to Achilles, the Aeacides *par excellence*. Then at J. 12.16.3 A's achievements are made to confer more honour upon Olympias than the achievements of any of the Aeacidae of the past and of the reigns of her father (Neoptolemus, the Molossian king), her brother (Alexander, the Molossian king) and her husband (Philip). There is clearly a determination to underplay the Macedonian side and to represent A as an Aeacid first and last. The passages where this determination is shown – 11.3.1, 11.4.5, 12.15.1 and 12.16.3 – came from a source who was not a Macedonian but someone hostile to Macedonia. He wrote perhaps when another Aeacid was making or had made his name, Pyrrhus.[12]

Another attempt to underplay the Macedonian element in A's career may be seen in J.'s account of what may be called the serpentine conception. At 12.16.2, just after A's death, J. writes as follows. 'On the night that Olympias conceived him, she seemed in the calm of sleep to roll in the embrace of an enormous serpent, nor was it a dream to deceive her, for assuredly she carried in her womb something more than human mortality.' On the day that the child, Alexander, was born, there were portents: two eagles soaring and settling on the roof of his father's house, signifying the conquest by Alexander of Europe and Asia, and news reaching Philip of two victories, over the Illyrians in battle and over all-comers at Olympia in the chariot race ('quadrigarum currus'),[13] signifying victory by Alexander over the whole world ('universarum terrarum victoriam'). Again, when A was at Siwa, he asked Zeus Ammon about his origin (J. 11.11.2f).

For his mother Olympias had confessed to her husband Philip that she had conceived A not from him but from a serpent of enormous size. Finally almost in the last period of his life Philip had stated openly that A was not his son. On this account he had got rid of Olympias by divorce as having been found guilty of adultery.

In these last words, 'velut stupri conpertam repudio dimiserat,' J. is resuming his earlier words at 9.5.9 'expulsa Alexandri matre Olympiade propter stupri suspitionem', words which referred there to 337 B.C., 'almost in the last period of his life' (11.11.4).

It seems, then, that not only 9.5.9 but also the longer passage at 12.16.2–6 which has the serpentine conception, the Aeacid connection and the portents of A's birth foreshadowing world conquest came from the same source. It is most probable that the source was Cleitarchus. For the enquiry at Siwa and the alleged replies of the god that he was the son not of Philip but of Zeus Ammon and that he would win possession of the world ('possessionemque terrarum dari') have generally been ascribed to Cleitarchus.[14] The god's reply achieved also what A had hoped for, the clearing of Olympias from the charge of adultery ('cupiens . . . simul et matrem infamia liberare' 11.11.6).

We are now able to name 'the source other than Satyrus' for 9.5.8 to 9.6.8 and also for 9.8.1–3 as Cleitarchus. His delight in describing as prostitutes women associated with the Macedonian kings, such as Thaïs at Persepolis, appears in the description of Philip's Larissaean wife as a dancing-girl at 9.8.2. To Cleitarchus we can attribute also the Aeacid connection at 11.3.1, 11.4.5, 12.15.1 and 12.16.3, and the serpentine conception at 11.11.2f. and 12.16.2. We shall resume these passages later.

We come next to J. 9.8.4–12 in which there is a contrast between Philip and Alexander which is highly charged with epigrams. As it incorporates judgements for which the evidence in A's case came later in books 11–12, it may well be a creation by J. himself or by Trogus originally.

When we compare J. 10 with Trogus, *Prologue* X, we can see that J. has omitted a great deal of what was in the account of Trogus, for instance the entire reign of Arses. Even so, where J. 10 overlaps with D. 17.5.3 – 6.3, there are great differences. In J. Darius Codomannus is elected by the people, and there is no mention of palace intrigues; in D. he owes his position primarily to the murderous activities of Bagoas. J. is alone in praising Darius for a long resistance to A 'magna virtute'. What they have in common is the single combat in Cadusia, in which Darius made his reputation for courage – an incident likely to appear in any author. We conclude that J.'s ultimate source was neither D. nor the source of D. (Diyllus on my interpretation).[15] One can propose only on general grounds that Deinon, *Persica*, may well have been the source and that his son Cleitarchus probably covered the overlap of Darius with A.

Consideration of Justin 11

To the period from the death of Philip to the departure of A for Asia J. devotes four chapters, 11.1–4. A comparison shows beyond doubt that Trogus had not obtained his material from the corresponding chapters of D. (17.2.1–3; 3–4; 8–14). The unevenness of content within these chapters is probably due entirely to J.; for the Prologues of Trogus show that Trogus gave much attention to wars and not least to those in the Balkans, whereas J. described the reduction of the rebels in the Balkans and the subjugation of Thebes in three sentences (11.2.4 and 11.3.7) although the mention of Triballi at 11.2.8 indicates that Trogus had described the Balkan campaign in some way. J. is much more interested in political situations, especially in Macedonia and at Athens, and in the pathetic appeal of the Theban Cleadas (11.4.1–6). Thus what J. has put into his epitome does not reveal the proportion of topics in the work of Trogus or in that of the source or sources of Trogus.

However, the strong characteristics of what J. has preserved in 11.1 – 11.4 are due most probably to the attitudes of the original source or sources: an overemphasis on Macedonia's weakness and on widespread discontent in Macedonia and in her empire, which was allayed only by A's tactful diplomacy and his remission of all dues except military service (11.1.1–10): an exaggeration of Athens' leadership (with Sparta coming second) and of Demosthenes' influence in the rising by the Greek states which ended with A's capture of Thebes (11.2.7–9 and 3.3–5): and the reporting of the debate in the Council of the Greek League with references to myths, Persian wars and present miseries (11.3.8 – 11.4.6). That these chapters came ultimately from one source only is strongly indicated by internal links: two allusions to the Aeacidae (11.3.1 and 11.4.5), two allusions to the (false) report of A's death (11.2.8 and 11.4.1) and the pro-Athenian stances (11.2.7 and 11.4.9–11).

We have already attributed to Trogus' use of Cleitarchus the stress on the Aeacid descent of A, as here in 11.3.1 and 11.4.5, and the depreciation of Macedonia, which appears here in 11.1.1–6 and 11.2.7–9. If Cleitarchus is the source also of J.'s account of Thebes, then that account should not be incompatible with the account of Thebes in D. 17.8.2 – 14, which on my analysis[16] was based on the account by Cleitarchus. In fact there are points of similarity: A offers a free pardon (11.3.6 and D. 17.9.4); the extreme sufferings, including rape (11.3.7 and 4.2–4, 'stupris'; and D. 17.13, μετὰ τῆς ἐσχάτης ὕβρεως);[17] Phocians, Plataeans, Thespians and Orchomenians joining in the sack and in the verdict (11.3.8 and D. 17.13.5 with 'some others' in place of 'Phocians').[18] The appeal by Cleadas is not found elsewhere. The sensational and pathetic tone is typical of Cleitarchus, the first of many to write of Thebes destroyed (e.g. Hegesias in *FGrH* 142 F 7, 9, 12, etc). Although the occasion appears to be a meeting of the Council of the Greek League, the appeal is addressed to the King throughout (e.g. 'rogat urbi parcat') and its failure is due to the anger of the King (11.4.7, 'sed potentior fuit ira quam preces'). This anger is a feature of A's attitude to Thebes in D. 17.9.6 (Cleitarchus). The case, then, for accepting Cleitarchus as the ultimate source behind J. 11.1 – 11.4 is very strong.

This case is reinforced by a difference between 11.4.10–12 (Cleitarchus) and the corresponding passage in D. 17.15 (Diyllus). According to J., Athens was ready to go to war rather than accept A's requests and in the end she 'banished her generals ['duces'], who joined Darius and were no small accession to the strength of Persia'.[19] According to Diodorus there was no readiness to go to war, and in the end Demades obtained from A the granting of *all* the requests of Athens. The difference is presumably due to the difference between Cleitarchus and Diyllus.

The preparations of A for the crossing to Asia follow in J. 11.5. The account is entirely different from that in D. 17.16 (Diyllus), and it is thus certain that Trogus did not draw either on Diodorus or on Diyllus. According to J., A killed all those relations of his step-mother whom Philip had promoted, and he did not spare 'his own [relations] who seemed fit for the throne';[20] and he took on service to Asia the more gifted of the tribute-paying kings and left their kingdoms in the hands of sluggish characters. When his army had mustered, he embarked the troops. Then, on seeing Asia from on board his fleet,[21] he was fired with incredible enthusiasm and set up altars to the twelve gods as dedications for the impending war. He divided all his inheritance in Macedonia and Europe among his Friends, declaring he was satisfied with Asia; and his Macedonians, heedless of wives and children,[22] thought only of winning the gold of Persia and the wealth of the entire Orient. Such exaggerated and emotional statements are compatible with Cleitarchus being the source behind 11.5.

Once in Asia A is said by J. 11.5.10–12 to have taken some of the actions which were mentioned in D. 17.1–3 (Diyllus) and as 'reports' ($\lambda\epsilon\gamma\acute{o}\mu\epsilon\nu\alpha$) in Arr. 1.11.7–8 and 12.1. These actions were probably mentioned by all early Alexander-historians, from Callisthenes onwards. In 11.6.1 the idea that Asia was his is adduced to explain A's order to his troops not to engage in pillaging; and this idea again is compatible with the outlook of Cleitarchus.

The numbers of A's forces at the crossing into Asia are given as 32,000 infantry, 4,500 cavalry and 182 warships. The first figure is also in D. 17.17.4 (Diyllus); the second is found there also but only as the incorrect total for the numbers of the individual units; and the third is unique. J.'s numbers did not come from Aristobulus, Ptolemy or Anaximenes, whose recorded figures are different.[23] It is possible that Trogus took the totals for infantry and cavalry from D.'s totals but it is unlikely because he seems not to have been using D. at this stage; rather, it is likely that these figures and that for the battle-fleet were in Cleitarchus. This is made practically certain by the appearance in the next sentence of the 'world-conquest' idea ('hac tam parva manu universum terrarum orbem' etc.), which was a speciality of Cleitarchus at the moment of A's entry into Asia. 'This small band' ('hac tam parva manu') was remarkable for the inclusion of Macedonian veterans, with every file-leader being a sexagenarian (11.6.4–7) and it is such veterans that received their accolade at Halicarnassus in D. 17.27 (Cleitarchus). On the other hand, Darius trusted in his military strength and scorned to use guile (11.6.8–9); and this seems to hark back to the praise of Darius as fighting 'magna virtute' at 10.3.6, which might have come from Cleitarchus as a source.

J. gave very short descriptions of the actual fighting in the three set battles against Persia at 11.6.10–13, 11.9.1–9 and 11.13.1 – 14.7, and he supplied huge numbers on the Persian side and tiny losses on the Macedonian side. As the same characteristics are found in D. and in Plutarch and in what Arrian gave as 'reports' (e.g. 3.8.6), it does not seem possible to distinguish the source or sources used by J. for these battle-passages. Nor is there any clue to the source in such short passages as 11.6.14–15 and 11.7.1–2.[24]

The story of the Gordian knot is told at considerable length and the historical background is supplied; here J. must have more or less reproduced Trogus, who, to judge from the Prologues, was interested in 'origins' and supplied the historical background here. The account in 11.7.3–16 ends with A, unable to find the ends of the knot, cutting it with his sword 'violentius oraculo', from which the reader is expected surely to infer that A lost his temper and did not undo the knot in the way required by the oracle. This ending differs from the account of Aristobulus but agrees with that of 'most' writers (PA 18.2) and of 'some' writers (Arr. 2.3.7). As sources for J. (Trogus) we can exclude the following: Ptolemy and Aristobulus; D., who did not mention the episode, and probably the source D. was using at that stage of his narrative, Diyllus; and perhaps Marsyas 'the Younger' who seems to have had A remove the yoke-pin and let the vine-shoot knot loosen in consequence[25] (FGrH 135/6 F 4); and Callisthenes who would have put a better interpretation on any action by A. This leaves a restricted choice, and Cleitarchus is one of them.[26]

The account in 11.8.3–9 of A's illness at Tarsus contains features which Arrian mentioned only as 'reported' (2.4.7–11). Thus they did not come from Ptolemy or Aristobulus; nor are they found in the shorter account in D. 17.31.4–6

97

(Diyllus). The J. version[27] may well have come from Cleitarchus; but there is no proof. In 11.9.1–11 the speeches and the actions on both sides which are reported by J. do not provide clues to the source or sources.

On the other hand, the dealings of A with the womenfolk of Darius in 11.9.11–16 do. That A alone enters the tent may not be significant, because J.'s account is so short that we cannot exclude the possibility that in the account of Trogus he was accompanied by someone. But the statement, that the women threw themselves down at A's feet and asked that their own execution should be delayed until they had buried Darius, is incompatible with the versions of Ptolemy and Aristobulus in Arr. 2.12, with that reported there as a 'story' (λόγος), and with the account in D. 17.37.3 – 38.3, which on my interpretation came from Diyllus. It is almost certain that this much more sensational version was obtained by Trogus from Cleitarchus, whose account of the earlier part of the looting of the camp is reflected in D. 17.35 and 36 (Cleitarchus).

The idea which follows in 11.10.1–3, that A began to deteriorate into luxury and venery after the battle of Issus, not found in Ptolemy, Aristobulus and D., has usually been attributed to the influence of Cleitarchus.[28] The story of the gardener made king of Sidon in 11.10.8–9 appears with some variations in D. 17.47. A comparison shows that Trogus did not take his version from D., but Trogus and D. did probably have a common source, namely Cleitarchus, who on my interpretation was used by D.

Tyre is disposed of in a mere five sections, 11.10.10–14. Justin must have disregarded whole chapters in Trogus to reduce the long siege to his own silly sentence: 'in no great time Tyre was captured by treachery' (11.10.14). But he does relate four points which were preliminary to the siege: the rage of A, his threat to destroy Tyre, the Tyrians' trust in Carthage and the evacuation of Tyrian women and children to Carthage. All four points occur in D.'s long account at 17.40.3, 40.1 and 46.4, where, on my interpretation, he was following Cleitarchus. We conclude that

Trogus used Cleitarchus for the episode of Tyre. At 18.3.18 J. referred to A as having taken Tyre by storm (this from Trogus being inconsistent with Justin's own silly sentence at 11.10.14) and having crucified all surviving fighters. Both points occur in D. 17.46.1–3 and 46.4 (Cleitarchus). Such massacres were a feature of Cleitarchus' narrative (*FGrH* 137 F 25).

The visit to Siwa in 11.2–11 has already been attributed to Cleitarchus as a source. The addition at 11.11.12, that from then onwards the arrogance and conceit of A grew remarkably, is also due to Cleitarchus. So too the placing of the foundation of Alexandria after this visit (11.11.13), a feature which is found also in D. 17.52.1–3 (Cleitarchus).[29]

J.'s report in 11.12 of three embassies sent by Darius to A raises some problems. Ptolemy and Aristobulus, as used by Arrian, had only two embassies: one soon after the battle of Issus with an offer of friendship and alliance (2.14), and the second during the siege of Tyre with the additional offer of 10,000 talents, the territory west of the Euphrates and the hand of a daughter; then when the second offer was rejected, Darius prepared for war (2.25.3). Two of J.'s three embassies are at the times of these two: after Issus with the offer of 'big money' ('magnam pecuniam', 11.12.1–2).; then, 'interiecto tempore', with the offer of a daughter in marriage and a portion of his kingdom, and on A's refusal Darius prepared for war (11.12.3–5). J.'s third embassy set out after the report of the death of Darius' wife in childbirth, which reached Darius during his march from his base (? Babylon or Susa). The negotiations ended shortly before the battle of Gaugamela. The offer this time was 'the greater portion of his kingdom as far as the Euphrates, his other daughter in marriage ['alteram filiam uxorem'] and 30,000 talents' (11.12.10). Thus each time Darius raised his offer. D. agreed only partly with J. He mentioned an embassy first soon after Issus at 17.39.1 (based on Cleitarchus). The offer was 'big money' ($\chi\rho\eta\mu\acute{\alpha}\tau\omega\nu$ $\pi\lambda\tilde{\eta}\vartheta\circ\varsigma$) and the territory west of the Halys; and when this was refused Darius prepared for war.

If, as we shall argue, D. and J. were drawing on the same source, then D. has telescoped the first two embassies into one and in the process has omitted the offer of a daughter in marriage. That this was an omission becomes clear when we move to D.'s next embassy at 17.54 (Cleitarchus). Then, just before the battle of Gaugamela the offer was the kingdom as far as the Euphrates, 30,000 talents of silver and 'his other daughter in marriage' (τὴν ἑτέραν τῶν ἑαυτοῦ θυγατέρων γυναῖκα, the equivalent of J.'s 'alteram filiam uxorem').[30] The similarity between D. and J. for this embassy in time, terms and phraseology[31] leaves no doubt that they were drawing on the same source, Cleitarchus, who had reported three embassies with increasing offers (1, big money; 2, territory to the Halys and a daughter in marriage; 3, territory to the Euphrates, 30,000 talents of silver and the second daughter in marriage).[32] D. mentioned at 17.54.1 that the earlier offer had been territory to the Halys and 20,000 talents of silver; so we should probably attach that sum to the second of Cleitarchus' embassies, the sum being just twice that recorded by Ptolemy and Aristobulus. Perhaps Cleitarchus' 'big money' of the first embassy was 10,000 talents. Finally, D. failed to mention the death of Darius' wife as the cause of the final embassy; so he tacked her death on at the end (17.54.7 ἅμα δὲ τούτοις κτλ.). Needless to say, the third embassy is unhistorical.

During the night before the battle of Gaugamela, according to J. 11.13.1–3, A overslept, was awakened by Parmenio and explained that sleep had come on his realising that Darius had brought all Persian forces together. The same points are made in D. 17.56.1–3 (Cleitarchus). In theory Trogus could have taken his version from D., making slight changes; but it is more likely that D. and Trogus had a common source, Cleitarchus. The speeches — which any rhetorical writer could make up — and the actions at Gaugamela in 11.13 and 11.14.1–7 do not betray their source except that the worthy behaviour of Darius at 11.14.3–4 fits the praise of him as fighting 'magna virtute' at 10.3.7, a passage we have attributed to Cleitarchus as source.

The story of the mutilated Greeks at 11.14.11–12 is told more fully in D. 17.69.2–9 (Cleitarchus). J. or rather Trogus may have got it from Cleitarchus; but it must have been told by many Hellenistic writers. The last chapter of the book is devoted to the end of the unfortunate Darius 'bound with fetters and chains of gold'; and the description is so full that the version of Trogus can have been only slightly abbreviated. Trogus did not get the story from D., who put it into a single sentence at 17.73.3 (Cleitarchus). According to J. a soldier of A 'while going to a nearby spring', found Darius pierced with many wounds but still breathing, and he, being a Persian-speaker, received and transmitted the dying words of Darius, which paid tribute to A and prayed that A would be victorious and win world-rule ('terrarum omnium victori contingat imperium'). Wishing to send a last handshake to A, Darius held out his hand and died. Later, A wept over him and gave him a royal funeral. All this is incompatible with the account of Ptolemy and Aristobulus, as reflected in Arr. 3.21.10. The sensational account and the prayer for continuous victory and world-rule are typical of Cleitarchus. The mention of 'the nearby spring' is pointless in Justin; its relevance is to be found in Plutarch's version (*Alex.* 43) and it serves to remind us that J.'s account is very much shorter than the original account of Cleitarchus.[33]

To summarise, there are very strong reasons to believe that Trogus used Cleitarchus as his source for the account of A's actions up to and including the death of Darius, except in the case of a few passages in J. where clues are lacking to distinguish possible sources (11.5.10–12; 6.10–15; 7.1–2; 9.1–10; 13.1 – 14.7; 14.11–12). In his epitome J. omitted entirely the origins and the kings of Caria, which Trogus had described (*Prologue* XI).

Consideration of Justin 12–13.1

This is a less satisfactory book for the source-critic, partly because much of the only earlier account, that of D., is missing for the period and mainly because J. has often reduced his account to a bare minimum. Thus a source-critic cannot make anything of the passages 1.1–3; 3.2–4; 5.9–13; 6.18; 7.1–3; 8.8–9; 9.1–3; 10.8–10; 12.8–10, in which some of the points or figures occur in D.[34] and others do not.[35]

Next, at 12.4, it is clear that Trogus or/and J. have introduced for A's training of the 'Epigoni' their own explanations which stem from the Roman practice of soldiers' sons joining the legions and the fathers of several sons being rewarded. The explanations which Justin gives are of course absurd in the context of 330 B.C., at which time sons born to soldiers serving in Asia would in general have been three years of age and under. The whole of 12.4 is a historically worthless example of anachronistic interpretation by Roman writers.

When we compare *Prologue* XII of Trogus with the order of events in J. 12, we find that J. has rearranged his material from Trogus so that the acts of Agis, Alexander the Molossian and Zopyrion come early in the book, at 12.1.4 – 2.17, and the acts of Archidamus and 'the Italian origins' are omitted altogether. It is obvious too that J. has omitted large runs of narrative about A which were in Trogus 12. However, let us concentrate on what we do have that is not too severely abbreviated, beginning with the acts of A.

At 12.3.3–7 Thalestris, the Amazon queen, escorted by 300 Amazons, visits A and lives with him for thirteen days in order to be made pregnant by him. These same details are in D. 17.77.1–3 (Cleitarchus). Further the name Thalestris is cited by Strabo as given by Cleitarchus; and in listing authors who gave this story as true Plutarch cited Cleitarchus first (*Alex.* 46.1). The source, then, is certainly Cleitarchus. The alternative name given by J. at 12.3.5, Minythyia, came presumably from another teller of the story, whom Trogus had consulted.[36]

At 12.3.8–10 J. gives the adoption by A of Darius' Persian dress and by his Friends of the Persian 'purple' dress on A's orders, and the taking over of Darius' harem of beautiful, high-born girls, who, A arranged, took turns with him during the nights. Both items appear in the same sequence in D. 17.77.4–7 (Cleitarchus).[37] The source was again Cleitarchus.

The betrayal of the mores of Philip and of the Macedonians which the adoption of these ways was taken to involve is advanced in 12.5.1-3 as the cause of the killing of Philotas and Parmenio, and the killings are cited as the beginning of A's deterioration: 'he begins to rage against his own people not with royal [emotion] but with the hatred [reserved] for an enemy', and he was made especially furious by the criticism of his new ways. As these ideas follow on from 12.3.8-10, they came presumably from Cleitarchus. No doubt he had mentioned the conspiracy of Dimnus; but it is his stress on A's real motives which J. has chosen to record. The corresponding account in D. 17.79 (Diyllus) is entirely different and in tone is sympathetic to A. Both J. 12.5.3 and D. 17.80.1-2 (Diyllus) declare that Philotas and Parmenio were tried and condemned; here, then, Cleitarchus and Diyllus were in agreement on what was a factual matter, no doubt historically correct.

'Universal discontent throughout the entire camp' was reported to A (12.5.4-5), who feared it might spread into Macedonia; so he tricked the soldiers into writing letters home, which he intercepted, so that he was able to select the malcontents and put them into one brigade. 'His intention was to destroy them [in action] or post them to colonies at the end of the world' (as later at 12.5.13). The whole affair is blown up, and sinister intentions are given to A in the manner rather of Cleitarchus. The version in D. 17.80.4 (Diyllus) makes much less of it.

In 12.6 comes the next example of 'A's rage against his own people', the killing of Cleitus. We know from Arr. 4.9.2 that many authors wrote accounts, and in particular that some authors — the less trustworthy since Arrian rejected them — said that A attempted to kill himself in his remorse (so J. 12.6.8), but that most authors denied that. Then too the remorse which A felt with regard to his nurse, the sister of Cleitus (so at 12.6.10) is said by Arrian to have been mentioned by 'most authors' (4.9.3). There is one point which appears in J.'s account and not in surviving accounts, namely that it was Callisthenes who did most to bring A to his senses

(12.6.17); for in Arr. 4.9.7 and PA 52 Anaxarchus got the credit, and in Plutarch at the expense of Callisthenes, who lost favour. J.'s account is excessively sensational, with A taunting the corpse of Cleitus in his rage, then embracing the corpse and fondling its wounds in his remorse, and finally recalling all his past crimes. No doubt Justin added a touch of rhetorical colour; but the list of A's victims at 12.6.14, for instance, includes persons Justin had not mentioned earlier and so must have come from Trogus.[38] It seems that Trogus himself used a highly rhetorical account by one of the authors Arrian regarded as less trustworthy. Cleitarchus is the most likely candidate.

At 12.7.4 the Indian campaign is introduced by the silvering of the soldiers' arms and the horses' bosses, and by the naming of the army as Argyraspides, i.e. Silvershielders (J. mistakenly extending the term to all the troops). Justin jumps next to Nysa, 'a city founded by Liber', i.e. Dionysus, where the army visited his sacred mountain, 'clothed in the beauties of nature, the vine and the ivy', was seized with a Dionysiac frenzy and engaged in a wild rout. Arrian (5.2.7) did not think the rout historical, but he said it was reported 'by some writers'. One of them was probably Cleitarchus (Arrian never mentioned him by name), and in fact a fragment of Cleitarchus mentioned the plant like ivy on mount Nysa[39] (FGrH 137 F 17). Also Justin makes A mention the expedition of Dionysus into India; that too was in the Cleitarchus fragment. It is very probable, then, that the source is Cleitarchus.

At 12.7.9–11, when Queen Cleophis surrendered to A, she regained by her charms what she had lost in war, produced a son by A who later ruled over Indians, and earned the name 'the royal harlot' for her promiscuity. This romance, like the story of the Amazon queen, is worthy of Cleitarchus. A then captured a remarkable rock-refuge which Heracles had been deterred by an earthquake from assaulting (12.7.12–13).[40] D. 17.85.2 mentioned 'the story' (λέγεται) that Heracles had been deterred by earthquakes, and he named the rock Aornus (86.1); so it is probable that D. and J. were derived from the same source, whom I have previously identified for D. as Cleitarchus (see p. 53).

The battle with Porus is remarkable for a personal combat between A and Porus on the challenge of Porus. In the course of it A's horse was wounded, A was thrown and he was saved only by the intervention of his Companions (12.8.3–4). Porus, overwhelmed with many a wound, was taken prisoner; but he refused food or medical treatment and wanted to die, until A persuaded him to live and to accept his kingdom back again. This highly coloured version of combat and reconciliation is not found elsewhere, and in particular not in D. 17.88.5–6 and 89.2 and 6 (Cleitarchus). It seems, then, that J.'s version came from a source other than Cleitarchus. At 12.8.10–17 the army turns back. This is the occasion for a pathetic appeal by the troops and then the construction of a camp more magnificent than usual to frighten the enemy and arouse the admiration of posterity. But the place is uncertain. It appears that the army had defeated an enemy force of 200,000 cavalry in the kingdom of Sophitis before it turned back upon its tracks (12.8.10 and 17). Except in a superficial way as regards the camp, Justin's account is entirely different from the account of D. 17.94–95.2 (Cleitarchus). I infer, then, that the source was someone other than Cleitarchus.

At 12.9.4–13 the story of A fighting alone and being severely wounded is told without the town (that of the Malli) being named. A was protected by the trunk of a tree (9); then, wounded by an arrow below the nipple, he dropped onto one knee ('genu posito'); but he killed the man who had shot the arrow. These details are in the account of D. 17.99.2–3 (Cleitarchus), but not in that of Arr. 6.10, which was derived from Ptolemy and Aristobulus. It is possible, then, that J. as well as D. drew his version ultimately from Cleitarchus.

A's curing of Ptolemy and others who had been wounded by poisoned arrows is explained as due to a herbal remedy in a drink, which had been revealed to the king in a dream (12.10.2–3). This is found also in D. 17.103.7–8 (Cleitarchus); so the source of J. is probably also Cleitarchus. In

12.10.4–6 A made libations to Oceanus and only later reached the mouth of the Indus, founded a city Barce there and set up altars; and the mouth of the Indus marked the end of his empire, like the end of a chariot-course. This last point seems to resume 12.7.4, where A set off for India 'in order to end his empire with Ocean and the farthest East', in a chapter which was ascribed generally to Cleitarchus as source (p. 104 above). The order of events is slightly different in D. 17.104: A sailed out into the Ocean and then offered his libations, erected altars to Tethys and Oceanus and returned to Pattala; and at the mouth of the Indus A regarded the projected expedition as being at an end. The differences are due to D.'s using Diyllus (p. 68 above). However, Cleitarchus and Diyllus both regarded the Indus mouth as the farthest limit of conquest.

In the description of A's return to Babylonia a sentence of Justin at 12.10.1 seems to have got misplaced in the text (although not noted by O. Seel in his excellent edition); for after recovering from his wound (at the city of the Malli far inland) A is made to embark on his fleet and 'traverse the shores of Ocean' ('Oceani litora peragrat'). This sentence should belong with the mention of the 'litorales Indi' at 12.10.6. Thus, after sending Polyperchon overland with an army to Babylonia, A explored the coast of Ocean and ordered wells to be dug,[41] because for his own land journey there were waterless places midway (12.10.1 and 12.10.7). J. has no account of any difficulties in the Gedrosian desert; for he merely says that 'a huge amount of sweet water was found and A returned to Babylonia'. Cleitarchus too made relatively little of troubles in the Gedrosian desert, if I am correct in regarding him as the source behind D. 17.105.6 (p. 70 above). If Trogus followed Cleitarchus here, we can understand why J. made little of it.

At 12.11.1 A promised to pay the debts of 'all' at his own expense. The debts amounted to 20,000 talents; the same sum for the debts of the army is found in Arr. 7.5.1–3. This is a different affair from the paying of debts for the 10,000 veterans whom A dismissed in D. 17.109.2 (Diyllus).[42] The account of the mutiny in 12.11.4–7 is close to that in Arr. 7.8.3, in that it was the Macedonians *not* dismissed (keeping the MSS μένουσι at 7.8.1) who demanded dismissal and told A to go campaigning with his father Ammon, and in that A jumped into the crowd and had thirteen men arrested for punishment (though J. exaggerated by making A lead them off 'with his own hand').[43] D. 17.109.2–3 is different: he puts the mutiny at Susa, mentions the Ammon jibe earlier (108.3) and does not give the number of men arrested. J., then, did not draw on D. or on D.'s source, Diyllus.

For the second part of his account J. provides a speech to the Persians (in oratio obliqua) and it is probable that the short passages at 12.11.5–7 are relics of fuller speeches by the rebels and by A, which were also in oratio obliqua in Trogus. For we know from 38.3.11 that this was the practice of Trogus. In the speech to the Persians A emphasises the fusion of customs and of marriages, whereby he put conquerors and conquered on the same level, and he says he will trust Persians as his personal guards.[44] Next, he selected 1,000 Persians to join the Companions, and he 'mixed' a portion of the Persian troops trained in Macedonian weapons into his army, i.e. into the phalanx ('exercitui suo miscet').[45] All this annoyed the Macedonians. They then became reconciled with him, and he ended by retiring 11,000 men from his service (12.12.7).

The second part of J.'s account is different from that in D. 17.109.3 (Diyllus), who mentioned only appointments of Persians to positions of high command (as in Arr. 7.11.1), and also from that in Arr. 7.11.3, where the giving of Macedonian regimental titles to Persian units was the final incident which led to the reconciliation. Thus we can exclude as sources for Trogus both D. and Diyllus, and probably Ptolemy and Aristobulus, Arrian's sources. Yet Trogus evidently had a full and detailed source. Cleitarchus is certainly probable.

In 12.12.11–12 J. mentioned the death of Hephaestion, 'very dear to the king, at first because of his dower of beauty and youth, and later because of his obsequiousness'; then the cost of the monument for Hephaestion, 12,000 talents; and the order of A that Hephaestion was to be worshipped as a god. D. made some of the same points: A loved Hephaestion most of all the Friends he held in affection (17.114.1); the cost of the monument 'they say' was over 12,000 talents (115.5); and Hephaestion was worshipped as a god (115.6). As we noted above (p. 75), the last two points differed from the reports of 'the majority of writers'. Thus it seems that J. and D. had a source in common. It is probable that Trogus, like D., drew on Ephippus, but perhaps through an intermediary, since the brevity of J. does not enable us to be sure that he drew directly.

In 12.13.1–5 we have the idea of world conquest, a Cleitarchan feature as we have noted, in connection with the embassies to A and the spread of A's reputation.[46] The prediction of 'a certain' Babylonian prophet then caused A to avoid Babylon and cross the Euphrates, so that he reached a deserted site called Borsipa; but later he was compelled by the philosopher Anaxarchus to reject the prediction. In D. 17.112–113 (Diyllus) the order of events is reversed. Trogus, then, did not follow D. or Diyllus; nor Ptolemy nor Aristobulus as used by Arr. 7.16.5 – 17.6, who had a group of prominent Chaldaeans meet A and divert him in accordance with an oracle of the god Belus, and who reported from Aristobulus that A failed to cross the Euphrates as the ground was too marshy. Again the source of Justin might be Cleitarchus.

At 12.13.6–10 J. moves quickly through festivities to a banquet to which Medius Thessalus invited A. There 'the King accepted a tankard, and, in the middle of drinking it down, he suddenly cried out as if pierced by a weapon, was carried out of the banquet half-conscious, and was racked with such pain that he called for a weapon to gain release and found any human touch as painful as a wound'. At this point J. disgresses in order to discuss the cause of this, and in particular to consider a story made up some time after the death of A. We shall consider this digression later, and continue now with J.'s narrative at 15.1. First, however, we should note that the drinking, and crying out, the half-consciousness and the pain are all as in D. 17.117.1–2 (Cleitarchus). The demand for a weapon is peculiar to J. but typical too of Cleitarchus (see p. 103 above on J. 12.6.8). Trogus' source so far, then, for A's illness is Cleitarchus. This is clearly so at 15.1, where the Aeacid connection and the implicit reference to Achilles dying young are due to Cleitarchus as source (see p. 91 above). The sensational and largely fictitious account runs on to 15.13, and it shares with the account of D. 17.117.3–4 (Cleitarchus) the giving of the ring by A to Perdiccas, the leaving of the kingdom 'to the best' (τῷ κρατίστῳ, and in J. 9 and 10 'dignissimum') and the prospect of a contest between the leading Friends for the succession (17.117.4 and J. 12.15.6 cf. 11).[47] J., in fact, has preserved more of the final scene as portrayed by Cleitarchus than D. has done.

In 12.16 the ultimate source, as we have seen (p. 92 above), is Cleitarchus, who depicted A as world-ruler and unconquered even in the face of death, 12.16.10–11. This continues into 13.1.2–3 and leads to the suicide of Sisygambis, with which D. closed his book on A (17.117.3, a passage which I ascribed to Diyllus as source). In any case it is certain that an entirely new source[48] was followed by Trogus for the reaction to the death of A among the Macedonians at 13.1.7–8; for the hatred of A there portrayed is incompatible with the picture of the weeping soldiers at 12.15.2–3.

We must now turn back to 12.13.10 and 12.14. The whole passage is an inset between the two stages of A's illness. It gives two explanations for the illness: excessive drinking ('intemperiem ebrietatis') according to the report spread by A's Friends,[49] and a poison-plot of which the disgrace was stifled by the power of the Successors ('infamiam successorum potentia oppressit'). These are not cumulative but mutually exclusive explanations, and J. plumps for the second as the true one ('re vera'). Now the poison-plot and the suppression of information are mentioned also by D. 17.117.5 and 118.2. D. stated that 'many historians' kept silent for fear of Antipater and Cassander (their power ended in 297 B.C. with the latter's death); and this is confirmed by the instance of

Onesicritus, who did not dare name those present at the party of Medius (*FGrH* 134 F 37 'fugiens simultatem').[50] However, for his account of the plot J. (Trogus) did not draw on Diodorus.[51] It is possible that they both drew on a common source. We can exclude as a candidate for such a source *The Alexander Romance* and the *Testamentum Alexandri*, conveniently published side by side by Merkelbach;[52] for there the story of the illness and the poison-plot are interwoven into a sensational narrative with three applications of poison and with fourteen of A's Friends out of twenty in the conspiracy!

The incidents cited by J. to explain the motivation of Antipater look like excerpts from a longer list and are not indicative of any special source. In J. the administering of the poison is arranged by Cassander, Philip and Iolas (only two of them in the *Alexander Romance*, henceforth *AR*), and the poison is so potent that it has to be stored in a horse's hoof (some form of hoof in PA 77.2, C. 10.10.16 and *AR*). In J. those in the know are the three brothers and Medius (many others in *AR* but only two brothers), and both Philip and Iolas were tasters and so both administered the poison (elsewhere, in D., C., Plutarch and *AR*, it is only one son). Arrian gave a summary of the various stories, in which incidentally he did not believe (7.27), and these stories include most of the points already mentioned: in particular the complicity of Medius as a lover of Iolas, and also Aristotle helping Antipater in the preparation of the poison and Roxane preventing A's attempt at suicide (the last is in *AR*). The fullest and most elaborate account of all is that of *AR*, and it is for that reason likely to be the latest in date as an original composition.[53]

The probable sequence of events is that Olympias in 317 B.C. started the attack on Antipater and his sons as poisoners of A.[54] However, she was killed by one of them, Cassander, before the idea passed into the writings of any Alexander-historian. Only after Cassander's death in 297 B.C. did the poison-plot enter into such writings.[55] The story then grew rapidly and reached the dimensions which we see in *AR*.

Somewhere along the line an author wrote a full account which was the common source most probably of D. and J. and was reponsible for some details in Curtius, Plutarch and Arrian. He was perhaps Satyrus, whose biographies of famous men surely included one of Alexander (so C. Müller supposed in *FHG* III Satyrus F 18); and Trogus had already used Satyrus for the alleged participation of Olympias and A himself in the killing of Philip (J. 9.7, as on p. 89 above). Moreover, the love-motif of the amour between Medius and Iolas is typical of Satyrus (e.g. F 1 and F 12).

We can now return to 12.1.4 – 2.17, in which the fates of Agis, Alexander the Molossian and Zopyrion were related. One feature links this group with the passage we have just been considering, the alleged poisoning of A in 12.14; for the prediction at 12.2.3 by the Delphic Oracle of a 'plot in Macedonia' against Alexander the Great cannot but refer to this very plot by Antipater in Macedonia and to the belief that the prediction was fulfilled. Now this oracle is knit together with that from Dodona about Alexander the Molossian. It follows that the passage from 12.2.3 to 12.2.4, where the oracle is said to have been fulfilled, came from a source who wrote after 297 B.C. (see p. 110 above) and who believed in the poisoning of A as true. We may then exclude Cleitarchus from consideration; for Cleitarchus did not believe in any such poisoning on my understanding of D. 17.117.1–4, being from Cleitarchus, and of 117.5, being from someone other than Cleitarchus.[56] On the other hand, if Satyrus is the source from whom Trogus derived the story of the poisoning, it is likely that 12.2.3–14 came from Satyrus. Moreover, Satyrus seems from 9.7.1 to have given a hostile picture of A; and here A is represented as rejoicing in the death of 'the rival kings' (12.1.5; cf. fear of a rival at 9.7.3, being from Satyrus) and 'pretending' to mourn for Alexander the Molossian (12.3.1). One of the few facts we know about Satyrus is that he wrote on ancient myths (F 22);[57] and in the account of the campaigns in Italy there is reference to early myths about Diomede, a hero of the Trojan War (12.2.7–10). Thus Satyrus is a strong candidate.

We must also compare Livy's account of Alexander the Molossian with that of J. According to Livy 8.24 Alexander met his death in the waters of the Acheron in fulfilment of the oracle; his corpse was mutilated, then recovered by a woman, then buried at Consentia in enemy territory; next his bones were sent to Metapontum in friendly territory and eventually reached Olympias and Cleopatra in Epirus. The death occurred when Alexandria in Egypt was founded (7.24.1), i.e. early in 331 B.C. According to J., Alexander was killed 'beside the city of Pandosia and the river Acheron'; his corpse was recovered at public expense and was buried by the people of Thurii (12.2.14–15). The news reached A in Parthia (12.3.1), i.e. late in 330 B.C. It is obvious that Livy and J. did not use one another or use a common source.

Who was Livy's source? He used someone who was writing also about A; for he introduces the Molossian Alexander alongside Alexander the Great at 8.3.6–7; dates his death by A's foundation of Alexandria at 8.24.1; brings in Olympias and Cleopatra as mother and sister of A at 8.24.17; contrasts the death of the Molossian with the revel of A's army through India and the defeat by A of Darius complete with harem, eunuchs and gold and purple dress, at 9.17.16–17; and makes the Molossian contrast the warfare he experienced with that of A 'against women' at 9.19.10–11. An author writing at considerable length about both Alexanders and not limiting himself to the Anabasis of A, as Ptolemy, Aristobulus and many others seem to have done, is very unusual and can hardly be other than Cleitarchus. Moreover, as we have seen already, it was Cleitarchus who concerned himself with Darius having a harem and eunuchs on his campaign, with Persian attire of gold and purple, with the rout of the revellers in India, with the deterioration of A under prosperity and his taking to Persian ways (so in Livy 9.18.1–3) and his Persian dress, his demand for 'proskynesis', his killing of his friends at banquets, his conceited lies about his origin (ibid. 4), his daily increasing love of wine and his fierce and boiling anger (ibid. 5).

112

Returning to Livy's description of the fate of the Molossian, we may note the emotional sensationalism which is typical of Cleitarchus in the description of the weeping woman facing the raging mob in her prayer to be given the corpse. The mutilation too of the corpse, sawn in two and pelted with javelins and stones, has a similarity with the mutilation of the corpse of Bessus and the hurling of the bits with slings in D. 17.83.9, a passage of which I reckoned the source to be Cleitarchus.[58] Thus on many grounds it seems that Livy drew on Cleitarchus for his accounts both of Alexander the Molossian and of Alexander the Great. As the author behind J.'s account was different from that behind Livy's account, we have a negative argument in favour of Satyrus as J.'s source.

The account in J. 12.1.9–11 of Agis' death, as occurring when Agis saw his own men in flight and stayed alone, is different from that in D. 17.63.4, where Agis was being carried away wounded and then at his own request fought alone resting on one knee. Thus J.'s source is again someone other than Cleitarchus, who (I have argued) is the source behind the passage in D. So it seems on several counts that Satyrus is the source behind 12.1.4 – 12.2.15.

Attributions and general conclusions

The sources we have suggested are as follows.

9.5–8 to 6.8	Philip's last summer		Cleitarchus
9.7	Plot instigated by Olympias		Satyrus
9.8.1–3	Sons of Philip		Cleitarchus
10	Persia		?Deinon
11.1–4.6	A in Europe		Cleitarchus
11.5.9 and 6.9	A in Asia		Cleitarchus
11.5.10–12 and 6.10 – 7.2		No suggestion	
11.7.3–16	Gordium		Cleitarchus
11.8			?Cleitarchus
11.9.1–10		No suggestion	
11.9.11–16	D's women		Cleitarchus
11.10.1–9	A deteriorates		Cleitarchus
	Abdalonymus		Cleitarchus
11.10.10–14	Tyre		Cleitarchus
11.11	Ammon, Alexandria		Cleitarchus
11.12	D's embassies		Cleitarchus
11.13.1–3	A oversleeps		Cleitarchus
11.13–14	Gaugamela to Persepolis	No suggestion	
11.15	D's death		Cleitarchus
12.1.1–3		No suggestion	
12.1.4 – 2.15	Agis, Alex. the Molossian		Satyrus
12.2.16–17 and 12.3.1–4		No suggestion	
12.3.5–7	Amazon		Cleitarchus
12.3.8–12	A orientalises		Cleitarchus
12.4	Epigoni	A Roman fabrication	
12.5.1–8	Philotas, Disorderlies		Cleitarchus
12.5.9–13		No suggestion	
12.6.1–17	Cleitus		Cleitarchus

12.6.18 – 7.3		No suggestion	
12.7.4–13	Nysa, Cleophis, Aornus		Cleitarchus
12.8.1–17	Porus and Hyphasis	No suggestion but not Cleitarchus	
12.9.1–3		No suggestion but not Cleitarchus	
12.9.4–13	A severely wounded		Cleitarchus
12.10.1–7	Curing of Ptolemy and return to Babylonia		Cleitarchus
12.10.8–10		No suggestion	
12.11–12.12.10	Debts and mutiny		?Cleitarchus
12.12.11–12	Hephaestion		?Cleitarchus
12.13.1–5	Embassies and Anaxarchus		following Ephippus
12.13.6–9 and 15	A's illness and death		Cleitarchus
12.14	Poisoning of A		Cleitarchus
12.16	Superhuman aspects of A		Satyrus
13.1.1–6	Sisygambis		Cleitarchus
13.1.7–15	Praise of Successors	Not Cleitarchus	Cleitarchus

Some firm conclusions may be drawn from this study. The first are of a negative nature. Trogus did not draw on the universal history of D., his immediate predecessor in the field. This is not surprising; for he had to write a different book if he was to obtain a contemporary readership. Nor did Trogus draw at all on the detailed history of Diyllus, which D. had used for much of his account of Alexander's period; for Trogus probably found Diyllus dull and factual, and too open-minded about Macedonia. Above all, Trogus kept clear of the Macedonian writers, such as Ptolemy, Aristobulus and Marsyas, who wrote favourably of their king and country; for Trogus, like his contemporary Roman historian, Livy, was anxious not to let the achievements of Macedonia even appear to rival those of Rome, the capital of the world.

The popular account of A in the late Republic and early Empire was that of Cleitarchus, which combined a highly sensational and colourful description of A's conquests and personality with a considerable animosity towards the Macedonians and with the picture of a world-conqueror corrupted by power. The outlook of Cleitarchus appealed to Trogus, and it was his account on which Trogus mainly drew. Cleitarchus had also been one of D.'s sources; but whereas the sensational effects of Cleitarchus had been underplayed by D., they were fully reproduced by Trogus (we may compare the death-scene of A, drawn from Cleitarchus, in D. 17.117.1–4 and in J. 12.13.6–9 and 15.1–12). In addition to Cleitarchus Trogus made use of a sensational biographer who had an even greater taste for scandal than

Cleitarchus and, being farther removed from events, wrote with a freer pen, namely Satyrus. For there is little doubt that Trogus took from Satyrus the exciting ideas that Olympias and A organised the killing of Philip, and that Antipater and his sons engineered the death by poisoning of A in his thirty-third year and brought to an end the possibility of world-conquest. Trogus found there too the sensational deaths of Agis and Alexander the Molossian. For affairs in India Trogus seems to have turned to a third writer, who was shorter than Cleitarchus; and if we may judge by the contents of Trogus, *Prologue* XII, Trogus wrote at less length on areas which lay beyond Parthia, the horizon then of Rome's ambition.[59]

It has emerged also that Trogus was capable of introducing anachronistic material of contemporary interest, as in his interpretation of the Epigoni at J. 12.4. That Trogus himself composed speeches in oratio obliqua for his history is known from the example preserved at J. 38.4f.; and we may suspect that there are traces of Trogus' freely composed speeches in such passages in J. as that describing the mutiny (12.11.5–12.3). And it is difficult to resist the thought that Trogus himself may have made the account of Cleitus' death and A's remorse even more sensational than it had been in Cleitarchus.

For a historian today it is a matter of crucial importance to know what were the sources of the statements in our two earlier extant accounts, those of D. and J. If the two enquiries which have been conducted so far are well founded in general, even if specific details are doubtful to varying degrees, the conclusions go a long way towards enabling us to see which material can be used and which can be discarded in writing on this period. No less important, we have obtained perhaps a fuller knowledge of the characteristics and the qualities of the ultimate sources whom we know directly only from their fragments — Cleitarchus, Diyllus and Satyrus. Armed with these conclusions and with this knowledge we are much better placed to consider the sources used by C. and to put names to the authors of what Arrian, the latest and the best writer on A, merely mentioned as λεγόμενα.

CHAPTER 4

THE SOURCES OF CURTIUS 3-6

Resemblances[1] in Diodorus and Curtius 3-4

The short account in D. 17.30.1-7 of Charidemus giving frank advice to Darius has analogies with the much longer account in C. 3.2.1-19. Both belong to the category of historical fiction which is composed with a moralising purpose. For if there was in fact any conference between Darius and his entourage – the 'purpurati' of C. 3.2.10 and the φίλοι of D. 17.30.1 and 4 – what was said cannot have been known to any Greek historian. The model for this form of literature was the description of the conference of Xerxes in Herodotus 7, and other echoes of that book are found in the numbering of the host by putting 10,000 at a time into a giant sheep-pen (C. 3.2.2 and Hdt. 7.60), in recording numbers of large units and in giving some detail of equipment (C. 2.2.4-9 and Hdt. 7.41 and 61f.).[2]

Some elements in the accounts are in common, as follows. Charidemus denounces the Persians as unmanly (D. 17.30.4 ὀνειδίσας τὴν Περσῶν ἀνανδρίαν; C. 3.2.16 telling Darius to hire real soldiers in Greece). The anger of the proud despot blinds him to the wisdom of Charidemus' words (D. 17.30.4 τοῦ θυμοῦ δὲ τὸ συμφέρον ἀφαιρουμένου and C. 3.2.11 'regiae superbiae' with 3.2.17 'maxime utilia suadentem'). Darius orders the immediate execution of Charidemus, who has the last word in foretelling the fall of Darius at Alexander's hands (D. 17.30.5 ἐπιδόντα τὴν κατάλυσιν τῆς βασιλείας and C. 3.2.18 'habeo paratum mortis meae ultorem'). His order fulfilled, Darius repents but too late (D. 17.30.6 ἀνέντος τοῦ θυμοῦ τὴν ψυχὴν μετενόησε ... ἀλλ' οὐ γὰρ ἦν δυνατὸν τὸ γεγονός ... ἀγένητον κατασκευάσαι and C. 3.2.19 'sera deinde paenitentia').

It is in theory possible that C. read D., borrowed the scene and greatly enlarged it out of his own imagination, but there is little evidence that C. drew directly on D. The alternative, that the common elements are due to their independent use of a common source, is more likely.[3] If so, the source is Cleitarchus (see above p. 41).

There are differences between the two accounts. D., living when republicanism and autocracy were in conflict, has the autocratic Darius misled by his advisers and then by his own anger. Writing as a Greek, D. draws Charidemus as a man admired among the Persians for his valour and ability, and then has him fall from the highest hopes to utter ruin because of ill-timed outspokenness. C., writing in a period when autocracy was established, was interested in the effect of autocratic power on the autocrat's psyche.[4] He portrays Darius as a man at first of happy, mild and amenable disposition, who is then corrupted by 'Fortuna', i.e. the position in which Chance has placed him, so much so that he disregards the rights of truth, hospitality and supplication. Darius is changed by the licence of supreme power (C. 3.2.10 and 17–18, 'licentia regni tam subito mutatus'). Charidemus alone speaks out. While the 'purpurati' flattered the autocrat, Charidemus disregarded the position Chance had given him and the arrogant pride of Darius, and thus brought death upon himself. But mindful of freedom, 'libertas', he uttered his prophetic words before the autocrat's lackeys cut his throat. Of the two authors D. is certainly closer to the attitude of a fourth-century Greek writing about Greeks and Persians; for C.'s portrait belongs to the period which Tacitus painted so vividly.

The battle of Issus provides a purple passage in both writers. D. disregarded the conditions of phalanx-warfare with Macedonian pikes and Persian or Greek mercenary spears.[5] Instead he writes as follows. 'When the forces were within missile range, the Persians hurled such a multitude of missiles that the weapons fouled one another, being so close-packed in the air, and the blows were too feeble.' Later, 'no javelin-cast, no sword-thrust failed, for the crowded ranks offered a ready target' (D. 17.33.2–7). Likewise C. makes the press of troops so dense that as soon as their missiles were hurled, they met one another in mid-course, became entangled in the air, and for the most part fell harm-lessly to the ground, and only a few inflicted on the enemy a light and ineffective blow. Forced therefore to join battle at close quarters, they drew their swords eagerly. Then truly there was a mass of blood shed, the two lines being so stuck into one another that shield beat upon shield and sword-points thrust at each other's faces.   (C. 3.11.4–5).

Both writers describe the fighting around Darius in similar terms, and they mention by name the same Persians — Oxathres, a mighty fighter killing 'many' (D. 17.34.2–4 and C. 3.11.8), Antixyes, Rheomithres and 'the satrap of Egypt' — and the four horses of Darius' chariot suffering many wounds, so that they 'tried to shake off their bits' (D. 17.34.6 τὰ χαλινὰ διεσείοντο) or 'tossed the yoke' (C. 31.11.11 'iugum quatere . . . coeperant'). D. goes one better than C. in having Darius transfer from this chariot to another chariot; but once in flight he transfers to a single horse in each account (D. 17.37.1 and C. 3.11.11).[6] Both then proceed to the looting of the camp with its vast riches (D. 17.35.4 τὴν ὑπερβολὴν τοῦ πλούτου καὶ τῆς τρυφῆς and C. 3.11.20 'ingens auri argentique pondus . . . luxuriae apparatum'), the pathetic agonies of the Persian ladies who were exposed to the violence and the lust of their captors (D. 17.35.5–7 and C. 3.11.21–22), and the despair of Darius' mother, wife and children (D. 17.36.2–4 and C. 3.11.24–6). They both tell of a report of Darius having been killed, the wailing of the royal women, the sending of Leonnatus by A, and then next day the visit by A and Hephaestion, the misunderstanding by the queen mother and A's remark: 'No matter, Mother; actually he also is Alexander' (D. 17.37.6 and C. 3.12.17).

It is evident that throughout the battle and its aftermath D. and C., who writes at much greater length, were drawing upon a common source.[7] If my identification is correct (see above, p. 20), they used Cleitarchus.

D. and C. are alike in their descriptions of the siege of Tyre in the following matters. The Tyrians hope for help from Carthage (D. 17.40.3 and C. 4.2.10), their island is 4 stades from the mainland (D. 17.40.4 and C. 4.2.7), and they taunt

A as a man hoping to defeat Poseidon (D. 17.41.1 and C. 4.2.20). They evacuate old men, women and children to Carthage (D. 17.41.1–2 and 46.4, and C. 4.3.20). There are divine events: a sea monster (D. 17.41.5 κῆτος and C. 4.4.3– 5 'belua'), bloody bread (D. 17.41.7 and C. 4.2.14) and the shackling of Apollo (D. 17.41.7–8 and C. 4.3.21–2). A storm does damage, and entire trees are used to repair it (D. 17.42.5–6 and C. 4.3.6–9). The Tyrians put three ships in front of the harbour (D. 17.43.3) or in front of the very walls (C. 4.3.12), which were naturally sunk by A (Arr. 2.20.9 enables us to understand the situation of the three ships); they build an inner wall (D. 17.43.3 and C. 4.3.13) and use burning sand on the attackers (D. 17.44.1–3 and C. 4.3.25–26). A is ready to abandon the siege (D. 17.45.7 and C. 4.4.1), but he wins, thanks to his own personal *aristeia* (D. 17.46.1–2 and C. 4.4.10–11), and he crucifies 2,000 Tyrian men (D. 17.46.4 and C. 4.4.17). So ended the seven months' siege (D. 17.46.5 and C. 4.4.19). These similarities in matters of which many are not found in other accounts are due to the use of a common source, namely Cleitarchus (see above, p. 42).[8]

The moralising story of the gardener Abdalonymus (Ballonymus in D. 17.46.6 being evidently a textual corruption), raised from poverty to kingship, is common to D. and C. 4.1.16–26. Again it seems probable that both used a common source, namely Cleitarchus (loc. cit. above). D., having omitted the story in its proper setting of King Straton at Sidon, could not resist telling it *after* his narrative of the siege of Tyre; so he put it in at 17.46.6 and moved the location and King Straton to Tyre. Otherwise the differences between D. and C. may be attributed to C.'s expansive style and his introduction of moral aphorisms in the manner of Seneca and of Rumour in the manner of Virgil.[9]

The journey of Amyntas with 4,000 Greek mercenaries from Issus via Tripolis and Cyprus to Egypt, his successes at Pelusium and Memphis, and then his death and that of his entire force are told in the same sequence by D. 17.48.2–5 and C. 4.1.27–33. As C. is longer and the situation he gives

119

is more intelligible (e.g. on Persians rather than 'the locals' issuing from Memphis at 4.1.32), we may deduce that C. is closer to their common source, namely Diyllus (loc. cit. above). Next, events follow in the same order in D. and C. First, there are the actions by other commanders of Darius' forces at Issus (much more detail in C. 4.1.34-35 and 4.5.13). The decision by the Council of 'the Greeks' to send a gold wreath and congratulations to A comes after the end of those actions (D. 17.48.6 putting it at the end of his year 332/1 and C. 4.5.11-12 after the fall of Tyre). The order in which these events are given may be due to D. and C. using a common source,[10] namely Diyllus (loc. cit. above).

Comparison between Justin and Curtius 3-4

C. 3.1.14-18 has A cut the knot at Gordium with his sword. Not so Aristobulus, Ptolemy and probably Marsyas (see above, p. 97); nor D., who omitted the episode altogether. J.'s epitome in the third or fourth century A.D. of Trogus, who wrote in the time of Augustus, is here unusually full. It has A cutting the knot in this way; and it is evident that Trogus was one of 'most writers' (PA 18.2) or of 'some writers' (Arr. 2.3.7) who ended their account with A cutting the knot. Now the differences between J. and C. suggest that Trogus was not followed by C. For in J. 11.7 A knew beforehand about the oracle; so when he captured the city, he asked for the whereabouts of the wagon. In C. A entered the temple of Jupiter, saw the wagon and learnt from the natives about the oracle ('incolis deinde affirmantibus'). In J. the end is briefly told; C. has the Phrygians and the Macedonians watching the over-confident king struggle in vain with the knots and fearing lest his failure should be an omen of defeat, and then his cutting of the knots either cheated the oracle or fulfilled it. If Trogus and C. used the same sources, namely Cleitarchus for Trogus (loc. cit. above), then C. treated it very freely. On the whole it is more likely that Trogus and C. used different sources.[11]

J. and C. attribute A's illness to a bathe in the Cydnus when he was 'plenus pulveris ac sudoris' (J. 11.8.3) or 'pulvere simul ac sudore perfusus' (C. 3.5.1). Aristobulus had a different account (Arr. 2.4.7). J. and C. both mention a report that Darius was approaching with a huge army and they say that A was cured after three days (J. 11.18.1 and 9 'quarta die', and C. 3.5.10 and 3.6.16, making it more dramatic by his 'quinto die' and 'post tertium diem'). Both have Parmenio send a letter to A; and when A takes his medicine he watches Philip read the letter and keeps his eyes on Philip's face (J. 11.8.8 and C. 3.6.9). This was not the version reported by Aristobulus (Arr. 2.4.7), and the meteoric recovery can hardly be historical. The resemblances between J. and C. are so strong that we may conclude Trogus and C. used the same source, probably Cleitarchus (see above p. 98).[12]

On the way to engage at Issus J. 11.9.3 has A address 'singulas gentes diversa oratione'; likewise C. 3.10.4 'varia oratione'. This can hardly be historical, and Arr. 2.7.3-7 and 2.10.2, in which A addressed his commanders on the previous day and exhorted leading men as he rode along the line before he reached position for battle, is to be preferred. A common source for Trogus and C. is probable, but the passage is too short for one to name the source.[13]

J. 11.10.8-9 gives the essence of the story of Abdalonymus, the poor gardener, who was made king of Sidon; C. tells the story at length (4.1.16-26). Both place it before the siege of Tyre. A common source is probable, and as we have seen with D.'s version it may well be Cleitarchus (see above, p. 43).

As regards Tyre J. 11.10.10-14 and C. 4.2.2-5 have the Tyrians send a golden crown to A and then counter A's request by saying that he should sacrifice to Heracles in Old Tyre. In both authors the Tyrians trust in Carthage (J. 'fiducia Carthaginiensium', and C. 4.2.10-11) and send non-combatants to Carthage (J., and C. 4.3.20). These are small points but significant, because none of them is in Arrian's account.[14] They may well be due to a common source, namely Cleitarchus (see above, p. 98).

J. 11.12 reports three offers of peace from Darius, and so does C.; but Arrian has only two offers. The first offer contains the promise of 'magnam pecuniam' in J.; and of 'enough money to fill all Macedonia' in C. 4.1.8. The second offer contains promise of a daughter in marriage and a part of the kingdom in J. and also in C. 4.5.1. A replies in J. that he is being offered his own property, and he requires Darius to come as a suppliant and entrust the decision about the kingdom to the victor ('sua sibi dari rescripsit; iussitque supplicem venire, et regni arbitria victori permittere'). A's reply in C. 4.5.7, a longer version, has two of these points[15] ('sibi aliena promittere', and 'leges autem a victoribus dici . . . quam primum Marte decerneret'). The third offer, dated by both to just before the battle of Gaugamela, was made in connection with the death of Darius' wife and the hope of Darius, that in the event of his own defeat A would be the victorious ruler (J. 11.12.8, and C. 4.10.34). This time Darius offered the land west of the Euphrates, the hand of a daughter and 30,000 talents (J. 11.12.10, and C. 4.11.5–6). This third offer is certainly not historical. The full agreement between J. and C. indicates that Trogus and C. went back to a common source,[16] namely Cleitarchus (see above p. 100). C., of course, has added much of his own in the speeches.

For the visit to Siwa J. and C. are in agreement on the following points. A accepted the priest's greeting of him as son of Zeus Ammon (J. 11.11.7, and C. 4.7.25). When A asked if all his father's murderers had been punished, he received the same answer (J. 11.11.9, and C. 4.7.27). He was promised rule over all lands (J. 11.11.10, and C. 4.7.26). His Companions were told to worship A as a god (J. 11.11.11, and C. 4.7.28). A founded Alexandria after the visit to Siwa. All these points of agreement mean that Trogus and C. had a common source,[17] namely Cleitarchus (see above p. 99).

A's anxiety before Gaugamela, his deep sleep, his being awakened by Parmenio, and his explanation that he was relieved to be facing Darius' forces in battle are found in

J. 11.13.3 and in C. 4.13.16–24. Speeches for Darius and A as they go into battle are provided in both accounts (J. 11.13.7–11, and C. 4.14.1–26); they have in common such points as Darius having more men but A more soldiers. In his flight Darius chose not to destroy the bridge over the river (J. 11.14.4 erroneously calling it the Cydnus, and C. correctly the Lycus); this story is peculiar to J. and C. The probable explanation for these agreements is the use of a common source by Trogus and C., and in the matter of Parmenio awakening A in J. the source is thought to be Cleitarchus (see above, p. 100).

The general result of this section is that where J., i.e. Trogus, and C. used a common source, whether certainly or probably, that common source was Cleitarchus.

Some comparisons between Curtius and Arrian

There are a number of passages in C. 3–4 where C. was demonstrably not following the sources of Arrian, namely Aristobulus and Ptolemy. Not, for instance, at the Cilician Gates, the battle of Issus, the siege of Tyre, the visit to Siwa, and the campaign and battle of Gaugamela. Further, there are many stories in C. which are mentioned by Arrian as λόγοι or λεγόμενα, that is as recorded by authors other than Aristobulus and Ptolemy: for instance, at Arr. 2.4.7–11 (at least not Aristobulus for the illness of A and the account of Philip the doctor), 2.12.6 (A and Hephaestion visiting the royal women), 3.2.1–2 (barley at Alexandria), 3.10.1 (Parmenio's proposal of a night attack), and 4.20.1–3 (Darius' surprise at A's continence, as on a different occasion in C. 4.10.32–34). There are enough of these passages to show that C. did not use as a regular source either Aristobulus or Ptolemy. Whether he drew occasionally on one or the other for a piece of description is another issue.

Sometimes C. and Arrian have the same facts, as is to be expected when they treat the same subject, but the striking thing is that C. used them in a different way. Thus A dreams of Heracles leading him into Tyre. In Arrian the dream is genuine and is interpreted as such by Aristander (2.18.1); but in C. it is a fake, invented by A who was 'by no means unskilled in the manipulation of his soldiers' minds' (4.2.17). At Tyre 8,000 Tyrian soldiers died. In Arrian they were killed in the street fighting, and the King and the leading men of Tyre and some Carthaginian envoys, having taken sanctuary, were granted a free pass by A (2.24.3–5); but in C. 2,000 of the 8,000 were crucified by a raging A, only the Carthaginian envoys are mentioned as being spared, and even then A declared war on Carthage (4.4.17).

At Gaza, when a mound had come close to the wall and the siege-engines were mounted, an omen occurred which was interpreted by Aristander: 'A would capture the city but for that day A must take care for himself.' In Arrian, i.e. according to Aristobulus and Ptolemy, a stone was dropped onto A's head by a carnivorous bird, when he was about to sacrifice the first victim and he himself was wearing a garland (2.26.4); and in accordance with Aristander's interpretation A did capture the city and he himself, failing to take care, was wounded by a catapult bolt (2.27.2). In C. 4.6.10f. the action had already started at Gaza and the Macedonians had suffered a serious reverse, so that A sounded the retreat and at dawn next day, when his army was about to attack the walls, he implored the help of the gods in a sacrifice. It was then that a crow dropped a clod which hit A on the head and spattered over him, and the bird then got caught in a mixture of bitumen and sulphur which coated a siege-tower. A, 'whose mind was not above superstitious belief', consulted the diviners and Aristander gave his interpretation, warning A not to begin the assault that day. So A gave the signal again for retreat. The sequel in C. is a near-miss by an Arab assassin, an arrow-wound (corresponding to the wound in Arrian), and a wound in the leg, caused by a hurled rock; this trio of events drives home C.'s moral that one cannot escape destiny ('ut opinor, inevitabile est fatum').

When Gaza's defences were breached, the defending soldiers were killed. In Arrian, based on Aristobulus and Ptolemy, the ruler of Gaza was a eunuch, Batis, who had brought in for himself a force of Arab mercenary soldiers, and with the Macedonians breaking into the city the defence kept together, fought on, and died there to a man, each at his post. The women and children were sold into slavery. C., however, has his commander, Batis, deserted by his soldiers (where did they go?), but with many wounds and his armour slippery with his own and his enemy's blood Batis fought on until he was taken captive. As A was already inflamed with rage (4.6.24), he now indulged his youthful, arrogant glee, his passion and frenzy, and his thirst for revenge by treating Batis grossly ('insolenti gaudio iuvenis elatus . . . ira, rabies, poena in hostem capienda'). And Batis was still alive when, tied by the heels to the chariot, he was dragged round the city while the King boasted that he was imitating his ancestor, Achilles.

How are we to account for the differences between Arrian and C.? Dreams, omens and Aristander's interpretations were original material, recorded surely in the *King's Journal* at the time and published (for these years) in the official history by Callisthenes. Nor is there any doubt that A, as a deeply religious king, believed in the divine nature of dreams and omens and in the interpretation of diviners, above all of Aristander. Historically Aristobulus and Ptolemy, Arrian's sources, were correct recorders of the dream at Tyre and the omen at Gaza. C.'s account in 4.2.17 and 4.6.12 is incorrect in depicting A as a cynical commander and inconsistent in making him a prey to superstition. The settings may be judged similarly. At Tyre the record of men killed in the capture of the city, the pardoning of the king and the leading men, and the respect for the Carthaginian envoys were surely recorded in the *King's Journal* and published by Callisthenes. Aristobulus and Ptolemy, Arrian's sources, are likely to have followed the official account. They mentioned too the fury of the Macedonians at the length of the siege and at an atrocity committed by the Tyrians. But C.'s account is suspect; for it contains the portrait of an angry A (as often in C.), a Greek form of execution, and a most improbable thing, a declaration of war by A on Carthage.

So too at Gaza the setting provided by Arrian has more claim to historicity than that provided by C. For instance, that the siege-engines came by sea from Tyre to Gaza and arrived only later (Arr. 2.27.3), is obviously correct; but it makes C.'s story of a bitumen-and-sulphur-coated siege-tower into an invention (not even plausible in itself). The two retreat-signals and the three dangers faced by A — especially the assassination-attempt by the Arab — look like dramatic frills. In Arrian Batis is described not as a commander appointed by Darius (like Hegesistratus at Miletus, Memnon at Halicarnassus and the satrap's troops at Celaenae in Arr. 1.18.4, 1.20.3 and 1.29.1) but as 'ruling the Gazaeans' city' (κρατῶν τῆς Γαζαίων πόλεως), a term appropriate rather to a dynast or tyrant, who then procured for himself a troop of Arab mercenaries (Ἀραβάς τε μισθωτοὺς ἐπαγαγόμενος). In C. 4.6.7f. Batis is a loyal officer of Darius, placed in charge of the city and supplied with only a modest garrison in relation to the size of the city. He had his moment of exultation when he thought A was killed (4.6.20); then we hear of his own *aristeia*, his unbroken and haughty spirit and his terrible end. And in C.'s account 'Persians[18] and Arabs' were killed at Gaza to the number of 10,000 — a number exceeding those killed at Tyre, and the more incredible as no number is given by Arrian.[19] The probability is that Aristobulus and Ptolemy, Arrian's sources, recorded the true facts (for they had no motive for falsifying the position of Batis), and that C. or/and his source indulged in the invention of a more sensational story.

C.'s version has echoes of Virgil in his view of 'inevitabile fatum' for A and in the description of Batis being dragged round the city walls (*Aen.* 2.273 'perque pedes traiectus lora tumentes', and 278–9 'vulneraque illa gerens, quae circum plurima muros | accepit patrios', and *Aen.* 1.475f., as compared with *Iliad* 22.395f. and C. 4.6.29). But is he only updating and improving on part of an earlier account which is known to us in a fragment of Hegesias, a third-century B.C. writer (*FGrH* 142 F 5)?

The passage is cited by Dionysius of Halicarnassus verbatim from Hegesias as an example of tasteless and ridiculous rhetoric. 'With this force the king was leading the way' (C. 'ad prima signa pervenit') when a man kneeling down seemed to A to be acting as a suppliant (C. has A order him as a suppliant to rise). When the man struck with his sword, A inclined a little (so too in C.) and the sword struck[20] the kirtle of A's cuirass (C. had introduced the cuirass 'quam raro induebat' in the preceding section, 14, but he does not follow it up, because in 16 he makes the man aim at the King's throat). A himself killed the man, hitting him on the head with his dagger (C. has A cut off the man's striking arm). A new anger fired the rest ... so that 'in response to that trumpet-call'[21] (C. had two 'signa', probably trumpet-calls, for retreat at 4.6.10 and 13) 6,000 barbarians were cut down (variant reading is 4,000; C. has 10,000). Batis[22] himself was brought to A by Leonnatus and Philotas. A saw him to be very fleshy, huge and very shaggy — swarthy too in complexion — and hated him for his plotting as well as for his appearance. So he gave orders that they should drive a bronze curb-chain through his feet and drag him naked in a circle; and as he was pounded against many hard places he shrieked at his sufferings ... And A declared that the fat and the bulk of the man's flesh made him another fat Babylonian beast. The crowd mocked.

The start of this passage, it seems, was read by Curtius, because the king in the lead, the cuirass, the kneeling suppliant and the inclination of A's body are so close to the text of Hegesias. But C. is already providing his own variations, with the man aiming at A's throat and having his arm cut off. The second part follows immediately in Hegesias; but A suffers two wounds before entering the city in C. So one has to assume that what follows in Hegesias is not consecutive citation (as Jacoby prints it), but a paraphrase by Dionysius, in which we have to understand from Dionysius' earlier words that Batis was dragged not by men but by the horses of a chariot.[23] Even so, the story in Hegesias is not the source of C.'s account, which is entirely different: for in Hegesias the men are angry, in C. it is A who is angry; the man is dragged in a circle, but in C. round the walls of the city; A mocks the fatness of his victim, but in C. he boasts he is imitating Achilles. Moreover, C. has a spirited conversation between Batis and A and says nothing of Batis' sorry physique. The conclusion must be that in this second part C. was following an author other than Hegesias. The *aristeia* of Batis, the portrayal of A possessed with furious rage, gleeful cruelty and thirst for revenge, the (fictional) interchange of remarks, the boast of A that he was imitating Achilles and the inflated number of enemy killed (inflated even beyond Hegesias' figure) are entirely consistent with the source being Cleitarchus. See above, pp. 91f., for Cleitarchus' development of the Achilles connection. If so, the division between Hegesias and Cleitarchus may be put at 4.6.17.

Summary of attributions for Curtius 3–4

To summarise our conclusions, it seems clear that C. made use of Cleitarchus as a regular source for books 3–4. This is seen to be so at the following passages: perhaps 3.1.14–18 (Gordium); 3.2.1–19 (Charidemus episode); 3.5.1–20 (A at Tarsus); 3.8.13 – 3.12.26 (Issus and the royal women); 4.1.7–14, 4.5.1–8; 4.11.1–22 (three offers of Darius); 4.1.16–26 (Abdalonymus); 4.6.17–30 (end of Gaza affair); 4.7.25–28 (part of Siwa); 4.8.1–6 (Alexandria); 4.13.16–24, 4.14.1–26, 4.16.8–9 (parts of Gaugamela). He used Diyllus as his source for 4.1.27–33 and 4.5.11–18 (Amyntas etc. and the Greek Council). And he used Hegesias for 4.6.14–16 (assassination-attempt at Gaza). He added minor variations, as in using Hegesias, and he imported many contemporary ideas and echoes of Roman literature and life. If C. read the relevant part of D. 17, he seems not to have drawn directly on D. On the other hand, he read Trogus and may well have borrowed some of Trogus' rhetorical touches for his own speeches; but in general he went to a source shared by Trogus and himself, mainly Cleitarchus.[24]

Sources in parts of Curtius 5-6

It seems impossible to pin down any source or sources for C. 5.1.1–35.[25] The next part, 5.1.36 – 5.3.15, covering the stay in Babylon and the advance into Sittacene, Susa and Uxiane may be taken in two groups, divided at the end of 5.2.15.

Although C. is much fuller than D. for the advance from Babylon to Susa, there is a remarkable similarity in the order of events and in the details which are common to them. The army spends 'more than 30 days' in Babylon (D. 17.64.4, while C. 5.1.39 has 34 days), appointments and bounties are detailed (D. 17.64.5–6 and C. 5.1.43–5, who alone mentions Mazaeus, Bagophanes and 2,000 soldiers for Menes and Apollodorus), reinforcements of the same sizes except one are given by the same areas (D. 17.65.1 and C. 5.1.40–1, giving a much smaller number of cavalry from the Peloponnese),[26] 50 young pages were sent to guard the king (D. 17.65.1 πρὸς τὴν σωματοφυλακίαν and C. 5.1.42 'ad custodiam corporis'), A delays in the rich province of Sittacene (D. 17.65.2 and C. 5.2.1–2) and reorganises his forces (D. 17.65.2–4 and C. 5.2.2–7 with much more detail), Abulites surrenders Susa perhaps on the orders of Darius (D. 17.65.5 and C. 5.2.8), and A obtains 50,000 talents (D. 17.66.1–2 'more than 40,000' plus 9,000, and C. 5.2.11) which had been accumulated by the kings over a long period of time (D. ibid. and C. ibid.).

There are some differences. As we have noted, C., being fuller, mentioned a few points at 5.1.43–5, and he has only 380 Peloponnesian cavalry, whereas D. gives 'less than a thousand' (an error by D.?). Each gives his own slant: C. sees corruption and degeneration of the army in Babylon (as of the Roman army in the East before Corbulo took it in hand), whereas D. has A granting a time of recuperation. C. sees the irony of kings saving for posterity only to be robbed on one day by a foreign king (5.2.12), whereas D.'s kings save 'against the unexpected turns of chance' (17.66.2).

When we compare the two narratives, there is no doubt that D. and C. were following a common source. On my analysis above (p. 55) the source for D., and so here for C., is Diyllus.

The story of A sitting on the throne of Darius is found only in D. 17.66.3–7 and C. 5.2.13–15, and it comes probably from a common source, because we find in the two accounts the details of the Page putting Darius' table under A's feet, the eunuch weeping, A intending to have the table removed, Philotas' insistence on the omen, and A's decision to keep it under his feet. The source on my interpretation was Diyllus (loc. cit. above). The moral of the story in D. is more appropriate to a Greek writer such as Diyllus, and the moral in C., that A was overcome with shame at abusing the gods of hospitality, seems to be a silly addition by C. himself.

C. 5.2.16 – 3.15 presents a special problem. C.'s appointments at Susa are not as in Arr. 3.16.9, the story of Sisygambis is unique, the campaign against Medates with the sieging of a city is unique but credible, and the relationship of Medates to Sisygambis explains why she interceded for him and obtained from A 'immunitas' for the combatants and freedom from tribute for the city. The account of the campaign is self-standing and complete; it illustrates the skill of Tauron (probably a brother of Harpalus), the daring of A and the policy of clemency towards brave Persians who surrendered and towards a relative of Darius, Medates. C. is alone in giving a full description of this campaign which was conducted against Persian forces and an Uxian city, evidently in the low-lying country of the Uxii;[27] for D. 17.67.4–5 has a brief and muddled account (perhaps mixing it with the campaign against the Uxii of the mountains) but concludes correctly with the reduction of 'all the cities in Uxiane' (C.'s 'regio Uxiorum'). Arrian mentioned only the conclusion:[28] 'those of the Uxii who inhabit the plains were obedient to the Persian satrap [i.e. resisted at first?] and then surrendered themselves to Alexander' (3.17.1, these being C.'s 'Uxiorum gens subacta' at 5.3.16).

Although this campaign was presumably described by Ptolemy and perhaps by Aristobulus, it is unlikely that C. took his account from either; for the appointments C. gives differ from those in Arrian, who used Ptolemy and Aristobulus. Yet it must have come from a full-scale work on A, and the probable candidate as author is Cleitarchus. Moreover, it has a Cleitarchan characteristic, that the Macedonians wanted to retire and A had to taunt them into standing their ground.

The campaign against the Uxii of the mountains, who were chiefly herdsmen and not city-dwellers, was described by Arrian (3.17.1–6). A trapped them in the open, inflicted heavy casualties and made them pay tribute (no 'immunities' for them); they were saved from expulsion only by the intercession of Sisygambis, a point recorded by Ptolemy (F 12). As neither D. nor C. mention this campaign, it is reasonable to assume that they were not following Aristobulus or Ptolemy.

At 5.3.16 C. takes us into Persis, where the Susian Gates were held by Ariobarzanes with 25,000 infantry. His narrative from 5.3.17 to 5.4.27, though much fuller, has the same points as that of D. 17.68.1–6. It is clear that C. was not drawing on D., but both were using a common source, namely on my interpretation Cleitarchus (see above, p. 56). While D. described the climax in one sentence, C. has a purple passage, which includes the (unhistorical) escape of Ariobarzanes' force of 5,000 infantry and 40 cavalrymen.[29] The advance to the Araxes in C. 5.5.1–4, being different from Arr. 3.18.6 but close to D. 17.69, came presumably from the same common source.

C. 5.5.5–24 and D. 17.69.2–9 (and briefly J. 11.14.11–12) are alone in telling the pathetic story of the mutilated Greeks whom A met on his march. The story, with the same details of clothing etc. at the climax,[30] originates in a common source, namely Cleitarchus on my interpretation (see above, p. 56). Next, C. 5.6.1–7 and D. 17.70 have A describe Persepolis as the most hostile city in the world and hand it over to wild looting by the soldiers, who fought one another for the spoil etc. — again due to a common source, Cleitarchus (loc. cit. above); and the same is true of the 120,000 talents on the citadel, and the camels and mules needed to transport it (D. 17.71.1–2 and C. 5.6.9).

The burning of the palace of Persepolis in the course of a drunken revel with the King throwing the first brand and Thaïs, the Athenian courtesan, playing a leading part is narrated in similar terms by C. 5.7.1–7 and D. 17.72, and it is generally agreed that they both drew on Cleitarchus (his F 11 mentioning Thaïs) but each added his own emphasis. C. is unique in describing at some length a winter campaign of one month's duration in inner Persis, where A showed his power of leadership and visited strange peoples (5.6.12–19). Some conquests by A in Persis are mentioned by D. 17.73.1 in a single sentence, whereas no other writer has such a campaign. It seems, then, that C. and D. took this from their common source, Cleitarchus. C. put it where it was in his source, i.e. between the looting of Persepolis and the burning of the palace,[31] and D. left it to be added in a note after the burning of the palace.

The rest of the book is concerned with the flight and end of Darius; it breaks off just before his death, because the last few sections are lost. What takes six chapters in C. is compressed into two sentences by D. (17.73.1–2), but they agree on two points, that Darius headed for Bactra and set out with 30,000 men 'both Persians and Greek mercenaries', the latter numbering 4,000 (D. ibid. and C. 5.8.3). C. adds some slingers, archers and 3,300 cavalry, who do not figure in D.'s abrupt account. This is of interest, because Arrian gave Darius about 3,000 cavalry but only 6,000 infantry. Thus C. and D. were not using Aristobulus or Ptolemy, but another source. The long account of Darius' flight and arrest (C. 5.8.6 – 5.12.20) is loaded with speeches and rhetoric probably of C.'s own invention. The pursuit by A in C. is from a source other than those used by Arrian (the messages, e.g. C. 5.13.3 and Arr. 3.21.2, the distances and the numbers are different); and the same is true of the climax of the pursuit.

That part of J. 11.14 which corresponds to C. 5.1.5 is exceedingly short. It shares with C. and D. three points: over

30 days of rest at Babylon, 40,000 talents 'in the city of Susa' (D. 17.66.1, with the additional 9,000 from another treasure-house, probably on the citadel; C. 5.2.11 has the total 50,000 from the treasure-houses, 'ex thesauris') and the story of the mutilated Greeks. This is compatible with Trogus having used the same source as C. and D. at each of these points; but there is not enough in J. to justify the identifying of a source (see above, p. 101). But J. 11.15 has important points in common with C.: Darius is bound with 'gold fetters', A reached the village in which Darius had been arrested (J. 'postera die'; C. 5.13.6 where a similar interval would explain C.'s account of the final pursuit), the advance force of 6,000 cavalry (C. adding 300 *dimachae*), the phalanx to follow ('exercitu' in J.), the fighting[32] (J.'s 'in itinere multa et periculosa praelia' being a loose summary, whereas C. has A's 3,000 leading cavalry kill almost 3,000 Persians and round up many more, although his men were badly outnumbered and weary), Darius with many wounds in a wagon, not at first discovered (how he came to be wounded is explained in C. but not in J.'s résumé) and one of the soldiers drinking water at a spring and finding Darius near death (J. 'spirantem adhuc'; C. 'semivivi'). It is obvious that Trogus and C. used the same source ultimately (C. may have drawn partly on Trogus for this scene); and that source on my interpretation of J. was Cleitarchus (loc. cit. above).

In book 6, when the text resumes after the lacuna, the last phase of the war between Antipater and Sparta and her allies is being described. The fact that this phase is reported after the death of Darius, i.e. after July 330, whereas in D. 17.62–63 it comes after the battle of Gaugamela i.e. after October 331, shows that C. and D. were following different sources. This is apparent also from the different figures for casualties on the Macedonian side, being 'not more than 1,000' in C. 6.1.16 and 3,500 in D. 17.63.3. On the other hand, D. adds at 17.63.4 a résumé of Agis' last fight which is obviously from the same source as C.'s account at 6.1.13–15 (even to the kneeling in D. ἐς γόνυ διαναστάς and in C. 'poplitibus semet excepit'). Thus either D. or C. changed source at this

133

point, D. at 17.63.4 or C. at 6.1.13; and, as we have seen above (p. 46), it was D. who changed from Diyllus to Cleitarchus at 17.63.4. Thus C. used Cleitarchus[33] for 6.1.1 to 6.1.16.

In C. 6.1.17-19 Antipater's fear of the jealous king looks like an addition by C. (we may compare Nero's jealousy of Corbulo); so too the statement that it was this fear which prompted Antipater to refer the settlement of terms to 'the Council of the Greeks' ('concilium Graecorum'). In fact, Antipater was following the principle of the Common Peace. C.'s source was well informed on the decisions of the Council (6.1.20); and it was presumably from him that C. made the remark that the war in Greece ended before the battle at Gaugamela, a remark so inconsistent with the place of the war in C.'s narrative that he must have found this information in another source than Cleitarchus.[34] The other passage which describes Antipater and the Council of the Greeks is D. 17.73.5-6, and the only decision D. records concerns the Spartans and their sending of envoys to A, as in C. 6.1.20. As the source of D. 17.73.5-6 is on my interpretation Diyllus (see above, p. 58), it is possible that C. drew on Diyllus at 6.1.17-20.

The next passage which is echoed in other writers concerns the return home of the Greek troops from Hecatompylus, the discontent of the Macedonians, A's speech and the agreement to proceed (6.2.15 - 4.1). To the Greeks he gave generous bounties (the same amounts per man in C. and D. 17.74.3).[35] His largesse totalled 12,000 talents (C. 6.2.10; D., including the value of clothing and goblets, 13,000 and J. 12.1.1 13,000); but an equal amount was embezzled (C. 6.2.10; D. 'even more, it was thought'). The Macedonians wanted to go home (C. 6.2.15-16; D. 17.74.3; J. 12.3.2), and A made a speech and persuaded them to continue (C. 6.2.18 - 4.1; D. ibid.; J. ibid.). The order of events and the similarities are the more significant, because Arrian put the dismissal of the Greek allies at Ecbatana *before* the pursuit of Darius and made the total bounty 2,000 talents, not 12,000 talents (3.19.5).[36] It seems, then, that C. and D.

followed the same source, who on my interpretation was Diyllus (see above, p. 58).

On entering Hyrcania A marched 150 stades and encamped at a spot where the river Stiboetes gushed out from the roots of the mountains and later ran underground for 300 stades (C. 6.4.1–5; D. 17.75.2). Later he reached the Caspian sea, remarkable for huge serpents and fish differently coloured from other fish (C. 6.4.18; D. 17.75.3). Further on, they came to an oak-like tree with honey-dew (C. 6.4.22; D. 17.75.6). A number of Persian commanders who had fled with Darius surrendered to A and were received kindly (scattered in C. 6.4.23 and 5.1; together in D. 17.76.1); so too the 1,500 Greek mercenaries of Darius, who were taken into A's forces (C. 6.5.10; D. 17.76.2). Next A attacked the Mardi who had made no approach to him, defeated them and drove them back into wild country (C. 6.5.11–17; D. 17.76.3–4). During the ravaging the natives captured A's horse, Bucephalas,[37] which used to kneel down for him alone (C. 'sponte genua submittens'; D. συγκαθίει τὸ σῶμα πρὸς τὴν ἀνάβασιν), but when A threatened to kill every man unless the horse was restored they brought the horse and also many gifts (C. 6.5.19–20; D. 17.76.8). Even so A cut down many trees (C. after the return of the horse, and D. before it; C. alone explained the use of trees as a fortification, at 6.5.13–14). On returning to his base (C. 6.5.22; D. 17.77.1 in Hyrcania) the Amazon queen Thalestris spent 13 days with A to become pregnant and then went home (C. 6.5.24–32; D. 17.77.1–3). As C. has many further points not in D., he did not use D. for all this narrative, but D. and C. drew on the same source, namely on my interpretation Cleitarchus (see above, p. 59). In considering D.'s narrative by itself, I left the matter of the Greek mercenaries and Bucephalas unallocated; but with the addition of C.'s narrative it seems most likely that Cleitarchus was used throughout.

J. describes only the visit of the Amazon queen. He gives her the same name, the same number of escorts (300), and the same length of stay to become pregnant. Thus Trogus and

C. go back to the same source, being Cleitarchus for Trogus, as we argued above (p. 102).

C. devotes two passages to the deterioration of A. The first (6.2.1–5), coming after the deaths of Darius and Agis, seems to be a free composition by C. himself; for it finds a psychological explanation for A's lapse into drunkenness, lechery and banqueting in the easing of tension after the deaths of Darius and Agis (in the same way Nero lapsed into excesses after the deaths of Agrippina and Seneca). For this passage C. used some points which came again in his second passage. The peculiarity of the second passage (6.6.1–11) is that it closely matches passages in D. and J. and is introduced at the same point in the narrative, namely after the sexual performance of A with the Amazon queen. Points in common are adoption of Persian court ceremonial (D. 17.77.4; C. 6.6.2–3), Persian gear and dress (D. 17.77.5; J. 12.3.8; C. 6.6.4), insolent extravagance (D. 17.77.4; C. 6.6.1 and 5), Friends and Companions forced into Persian dress (D. 17.77.5; J. 12.3.9; C. 6.6.7), concubines on night duty (D. 17.77.6; J. 12.3.10; C. 6.6.8), Macedonian resentment and A's recourse to gifts (D. 17.78.1; J. 12.4; C. 6.6.9–11). All three come clearly from a common source, namely on my interpretation Cleitarchus (see above, p. 59 and p. 102). Arrian does not cite Aristobulus and Ptolemy in this matter, but writing in the first person he mentions A's adoption of Persian dress and implies A's loss of self-control (4.7.4–5) and he records as a λόγος the changes in dress and court ceremonial as due to A's admiration for Persian ways and his demand for obeisance as due to his belief in his own descent from Ammon, not Philip (4.9.9). It may well be that Arrian took this from Cleitarchus.

As D. 17.78 is too concise to prove the use of a common source with C. 6.6.13–36, we turn next to the so-called conspiracy of Philotas. C. devoted the rest of the book to a very lengthy account of the conspiracy, full of fictitious conversations and speeches. There are a few points of similarity with D.'s single chapter (17.79), but they are such as might have occurred in many accounts[38] of what was evidently a stock theme for sensational writers. J. 12.5.2–3 is even briefer.

Summary of attributions for Curtius 5–6

To summarise our conclusions for these two books, C. used Diyllus for 5.1.36 – 3.15 (Babylon to Uxiane), 5.2.13–15 (A on Darius' throne), 6.17–20 (Antipater and the Greek Council) and 6.2.15 – 4.1 (Greeks return home, etc.). The first passage is more precise and detailed than most of 5–6, and the others are unsensational, not unfavourable to A and interested especially in Greek affairs. C. made greater use of Cleitarchus, whom he drew upon probably at 5.2.16 – 3.15 (Sisygambis and the campaign against Medates where Sisygambis obtained lenient terms), and then at 5.3.16 – 5.4 (campaign against Ariobarzanes), 5.5.5–24 (mutilated Greeks), 5.6.1–7 (sack of Persepolis town), 5.6.12–19 (winter campaign in Persis), 5.7.1–7 (burning of the palace), 5.8.1 – 5.13.25 (flight and death of Darius), 6.1.1–16 (death of Agis), 6.4.1 – 5.32 (Hyrcania and the Amazon queen) and 6.6.1–12 (deterioration of A). These passages show an interest in Sisygambis, a knowledge of Persian customs, a qualified opinion of Macedonians in battle, sensational looting, extreme drunkenness, treachery, pathos, heroism, generosity in A to suppliants, and then deterioration of A — in fact a great deal of sensational and sometimes fictional writing, to which C. has added contemporary Roman ideas and his own rhetorical flavouring.

CHAPTER 5

THE SOURCES OF CURTIUS 7–10

Sources in parts of Curtius 7–8

C.'s account of the trial of Alexander Lyncestes has a reference to the early part of C.'s history which is missing (7.1.6). This dates the arrest to a time before A reached Celaenae, i.e. to before early summer 333. Thus C.'s timing of the arrest is compatible with Arr. 1.25.10 but incompatible with D. 17.32.1, of which the source on my interpretation was Cleitarchus (see above, p. 41). So the source of C. 7.1.5–9 was not Cleitarchus. A shorter version of C.'s account appears in D. 17.80.2 with the same main features: a plot against A, a three-year spell under arrest,[1] kinship with a leading Macedonian (I take Antigonus in D. to be a not untypical error for Antipater), inability to make a defence, and execution. Thus C. and D. probably had a common source, who on my interpretation was Diyllus (see above, p. 60). I take it, then, that Diyllus was the source used by C. at 7.1.5–9.

Next comes the trial of Amyntas and his brothers, for which C. provided highly rhetorical speeches. It was omitted by D. and J., no doubt for reasons of space, but it is covered by Arrian, who himself had omitted the trial of Alexander Lyncestes. For this trial Arrian cites Ptolemy and Aristobulus, who were evidently in agreement (3.27.1, with 26.1 providing the subject of λέγουσι). The differences are illuminating. C. does not mention the additional brother, Attalus, who figures in Arrian; C. has Polemon run away, whereas Arrian has 'he ran away to the enemy' (ἔφυγεν ἐς τοὺς πολεμίους); C. has other persons bring Polemon back, whereas Arrian has Amyntas go and fetch Polemon with the permission of the Macedonians on his own acquittal. The unsensational nature of C.'s events is compatible with Diyllus being the source for the facts presented in C. 7.1.10 to 7.2.10.

In 7.2.11 – 7.3.5 there are no clues to C.'s source or sources, because the comparable passages in D., J., Arrian and Strabo 724 are too brief. C. has added unhistorical tête-à-tête conversations, probably of his own invention (e.g. 7.2.13). But in 7.3.5–18, which strongly resembles D. 17.82 (land of the Paropanisadae), and again in 7.3.19–23, which has in common with D. 17.83.1–2 the 16 or 17 days' crossing of the Caucasus, the rock of Prometheus, and an Alexandria founded with 7,000 natives and a number of non-natives, there is clear evidence of a common source for C. and D., namely Cleitarchus on my interpretation above (p. 60). The cautionary tale of Bessus and Gobares in 7.4.1–19 has only a faint echo in D. 17.83.7.[2] The points about the crossing of the Caucasus in 7.4.22–25, being additional to those in 7.3.19–23, come from a source other than Cleitarchus on my interpretation. They are concerned with the lack of wheat and the eating of fish, 'herbs' and draught-animals. What 'herbs' were they? Arrian cites Aristobulus as saying that nothing grew on the Caucasus except terebinth and silphium. So the 'herbs' were silphium, and it is evident that C. was drawing here on Aristobulus. Strabo 725 also mentioned the eating of silphium and draught-animals during the crossing of the Caucasus, which he said took 15 days (not 16 or 17 days, as above). All this indicates that Strabo's source here was probably Aristobulus, not Cleitarchus.

The descriptions of the fight after a challenge between Satibarzanes and Erigyius in C. 7.4.33–40 and D. 17.83.4–6 have sufficient points in common (evenly matched battle with 'utrimque aequis viribus' corresponding to ἰσόμαχον ποιούντων τὸν κίνδυνον; Satibarzanes bares his head; the Asians surrender) to show that C. and D. had the same source, namely Cleitarchus on my interpretation for D. (loc. cit. above). This is supported by the fact that Arrian's account, being from Ptolemy and Aristobulus, is different, in that it was during a bitter battle that Satibarzanes 'fell in with'[3] Erigyius and on his death the Asians broke and fled headlong (3.28.2–3).

The report of this event is tied up with two other pieces of news which were said by C. 7.4.32 to have reached A at the same time, i.e. when he had crossed the Caucasus and was at Bactra in early summer 329. One piece of news was that the Scythians from beyond the Tanaïs were on the way to join Bessus (this picks up 7.4.6 in the Bessus–Gobares story, but the Scythians do not arrive in C.'s later text); it may be fiction. The other piece of news is the report of war having broken out in Greece; and attached to this is an anecdote at 7.4.39, that on hearing the news A said Sparta had waited until she knew he had come 'to the borders of India'. This piece of news is wrong by about a year (see n. 34 to chapter 4), and the anecdote is ridiculous. Only Cleitarchus could be so far out, or else so eager to produce a triplet of news. If, then, Cleitarchus is C.'s source here at 7.4.32–40, the link with the Bessus–Gobares story shows that that story also came from Cleitarchus. This means that the echo of that story in D. 17.83.7 should come from Cleitarchus; and we have in fact already attributed D. 17.83 to Cleitarchus (loc. cit. above). On the other hand, the sensible sections about Bactria, C. 7.4.26–31, will come together with 7.4.22–5 from Aristobulus.

C. himself at 7.5.2 refers back to 7.4.27. This suggests that C. has returned to Aristobulus. The suggestion is confirmed by the similar outlook between 7.4.22–31 and 7.5.1–18 in regard to details of supply — oil or sesame oil, wine, lack of water — and travel by night in the desert. I conclude, then, that we owe to Aristobulus this account, which includes A giving back a cup of water and waiting unrefreshed to see the last man reach camp.[4]

C.'s story of Bessus (7.5.19–26 and 7.5.36–43) cannot come from Ptolemy or from Aristobulus (Arr. 3.29.6 – 30.5), because it differs on so many points (Spitamenes and Catanes bringing Bessus 'on a chain fixed into his neck' to Alexander; no mention of Ptolemy). On the other hand, it agrees with the brief account of D. 17.83.8–9, drawn from Cleitarchus (loc. cit. above). One point of this agreement is illuminating. In C. 7.5.40 Alexander *ordered* the brother of Darius to mutilate Bessus, have him pierced with arrows and keep the birds off the crucified corpse — and in the source, no doubt, this did happen, with Catanes showing his skill in archery and with gifts being given to the deliverers of Bessus. In D. (Cleitarchus) the deed was done: 'Darius' brother and his Kinsmen inflicted every outrage and torment, cut up his body bit by bit and catapulted the dismembered parts.' In C., however, this did not happen. In the last sentence of 7.5.43 C. thought better of it: he had Bessus wait to be killed at the scene of Darius' death.[5] Even that was a mistake; for at 7.10.10 he had him killed at Ecbatana, correctly as we see in Arr. 4.7.3, based on Ptolemy and Aristobulus.

The story of Bessus is interrupted by a short passage recording the discharge of 900 men with different bounties for cavalrymen and infantrymen, an exhortation to beget children, and the promise given by the rest of the army to complete the war (7.5.27). This certainly covers the discharge of the oldest of the Macedonians and the Thessalian volunteers (cavalrymen) recorded by Arrian (3.29.5). There is, however, a difference: C. placed it after the crossing of the Oxus, Arrian before the crossing. Either C. made a mistake; or Arrian, faced with a difference between Ptolemy and Aristobulus, did not trouble to record it but followed Ptolemy, while C. followed Aristobulus. It is probable that the latter is correct. C., then, was probably following Aristobulus.

After the interruption C. resumed his previous source, Cleitarchus, with the connecting phrase 'dum Bessus perducitur'[6] which looks back to 'Alexandro tradituri ducunt'. He now tells the story of the massacre of the Branchidae as a punishment exacted for sacrilege. As Pearson has pointed out,[7] the story serves 'the author's dramatic purpose of showing how Alexander punishes Greek traitors before he punishes the traitor Bessus'. It belongs, then, to the story of Bessus, and therefore comes also from Cleitarchus. Such an origin is consistent with its appearance in only one of our chief sources, namely D. (in the list of contents of book 17); for he too was using Cleitarchus just before the lacuna in the text of book 17. The destruction of the city of the Branchidae, recorded by Strabo 517/18, may well have come from Cleitarchus; for Strabo made use of Cleitarchus elsewhere, e.g. at 505 and 718. That the story is a fiction is most probable.[8] Cleitarchus was no respecter of the truth, he had a predilection for a massacre and a cautionary tale, and he introduced the Branchidae here for a sensational and dramatic purpose.

In 7.6.6-10 C. gives a description of the wounding of A and its consequences which is at variance with that of Arr. 3.30.10-11. In C. the wounded bone is different, the natives send envoys to see the wound and regret their impiety in warring 'with the gods', and A accepts their surrender. In Arrian the wounded A went on to capture the fastness, and only 8,000 of the 30,000 defenders escaped. C.'s source is romancing; Ptolemy and Aristobulus recorded what happened. Thus C. drew on Cleitarchus. He probably went on to take from Cleitarchus the story of the rivalry to carry the wounded king on a litter ('lectica militari').

C. 7.6.11-23 has much in common with Arr. 4.1.1 - 4.3.5. C. contracts the military side and causes some confusion, but he expands the psychological interest, for instance by depicting the just Scythians, the Abii, in these words: 'interpreting freedom as self-control and egalitarianism, they had put the leaders on the same level as the lower class'. Arrian gives a precise and systematic account of the military operations. C. puts the wounding of Alexander at the city of the Memaceni,[9] Arrian at Cyropolis. The similarities and the minor differences may be explained on the supposition that both C. and Arrian used Aristobulus but Arrian alone used Ptolemy as well. At the same time we must allow C. his own ability to elaborate and invent.

For the foundation of Alexandria on the Tanaïs C. 7.6.25-7 has the same figures as J. 12.5.12: seventeen days in the building, and walls 60 stades long (= 6 Roman miles in J.). Arr. 4.4.1 has 20 days of building and adds sacrifices and games. Again, it may be a case of C. using Aristobulus, and of Arrian correcting from Ptolemy. When I considered J.

12.5.4–5 (p. 103) I offered no suggestion. The details of the settlers in the three accounts seem to be complementary: each writer took what interested him from a long description.

The episode of Menedemus in C. 7.6.24 and 7.7.31–9 has all the marks of Cleitarchus as source: ambush, horse with two riders, *aristeia* of Menedemus on his mighty horse, *aristeia* of Hypsicles, disaster concealed by Alexander's threat to kill anyone reporting it. The force of Menedemus is given as 800 cavalry and 3,000 infantry, and of these 300 cavalry and 2,000 infantry were killed, so that (we infer) 500 cavalry and 1,000 infantry escaped. The account in Arr. 4.3.7 and 4.5.2 – 4.6.2 is entirely different; it is due to Ptolemy, since Arrian gives a variant from Aristobulus. Although C. shares an ambush with Aristobulus, C.'s account certainly does not come from Aristobulus. It seems clear that C. used Cleitarchus, the earliest to write on the subject: that Aristobulus wrote next; and that Ptolemy wrote last, using the *King's Journal.* Arrian had the good sense to accept Ptolemy's account.[10] Later, A reached the scene of the disaster in four days, covered the bones of the dead with a tumulus and sacrificed to the dead 'in the traditional way' (C. 7.9.20–1). According to Arrian, A reached Samarcand in three full days and a bit, and pursuing Spitamenes closely he came to the scene of disaster, where he buried the soldiers as best he could under the circumstances, evidently on the fourth day, as the close pursuit cannot have exceeded a few hours after such forced marching.[11] The common source here for C. and Arrian was evidently Aristobulus.

The Scythian episode is written up with great elaboration by C. (7.7.1–29; 7.8 – 7.9.19). The themes of 'fortuna, gloria, superstitio and ira' are treated in a Roman manner, and the fictitious speeches, although said at one point to be of traditional content (7.8.11), are packed with Senecan epigrams, such as 'bellum vitando alemus', 'firmissima est inter pares amicitia' and 'qui non reverentur homines, fallunt deos'. C. certainly did not use the sources of Arrian, i.e. Ptolemy and Aristobulus; for Arrian's account is entirely different. On the other hand, C.'s narrative has features found in Cleitarchus: the sensational effect of A's wound (7.7.9,18,20; 7.8.7; 7.9.11,14); the terror of Aristander and his change of interpretation (7.7.29; contrast Arr. 4.4.3 and 9); A's sleepless night, as at Gaugamela (7.8.1); A peeping through his tent-flaps to estimate from the twinkling fires the number of an enemy whom he had seen clearly by daylight; the fictitious envoys and their philosophical negotiations; and a complete failure to understand how the victory was won. It is enough for C. and his source that each Macedonian shield had been pierced by many arrows at the same moment (7.9.8), and that when the barbarians could not endure 'the expression, the weapons and the shout of the Macedonians' they fled.[12]

In C. 7.10.1-3 the description of Sogdiana and the river Polytimetus might come from any source. The story of the Sogdian captives in 7.10.4-9 was told also by Diodorus (in the list of contents); as Arrian, following Ptolemy and Aristobulus, does not give the story, we may infer that C. probably took it from Cleitarchus. The figures for troops left in Sogdiana and for reinforcements may come from Aristobulus (Arr. 4.7.2 gave more names but omitted figures, perhaps because they were not the same in his two sources), and this is confirmed by the mention of Bessus being brought to Ecbatana (see above p. 141). The story of the spring of water in A's tent (Arr. 4.15.7-8 has a slightly different account, evidently from Ptolemy whom he cites for the message to A) may well have come from Aristobulus.

The bold ascent of the Rock of Ariamazes, which Arrian called 'the Rock in Sogdiana', has many details shared by C. 7.11.1-26 with Arr. 4.18.4 - 19.3 but some slight differences (iron wedges instead of tent-pegs, and different-sized prizes). The best explanation is that C. drew on Aristobulus, and this is made more probable by the mention of A's 'cupido', corresponding to πόθος in Arrian, a characteristic of A usually thought to have been reported by Aristobulus. C. has, of course, expanded the episode and added a speech and perhaps a cave.

However, the sequel in C. 7.11.26-9 is entirely at variance with that in Arrian. C. has the leaders scourged and crucified; Arrian has A fall in love with Roxane and accept her father, Oxyartes, one of the leaders. In C.'s narrative Roxane appears first in 8.4.23 after the surrender of the Rock of Sisimithres, which Arrian calls 'the Rock of Chorienes' (4.21.1). This accords with Strabo's attribution of Roxane to the Rock of Sisimithres, and Strabo, like C., has the name 'Rock of Ariamazes' as a variant given by 'some' for the Rock of Sogdiana (Str. 517). One source used by Strabo was thus the same as that used by C., since the names and sequences were the same: Rock of Ariamazes, Rock of Sisimithres, appearance of Roxane; D. (in the list of contents) had that sequence and so shared that source. The likely candidate is Cleitarchus, not least because the scourging and the crucifying of the leaders at C. 7.11.28 are consistent with Cleitarchus' version of the end of Batis (see p. 128 above on C. 4.6.29). I conclude, then, that C. followed Aristobulus for the climbing of the Rock[13] but switched to Cleitarchus for the sequel.

In 8.1.1-6 and Arr. 4.16.1 - 17.2 there are two widely differing accounts of what were presumably the same incidents. These involved A dividing his army (C. into 3 parts, Arrian into 5), refugees and Massagetae (Bactrian in C., Sogdian in Arrian, 900 Massagetae in C., 600 in Arrian), an ambush (all killed in C., seven Companions and sixty mercenary cavalry in Arrian), and a success by Craterus (1,000 Dahae killed in C., 150 Scythians in Arrian). The discrepancies are too great to permit of Aristobulus being the source of one and Ptolemy of the other. Either Cleitarchus or some other writer must be the source of C. The next sections, 8.1.7-9, and Arr. 4.15.1-6 give the same message from the Scythian envoys but have different things to say of the Chorasmii; again, C.'s source may be Cleitarchus or another. In 8.1.11-19 the whole army goes a-hunting, kills 4,000 wild beasts and has a mighty banquet, and there are stories about A and Lysimachus. There is none of this in Arrian but the hunt appeared in D. (list of contents).[14]

The long account of Cleitus and his death in 8.1.20 – 2.12 certainly does not come from either Aristobulus (see especially Arr. 4.8.9) or Ptolemy, whose removal of Cleitus is not mentioned; nor does it share a common source with PA 50–1, whose source is generally held to be Chares. It is a masterpiece of Roman rhetoric, comparable to the much shorter version of J. 12.6, which has some points in common. As I remarked in the case of J. (p. 104 above), Cleitarchus is the most likely candidate. But there is no clear evidence.

Next comes the Rock of Chorienes, as Arrian calls it, or of Sisimithres, as C. calls it. Their accounts in 4.21.1–9 and 8.2.14–33 are about the same place (compare 4.21.2–6 with 8.2.23–24) and end alike (4.21.8–9 and 8.2.31–2), but they are concerned with such different aspects that they cannot be from the same source. In other words C. did not depend on Ptolemy or Aristobulus. The name 'Rock of Sisimithres' is found also in Strabo 517 and in PA 58.3, and both these writers say that it fell through surrender (Strabo ἐκ προδοσίας meaning rather 'abandonment' than betrayal, and Plutarch 'by frightening Sisimithres out of his wits'). C. too pictures the natives as struck with 'a huge panic', as 'trepidum diffidentemque'. It is apparent, then, that these three writers drew on the same source, namely Cleitarchus, who, we suggested above (p. 142), was the source of Strabo.

This same Sisimithres, whose incestuous habits delighted Cleitarchus, figures again in 8.4.19–20 as helping A. This passage is followed by the story of Oxyartes[15] and Roxane. Now, although C. does not name the location, he supplies the extravagant banquet ('barbara opulentia convivium') which Strabo mentioned (ξενίας πολυτελοῦς), and it was at this banquet that one of the thirty high-born girls on parade caught the eye of A: she was Roxane. Here too, then, C. draws on Cleitarchus. The analogy of Achilles, A's ancestor, cohabiting with a captive girl is adduced by C.; and this too is typical of Cleitarchus (see p. 91f. above).[16]

The story of Sisimithres is followed by that of Lysimachus' brother, called Philip (C. 8.2.34–39), a royal page who over-exerted himself in the King's service and died in the

King's arms. It is a trivial incident in itself, and the motive for reporting it was presumably to please Lysimachus, whose offer of a horse at the time is mentioned. Another story involving Lysimachus was introduced into the great hunt of C. 8.1.11–19. The most likely source for such stories of Lysimachus is Onesicritus, who read his works to Lysimachus at the court of Lysimachus (*FGrH* 134 F 8 = P*A* 46.4).

In Arr. 4.17.7 the last followers of Spitamenes, the Scythian Massagetae, cut off his head and sent it to A. Arrian's sources for this were presumably Ptolemy and Aristobulus. C., however, has a fantastic story of the love-life of Spitamenes, the wiles of his beautiful but exhausted wife, the murder in the marital bed, the head of the husband presented by the murderers to Alexander, and his dismissal of her from his camp, lest she should affect 'the character and the mild disposition of the Greeks' (8.3.1–15). This is cited as an example of Fortuna doing a job for A, 'as in most other things' (8.3.1). It all reads very like Cleitarchus, with tête-à-tête interchanges between Spitamenes and his wife which no one can have known and the moral that the Greeks behaved better than these barbarians. The next story, 8.4.1–19, is equally extraordinary: the army shattered by lightning everywhere, tornado winds from every quarter, torrential rain turning into ice, men stuck to trees who were in fact dead but looked as if they were conversing with one another, and A lifting up the fallen and even putting a soldier on his own royal seat which led to a quoted speech, contrasting Persian autocracy with A's readiness to save a soldier; and, to cap it all, the good Sisimithres sent huge gifts of stock to make good the losses of the army. The nature of the story and the return to Sisimithres smack of Cleitarchus.

In C. 8.5.1–5 A prepared for the campaign in India. Among the items which C. puts together are the addition of gold and silver to the equipment of his army – this occurs also in J. 12.7.4 – and the remark that 120,000 men followed A on that campaign. The true context of the figure 120,000 is given in Arr. *Ind.* 19.5, where Nearchus was the source

(*PA* 66.5 mentioned it *en passant*). It is not possible to say what source C. used here.

C. devoted much space — from 8.5.5 to 8.8.23 — to the events in which Callisthenes figured, because C. saw in them the topical theme of autocracy and liberty. His account is overlaid with matters calculated to appeal to readers in the middle period of the first century A.D. 'As a champion of public liberty Callisthenes was heard with ready attention' (8.5.20), while A, like Agrippina, hid behind a curtain to overhear his words.[17] The trial-scene is loaded with speeches palpably composed by C. It is not possible to see through this overlay to the sources on which C. must have drawn to produce his amalgam. The same can be said of the description of India in 8.9, which includes much that was known only after the time of A.

The invasion of India starts at 8.10 without mention of the crossing of the Caucasus but with a number of facts common to Arr. 4.22.6 – 23.5. There are, however, additions: the precedents of Dionysus and Heracles but A seen in person (cf. Strabo 688, attributed to A's flatterers), and the boats in sections carried on wagons. At the first city he captured A is said to have killed all the natives and vented his rage on the buildings, as an act of terrorism (in Arr. 4.23.5 the Macedonians took no prisoners because they were angry at the wounding of A, but most of the natives escaped). The same policy was stated by D. (in the list of contents: ἀναίρεσις ἄρδην τοῦ πρώτου ἔθνους πρὸς κατάπληξιν τῶν ἄλλων). The source common to C. and D. is likely to be Cleitarchus, and we know that Cleitarchus made much of Dionysus in India. Next in D. in the list of contents and next in the narrative of C. comes the surrender of Nysa founded by Dionysus and the sparing of the city; so too in J. 12.7.6. The visit of the whole army and the Bacchic revel on the holy mountain are both in C. and in J.; as remarked above (p. 104), the source is very probably Cleitarchus (cf. *FGrH* 137 F 17).

The same order continues in J. and C.: 'montes Daedali, regnaque Cleophidis reginae'. The siege of Massaga, described in some detail, ended with the defenders believing the siege-engines to be powered by the gods, envoys asking for pardon, the queen with her little son acting as a suppliant (in fact the child was her grandson), and the sparing of the city by A. The description of the siege is incompatible with that of Arr. 4.26 – 27.2, so that C.'s source is other than Ptolemy and Aristobulus. The likely candidate is Cleitarchus, as we suggested for J. and for D. 17.84.1, which picks up the story at the terms of surrender. C. rounded off the story with the broad hint of a love-affair between Cleophis, the queen, and A, and a son of the union who was called A. This was roundly said by J. 12.7.9–11 to be so; but D. was content to say she 'admired the greatheartedness of Alexander' and sent him gifts. D. alone reports the massacre of the Indian mercenaries after the treaty at Massaga; his source then was certainly Cleitarchus (see p. 53 above). We can see, then, that each secondary author took from Cleitarchus' long account what he preferred: D. the massacre, J. the love-affair, and C. a broad hint of the love-affair. Thus C. backed off from the ending of Cleitarchus' account, as he had done at 7.5.43 in the matter of Bessus' death.

For the attack on the rock called Aornus we have a clear account in Arr. 4.28.30, which came from Ptolemy who commanded one group. D. gave an account which differed in many respects (17.85); we have attributed it to Cleitarchus as source. C. 8.11 begins like D., but he then provides acts of heroism by A himself, a like-named officer[18] and another officer, Charus, which are neither in Arrian nor in D. It is probable that C. used two sources, Cleitarchus and then another, perhaps Chares (*FGrH* 125 F 16), who described the use of snow and stakes to fill up cavities (ὀρύγματα corresponding to C.'s 'cavernas' at 8.11.9). If we are correct in these attributions, Chares gave credit to the officers Alexander and Charus and not to Ptolemy. The brief remarks in J. 12.7.12–13 came probably from Cleitarchus (see p. 104 above).

C. 8.12.1–16 and D. 17.86 have the same events in the same sequence: one Erices (Aphrices in D.) with 20,000 men, his head cut off by his men, then sent to A, Indus bridged already, Omphis (Mophis in D.) parades his army and alarms A, but the kings meet and exchange gifts. As this is not in Arrian, it is from a source other than Ptolemy and Aristobulus. C. gives more information about Omphis than D. does about Mophis; but the conclusion is the same, that A restored his kingdom to him and Omphis (Mophis) changed his name to Taxiles. The source may well be Cleitarchus, as I suggested in considering D.'s account (p. 53 above). C.'s tailpiece to the story of Taxiles at 8.12.17–18 is found also in PA 59.5, a passage which Berve attributed tentatively to Onesicritus (2.370 n. 3).

In 8.13.2–5 C. reports events not found elsewhere: diplomatic negotiations with Porus, capture of 30 elephants and of Barsaentes and Damaxarus, and retention under guard of the two men. Then in 8.13.5 – 14.46 he devotes himself to the campaign and battle of the Hydaspes river. His long and rambling account has very little in common with the accounts of D., PA and Arrian. At one point to our knowledge, and probably elsewhere, C. did not use Ptolemy (8.14.2; Arr. 5.14.6), Aristobulus (8.14.2; Arr. 8.14.3) or Plutarch's source, namely A's letters (8.14.2; PA 60.8). If we are correct in attributing D. 17.87–89.3 to Cleitarchus as source, we may note one point which is found only in D. and C.: A decided to attack Porus before Abisares' troops could join Porus (17.87.2–3), and, when A did attack, Porus was still hoping for these troops under a special agreement (Abisares' envoys having tricked A at 8.13.1, 'ut mandatum erat', and 8.14.1 'ita convenerat'). Otherwise C. has merely an odd phrase in common with D., notably the simile of the elephants in the battle-line being like towers on a circuit-wall (8.14.3, cf. 8.12.8; D. 17.87.5).[19] In short, it seems probable that C. made use of Cleitarchus and of other unidentifiable and equally undependable sources, and failed to use Ptolemy, Aristobulus and A's letters to any noticeable degree.[20]

Summary of attributions for Curtius 7-8

We may summarise our suggestions of sources in this section as follows.

> Aristobulus for 7.4.22-31, 7.5.1-18, 7.5.27, 7.6.21-3, 7.9.20-1, 7.10.10-14, 7.11.1-26.
>
> Cleitarchus for 7.3.5-23, 7.4.1-19, 7.4.33-40, 7.5.19-26, 7.5.28-43, 7.6.6-10, 7.7.1-39, 7.8.1 - 7.10.4-9, 7.11.26-9, 8.1.1-9 (or another), 8.1.20 - 8.2.33, 8.3.1-15, 8.4.1-30, 8.10.1-36, 8.11.1-25 (perhaps together with Chares), 8.12.1-16, 8.13 and 8.14.
>
> Diyllus for 7.1.5 - 7.2.10.
>
> Onesicritus for 8.1.11-19, 8.2.34-9 and 8.12.17-18.
>
> Chares perhaps for 8.11, together with Cleitarchus.

It must be borne in mind that C. introduced speeches of his own composition and treated his source-material with considerable freedom.

Sources in parts of Curtius 9-10

There is every indication that a common source lay behind C. 9.1.6 - 9.2.7 and D. 17.90-93.3.[21] Such differences as there are may be attributed to the fact that C. wrote much more fully (e.g. contrast C. 9.1.15-23 with D. 17.91.2) and that each tells a story in his own way (e.g. that of the lion and the dogs at C. 9.1.31-34 and D. 17.92). As we noted above (pp. 62-3), D. was following Cleitarchus. C., then, used Cleitarchus.

When the army came to the Hyphasis, C. reflected upon the motives and the fears of A and the problems of the soldiers (9.2.8-11) and then produced a speech of his own composition for A to deliver to the assembled Macedonian soldiers (9.2.12-34). This is very different from Arr. 5.25.3 - 26.8, where A talks only to the leading officers. In C. the soldiers stayed silent, the terrified generals gazed upon the ground, and then everyone, including the King, wept copiously (9.3.3 'universa contione effusius flente'), and Coenus came forward to deliver a speech of C.'s own composition (9.3.5-15, again unlike the speech of Coenus in the meeting of officers in Arr. 5.27.2-9). All this looks like C.'s own invention, and we may add too the effect of Coenus' speech on the troops at 9.3.16–18. Alleged facts return with two days of rage, the twelve altars, the enlarged camp and the huge bunks of 9.3.19, which are found also in D. 17.95.1–2, based on Cleitarchus (see p. 64 above). Thus C. still has Cleitarchus to hand.

In 9.3.20–4 the narrative jumps from the Hyphasis to the Acesines river, and it is brief. It resembles D. 95.3–5 closely (Acesines, fleet ready, 25,000 ornate panoplies, 1,000 or so ships, naming of two cities), but C., as often, has additional points (death of Coenus, alliance of Porus and Taxiles, order of marching and sailing). C. and D. used the same source here, most notably in the naming of the two cities as Nicaea and Bucephala. Earlier in the narratives C. and D. had mentioned the founding of the two cities and explained their positions (C. 9.1.6 and D. 17.89.4); so it seems that there too they were following the same source — one which reported the first stage after the battle and the final stage (the naming) after the return to the Hydaspes. As we argued in the case of D., the source was Diyllus (above, p. 62). There is, however, a difficulty in their reports of the reinforcements. While the cavalry figures are near enough (C. has 5,000 and D. not much short of 6,000), the difference between the infantry figures is huge: C. 7,000 and D. more than 30,000. An explanation may be found in the words 'praeter eos' in the text of C.: 'equitum v milia, praeter eos ab Harpalo peditum vii milia adduxerat'. C. normally contrasts or couples 'equites' and 'pedites'[22] It seems, then, that sentences defining the origins of other infantry groups have disappeared in the transmission of the text. We conclude that C. made use of Diyllus at 9.1.1–6 and 9.3.20–4.

When A returned from the Hyphasis, he came first to the Acesines and then to the Hydaspes (Arr. 5.29.2 and 5), where he found his fleet ready on the river (Arr. 6.1.1). In C. 9.3.20, D. 17.95.3 and J. 12.9.1 A comes to the Acesines and finds the fleet afloat there. The error may go back to each writer's source: Diyllus on my interpretation for C. and D., and someone other than Cleitarchus for J. (p. 105 above). It was an easy mistake to make in the absence of maps. The source or sources for this mistake cannot be the same as the source which made the Acesines, the Hydaspes and the Indus all meet for the first time in a giant and turbulent confluence (C. 9.4.8 and D. 17.97.1), namely Cleitarchus; but we anticipate.

C. 9.4.1–8 and D. 17.96.1–5 are similar to one another in the sequence of the Acesines joining the Hydaspes, the Sibi, the descendants of Heracles' followers, 40,000 infantry in opposition, survivors sold as slaves, the burning of a city and yet the safe survival of its citadel. There are other items in C., which is natural, as he writes at greater length. What is strange is that C. gives a different explanation for some of Heracles' followers being left behind (being sick, whereas D. has them fail in an attack on the rock of Aornus) and for the firing of the city (by the Indians themselves, whereas D. has an enraged A burn it and the people). The probable explanation is that C. and D. were still using a common source, Diyllus (see p. 64 above for him being D.'s source here), but each added from another source a version which he personally preferred, C. adding the sickness of Heracles' troops and D. the rage of A. If my argument for D. is correct (pp. 61–2 above), the other source was Cleitarchus.

C. 9.4.8 and D. 17.97.1 now produce their triple confluence of Acesines, Hydaspes and Indus, the sinking of two ships, the peril of the naked A, his Friends swimming alongside, A's narrow escape and his sacrifice. The belief of A that he, like Achilles, had fought with the river (*Iliad* 21.228f.) is stated by D., but it is watered down into a 'you might think' by C. The source for this wild stuff is clearly Cleitarchus (see for D. loc. cit. above).

The same sensational style runs on in C. 9.4.15 – 9.5.20 with huge numbers of united enemies (90,000 infantry), psychological study of A and of his soldiers, a near-mutiny, a report of A's speech, a manic change in the soldiers to euphoria, a warning prophecy by Demophon, A's reprimand of Demophon and then the attack on a city of the 'Sudracae'. C. then takes A straight onto the wall, whereas D. has him first break in through a postern-gate. Thereafter they have the same sequence of exciting details. A on the crown of the wall is peppered with missiles, and two ladders break under the weight of the men; A jumps down alone into the city, he is protected by a tree, is the target of vast numbers of weapons, is struck down by an arrow; yet fights on one knee, kills the firer of the arrow, hoists himself up on a branch and challenges the enemy. Enter Peucestas from a different ladder. C. and D. certainly drew on the same source, namely Cleitarchus as we argued for D. (p. 65 above).

While D. brings his account to an end with the fall of the city and the massacre of all the inhabitants, C. continues in the same vein with the treatment of A's wound by a terrified Greek doctor, Critobulus (9.5.22–30) — no doubt from Cleitarchus. Neither C. nor D. included Ptolemy among those who fought alongside A; but C. 9.5.21 notes that Cleitarchus and Timagenes had included him in their accounts, but that Ptolemy himself had denied being present and had put his denial in writing. Cleitarchus, then, wrote of this affair and he published his account before Ptolemy wrote his work. C. and D. knew of Ptolemy's famous refutation, and therefore omitted Cleitarchus' mention of Ptolemy. C. gave a display of one-upmanship in censuring Timagenes, a writer of the late 1st century B.C., for repeating this lie. Arrian evidently had the mistakes of Cleitarchus in mind, when he drew attention to the confusion of 'Oxydracae' for Malli, the story of the Greek physician (Critodemus, a variant of Critobulus), the haemorrhage and the fainting (6.11.1–3).

In 9.6 C. seems to have indulged in some free composition of his own in order to portray concern for the king, namely a rhetorical *tour de force* by Craterus and a reply by A (9.6.6–27). In 9.7.1 Curtius recounts a rising by the Greeks 'around Bactra and the Scythian borders' (9.7.11), and it ends in the leader and others reaching Greece. D. 17.99.5–6 has the same basic facts. C. gave much the longer story. It came certainly from a Greek source, presumably Cleitarchus, to whom responsibility for D. 17.99.5 has been tentatively attributed (p. 66 above). In 9.7.12–26 C. gives a glorified version of what appears in D. 17.100–101, a banquet and the combat of a Macedonian and a Greek, and the suicide later of the Greek. Both draw on the same source, Cleitarchus on my interpretation of D. (loc. cit. above). In C. 9.8.1–7 and D. 17.102.1–4 the same events are recorded: A's force on board and the army marching alongside, Sambagrae (in D. Sambastae) a democratic self-governing people, forces of 60,000 infantry, 6,000 cavalry, 500 war-chariots; but, overcome by the sight of the fleet, they give in. On my interpretation the common source is still Cleitarchus.

C. and D. continue to give the same sequence of incidents (submission of next people, Alexandria founded, Musicani and Musicanus, Porticanus killed fighting, destruction wrought by A, Sambus, 80,000 killed in this region – C. citing Cleitarchus as the authority for the number – second revolt of Musicani = Brahmans in C., and the ruse of the 500 light-armed which brings out 3,000, whom A defeated). Each has a few additional points, not common to one another, but it is clear that both are drawing on the same (full) source; and that source is Cleitarchus on my interpretation of D. (loc. cit. above). The famous story of poisoned weapons, the illness of the beloved Ptolemy, the dream of A, the curing of Ptolemy and other sick men, and the surrender of the people (of Harmatelia in D.) is told both by C. and by D., again from Cleitarchus. Thus we attribute C. 9.8.8–30 to Cleitarchus as source. So too the short account of J. 12.10.2–3 (p. 105 above).

In 9.9 C. provides a long and elaborated account of A sailing down the Indus into the sea. There is no comparison now with D. who is very brief, and C.'s account differs from that of Arr. 6.18.3 – 19.5. We cannot tell who is C.'s source; but probably not Diyllus, who was proposed for the source of D. 17.104.1–2 (p. 68 above).

The accounts of A's return from India in C. 9.10 and D. 17.104–106.1 are similar in the vagueness of the geography and the cursory description of events. A tripartite division of forces between A, Ptolemy and Leonnatus is peculiar to C. and D., and it is to be noted that Ptolemy does not figure in Arrian's account; this is an indication that the source is Cleitarchus, always ready to give a role to Ptolemy. The description of the fish-eating aborigines is a commonplace, and the suffering in the Gedrosian desert is written up with much more rhetorical colouring in C. than in D. As with D. (see p. 70 above) the source may be Cleitarchus. The sending of food on camels to relieve the troops in Gedrosia is dated earlier in C. and D. than in Arrian (C. 9.10.17–18, D. 17.105.7–8 and Arr. 6.27.6); and considerations of time and distance make it unhistorical. The rout or 'komos' in honour of Dionysus with seven days of drunken festivity forms a sensational climax in C. and D. As we have seen in the case of D. (p. 70 above) the probable source is Cleitarchus. Arrian made a point of denying the historicity of the 'komos' which was reported, he wrote, neither by Ptolemy nor Aristobulus nor by any author worthy of credence. This remark is consistent with Cleitarchus being the source behind the 'komos' in C.; for Arrian scorned even to mention the name of Cleitarchus.

There is no clue to C.'s source for the punishment of satraps and officers for rebellion and misconduct, except that the names of the offenders are often different from those in Arrian, his being derived from Ptolemy and Aristobulus. C. added much contemporary Roman colouring with aphorisms reminiscent to us of Tacitean writing (e.g. 10.1.6 'power gained through crime is not lasting' as in T. *Ann.* 13.19.1). The arrival of Nearchus and Onesicritus and their report in C. 10.1.10–16 are not from Nearchus, whose account of himself and Archias coming overland to A in Arr. *Ind.* 34.7 (cf. *Anab.* 6.28.5) is entirely different. The arrival in C. appears to be that of the fleet,[23] as it is expressly in D. 17.106.4; and in both C. and D. the next commission of Nearchus is to sail to the Euphrates, whereas in Arrian it is to go to Susa on the Pasitigris. Thus C. and D. were probably following the same source, who, it was suggested in the case of D. (p. 71 above), was Cleitarchus.

In C. 10.1.17 grandiose plans for the future are attributed to A at a much earlier date than elsewhere. They include his hostility to Carthage, which had been developed in C.'s description of the siege of Tyre, especially at 4.4.18, a description which we attributed to Cleitarchus as source (p. 119 above). Next, the cutting of timber in the Lebanon and the transporting of it to Thapsacus and the laying of the keels of 700 septiremes are both pre-dated and grossly exaggerated (cf. Arr. 7.19.3, citing Aristobulus). At 10.1.22–42 C. tells a highly ornate and sensational story of the excessively wealthy Orsines, the intrigue of the eunuch boy Bagoas as A's darling, the robbing of Cyrus' tomb, the attribution of this to Orsines by Bagoas, and the execution of Orsines by a rapidly degenerating A 'at the caprice of a catamite' ('arbitrio scorti'). Now this Bagoas had already appeared in C. 6.5.23 as the royal catamite ('specie singulari spado') who moved A to pardon Nabarzanes. That was within a long passage which we ascribed to Cleitarchus as source (see p. 135 above).[24] There can be little doubt that all these passages were drawn from Cleitarchus by C., who added his own colouring and exaggeration. Aristobulus put the facts right about the building of ships and the robbing of the tomb of Cyrus (Arr. 6.29.4), and he may be the source of the reasons which led to the execution of Orsines at Arr. 6.30.2. As we have already noted, Aristobulus wrote after Cleitarchus.

After a lacuna the text of C. opens with Harpalus and his mercenaries crossing to Sunium in Attica. There he used his money to buy the support of some leading men but was ordered by the assembly to depart. Crossing to Crete Harpalus was killed by one of his friends. Next comes the order of A ('iussit') to the Greek states to restore the exiles except those guilty of 'civilian bloodshed', an order obeyed by the Greeks generally, who even restored property, but flouted by Athens. The same juxtaposition of topics and some of the same points occur also in D. 17.108.6 – 109.1, and the tone of both is unsensational and expressive of the Greek viewpoint. C. and D. seem to be drawing on the same source, whom we have identified in the case of D. as Diyllus (see p. 72 above).

The background to the mutiny comes next: the oldest soldiers due to be sent home, the payment of the debts of all soldiers ('omnes milites') to a total of 9,870 talents, and the news that some were to be sent home and others to be retained in Asia. The payment of the debts of all soldiers is reported by Arrian (7.5.3) as 'said to amount to 20,000 talents'; and it is placed by him some weeks before the question arose of sending unfit soldiers home (7.8.1). D. 17.109.1–2 has the same sequence as C. and the same amount of talents, 'a little short of 10,000', as C.; it is probably D.'s mistake that he has the debts only of the oldest soldiers paid.

In C. and D. it was the troops who were to be retained in Asia that became mutinous – thinking in C. that A would establish 'the seat of the kingdom in Asia' and saying they would not go anywhere except to Macedonia; whereas in Arrian's account it was those who were being sent home who started the mutiny (7.8.3), feeling that they were despised by A (7.8.2). In quelling the mutiny C. and D. have A arrest thirteen men with his own hands (10.2.30 'manu corripuit' and 17.109.2 ταῖς ἰδίαις χερσί), whereas Arrian has A point out the ringleaders and make the officers arrest them (7.8.3). It seems, then, that C. and D. followed the same source in these respects. The mutiny offered a marvellous opportunity for C. to deploy his rhetorical talent and he provided three specimens of direct speech (10.2.15–29, 10.3.7–14 and 10.4.1, a protest by a prisoner). It is probable that he introduced the hyperbole into the narrative at 10.3.4, where the execution of the ringleaders made the men step up their own obedience and loyalty, and later the men themselves offered their bodies for execution at 10.4.3. If we allow for C.'s own embroidery of the theme, the source behind C. and D. is the same, and we have already identified the likely source of D. as Diyllus (p. 73 above).

After another lacuna the text starts with the soldiers seeing A on his death-bed (10.5.1). This account is not taken from the *Journal* nor from an author who used the *Journal*; for there A could not speak, but in C. he goes on talking. Two of the alleged remarks appear also in D.'s very brief account: that he left his kingdom to the best man, and that he foresaw great funerary contests. All we can say is that C. did not draw on the *Journal* or Ptolemy or Aristobulus. The long description of mourning and confusion provides no clue to the source (10.5.7–25) except that the climax, the self-imposed death of Sisygambis on the fifth day after she took the resolve, is common to C. and to D. Since it was meant to shed glory on A, it may have come from Diyllus, as I suggested in the case of D.'s ending.

Summary of attributions for parts of Curtius 9–10

We end this section with a summary of our conclusions. C. made use of Cleitarchus for 9.1.6 – 9.3.19, 9.4.8 – 9.5.30, 9.7.1 – 9.8.30 and 9.10.1–30; and of Diyllus for 9.3.20–4 and 9.4.1–8 (with a slight mix of Cleitarchus). In book 10 C. used Cleitarchus for 10.1.10–42 and Diyllus for 10.2.1 – 10.4.3. C. himself wrote quite a lot, especially speeches, out of his own head but making use of wide reading. In some passages we can say only what sources he did not follow; and these include Ptolemy and Aristobulus and the *Journal*.

CHAPTER 6

SOME GENERAL CONCLUSIONS

The methods of working of Diodorus, Justin (Trogus) and Curtius

The conclusions which we have reached in considering the accounts of D., J. and C. individually may now be drawn together into a general picture. Let us begin with Diyllus as the author whom D. and C. used predominantly for Greek affairs. There was one negative reason for their choice, namely that the author whom they used mainly for Asian affairs, Cleitarchus, had written the *Histories of Alexander* which concentrated on the adventurous and sensational aspects of A in Asia; indeed it seems that Cleitarchus did not treat of A's campaign in Europe at all, nor of his involvement in Greek affairs in any detail apart from the destruction of Thebes. For this reason alone D. had to look to another author. A positive reason for choosing Diyllus was that Diyllus had written a 'universal history' (D. 21.5.1, κοινὰς πράξεις συντάξας), and this was what D. himself claimed to be doing.[1] In addition, D. was already familiar with Diyllus, since he had used his work in book 16 from the point where the work of the other 'universal historian', Ephorus, came to an end. It has been maintained by Schubert that D. used the work of Diyllus in book 18 for Greek affairs; and it may well be that he did so for later books too. For D.'s own references to the work of Diyllus are important pointers. D. reported three stages in Diyllus' work of 26 books at 16.14.5, 16.76.5 and 21.5.1, the last marking its end in 297 B.C.

On my interpretation[2] D. used Diyllus in book 16 for Greek affairs and for the intertwined activities of Philip II and the Greeks (Social War, Olynthian War, Siege of Byzantium and events in 338–336 B.C.). D. used him in book 17 for A's first two years, the siege of Miletus, Greeks and Carians in Caria, the Aegean, Memnon, A's Greek doctor, Agis, Sparta and the sending back of the Greek allied troops.

C. faced the same problem, but it mattered less to him because he was writing *Histories of Alexander the Great* and not a universal history. He drew upon Diyllus for Greek affairs at 4.1.27–33 (the 4,000 Greeks with Amyntas), 4.5.11–18 (mainly naval warfare), 6.2.15 – 4.1 (return of Greek troops) and 10.2.1–7 (Harpalus and Athens). On the other hand, J. (Trogus) made no use of Diyllus.

Both D. and C. used the work of Diyllus for some parts of A's progress in Asia. Thus D. for events from Babylon to Susa (64.5 – 67.1) and C. from Babylon via Susa to Uxiane (5.1.36 – 3.15). D. for the trial of Philotas and the advance to the Ariaspi (79–81); C. for the trials of Alexander Lyncestes, Amyntas and Simmias (7.1.5 – 2.10). D. for the return from the Hyphasis and the voyage down to the confluence of three great rivers (95.3 – 96); C. for the same stretch (9.3.20 – 4.8). D. for the scene at the mouth of the Indus (104.1–2). Then again D. for events from A's return to Susa until the death of Hephaestion (107–114). C. for the mutiny (10.2.8 – 4.3), an event within D.'s span in 107–114. Both D. and C. gave from Diyllus the death of Sisygambis as a tail-piece to the death of A (118.3 and 10.5.19–25).

The reasons which prompted D. and C. to make these uses of Diyllus' work can only be conjectured. Presumably D. thought that Cleitarchus' accounts of events from Babylon to Susa, from the Hyphasis to the confluence, and from the return to Susa until the death of Hephaestion were either unsatisfactory in themselves or too long for D.'s purpose. The latter explanation is certainly appropriate for the last section; for book 17 was already at 106 going to be considerably longer than book 16 and book 18. C. may have found Cleitarchus' accounts of events unsatisfactory and therefore preferred Diyllus. They both liked the death of Sisygambis as a (rather sentimental) conclusion. Otherwise each had his own reasons of personal preference: D. for the trial of Philotas and the scene at the mouth of the Indus; and C. for other trials and the mutiny.

The fullest use of Cleitarchus is found in J., who epitomised the 'Universal History' of Trogus, a work comparable rather to D. than to C. It suited Trogus to follow Cleitarchus from the beginning of A's reign, indeed from Philip's last summer, down to the death of Darius except for one version of a plot behind Philip's death and for a passage on Persia (due probably to Deinon, but transmitted perhaps through Cleitarchus). For the period from then to the death of A he used Cleitarchus for the outstanding events but he made more use of other writers, e.g. for the Battle of the Hydaspes and the halt at the Hyphasis river and for one version of A's death. Trogus probably found in Cleitarchus such congenial traits as a dislike of autocratic rule, an antipathy towards the Macedonians and a taste for sensation of all kinds.

Of the three D. made proportionately less use of Cleitarchus, because he had a naive admiration for A.[3] But he too wanted exciting descriptions and he turned to Cleitarchus for the great sieges, the great battles, the great feats of daring, the single combats, the portents and the circumstances of A's death. And these, of course, occupied the greater part of his book 17. D. had already cited Cleitarchus in 2.7.3 for the measurement of the walls of Babylon, and it was natural that he should turn now to Cleitarchus as the famous writer on Alexander in Asia.

C.'s use of Cleitarchus is more complex. C. was an original writer. He introduced into his work many speeches of his own composition, many aspects of events which had a contemporary topical allusion and some passages in which he mixed his own ideas with what he had read in more than one source and then produced a sophisticated amalgam (e.g. 8.5.5 – 8.8.23 on Callisthenes and the Pages' Conspiracy). However, it is certain that he took a great deal directly from Cleitarchus. This is most noticeable in the invasion of India up to the river Hyphasis (8.10 to 9.3.19) and in the return westwards from the Indus to Carmania (9.10.1–30). To his contemporary readers this was almost a fairyland; for Roman ambitions did not reach then beyond Armenia, Parthia and the Euphrates. C. probably had no hesitation in using

Cleitarchus. His own ability to invent shows that his concern for historical truth was far from absolute, and he found in Cleitarchus the same congenial traits as Trogus had done.

Turning to sources other than Diyllus and Cleitarchus, we can see that J. (Trogus) must have used many writers. For instance, the Prologues of Trogus include the 'origins' of diverse peoples,[4] which could have been ascertained only by wide reading. Even within the narrative which we have considered in J., Trogus used Satyrus, probably Deinon, and two unidentified authors, one for India (at 12.9.4–13 and 9.1–3) and another for praise of the Successors (13.1.7–15). Trogus was more ambitious, or at least more pretentious, than D., and the contrast is heightened by the fact that D. consulted far fewer sources. On our findings for book 17 D. contented himself almost entirely with Diyllus and Cleitarchus. Early in the book (7.4–7) and late in it (103.4–5) he evidently consulted specialist works on solar phenomena and snake poisons;[5] and he may have borrowed from Diades of Pella on siegecraft, Ephippus on the funeral of Hephaestion and Hieronymus on the poisoning of A. But these are small exceptions. The general rule of D. was to excerpt from two authors, Diyllus and Cleitarchus, one for Europe and the other for Asia; but at times he used Diyllus (who as a universal historian wrote also on Asia) for some affairs in the East where he found Diyllus more acceptable or/and concise than Cleitarchus.

It is certain that C. had read widely in Latin literature, both Augustan and post-Augustan,[6] and in much of the literature concerning A, including his predecessors D. and Trogus. We have identified Hegesias, Aristobulus and Onesicritus as authors from whom C. obtained information, and we add Timagenes (9.5.21) and as probabilities Marsyas of Pella and Chares; but the actual list was probably considerably longer. But this does not obscure the fact that C. used only one major source, Cleitarchus, and one minor source (mainly for Greek affairs), Diyllus. He had, after all, the same problem as D. had had, to obtain the basic information about the expedition of Alexander, and also, because he was himself interested in it, to learn what was happening concurrently in Greece and Macedonia. Thus he had to supplement Cleitarchus with Diyllus.

Why did none of these authors choose as a main source the Macedonian writers (Marsyas of Pella down to 331, Callisthenes down to a little later, Aristobulus and Ptolemy)? They certainly represented A as a Macedonian and as a king who brought glory to himself and his people and won the devotion of his soldiers and of most of his officers. Because D. had an admiration for A, he might have been tempted to use one or more of the Macedonian writers; but those for whom he wrote in the lifetime of Trogus and Livy did not want praise of the Macedonians and of kingship. Trogus and C. were reluctant to use a Macedonian writer; they were more interested in the corruption of absolute power and the deterioration of A. Cleitarchus provided what they wanted; and for D. and C. Diyllus was sufficiently neutral for their purposes.

That these writers went directly to Cleitarchus and Diyllus seems to be obvious. We know from Cicero and others that the work of Cleitarchus was widely known among the literati of the first century B.C., a relatively small group, and that any would-be historian of A would be bound to read that work. Indeed we have one piece of evidence which shows that in that period Timagenes did read the work of Cleitarchus; for he adopted the statement made by Cleitarchus that Ptolemy had been among those who saved the life of A (at the city of the Malli). We learn this from C. 9.5.21, 'Ptolomaeum ... huic pugnae adfuisse auctor est Clitarchus et Timagenes.' Now this story was started by Cleitarchus, and it was denied by Ptolemy himself in writing (Arr. 6.11.8). Anyone aware of Ptolemy's statement would drop this lie by Cleitarchus. D., C. and Arrian did so.[7] Since Timagenes did not, he had not read the work of Ptolemy. Arrian mentioned, without naming them, authors who made this misstatement; and it is clear that Cleitarchus and Timagenes were either those or among those he had in mind. The passage in C. has a further value: it shows that C. went direct to both writers.[8]

From time to time it has been suggested that one or all of D., J. and C. used an intermediary author who had already made an amalgam of the earlier writers whom we have been considering, and that D., J. (Trogus) and C. did not consult those earlier writers direct. This hypothetical intermediary has been identified as Timagenes. However, there are great obstacles in the way of this hypothesis. Timagenes' work *On Kings* could not have contained the full-dress account of A's life which we find in D.'s or C.'s passages based on Cleitarchus; and this is so too, if Timagenes wrote a 'general history', as Atkinson 59 suggests. Then the timing makes it wellnigh impossible. Timagenes was an exact contemporary of D., and he overlapped towards the end of his writing with Trogus.[9] Why should Timagenes alone have had access to these earlier writers? Why should his contemporaries, D. and Trogus, not have had access? Even if we suppose for argument's sake that Timagenes did write not a general history but a history of A based on these earlier writers, it is hardly possible that both D. and Trogus simply excerpted or reproduced with stylistic changes the book of a living contemporary. It would be as if a writer today were to sit down and reproduce Lane Fox's book on Alexander with only a few stylistic changes. *Cui bono?*

The Timagenes-hypothesis was introduced in order to account for those similarities between D., J. and C. or between any two of them which we have noted in the course of this book. In fact, however, the differences are equally significant; and they alone should put the Timagenes-hypothesis out of court. As I see it, the similarities are due rather to the fact that D., J. and C. all used Cleitarchus in some or most parts of their respective works and that D. and C. used Diyllus in a few parts of their works, in some of which the topic was the same. The differences are due to the fact that each took his own preferred passages; that these were not always the same in the case of Cleitarchus for D., J. and C., and in the case of Diyllus for D. and C. (J. did not use Diyllus); and that each used different additional sources.

Some consequences for the modern historian

It has been said time and again that 'the main problem in any serious interpretation of Alexander is, of course, that of the sources'.[10] In my book on Alexander I indicated the problem, gave numerous examples of conflicting evidence, passed judgement on their historical value and described A's career accordingly. The research which underlay those judgements has been carried farther in regard to D., J. and C. and has resulted in this book. What I hope that it has demonstrated to modern historians is that there is no short cut which will solve 'the main problem', and that to take refuge in 'The Vulgate' and to use a blanket term such as 'The Vulgate Tradition' as if it were the single-minded product of a single author is only to gloss over the difficulties and to postulate a simplistic solution. So too in the case of the authors treated in this book it has been demonstrated that there was not just one source on which D. or J. or C. drew. One must accordingly reject, for instance, what has become for some a conviction that D. used only one source throughout his book 17.[11]

There has been a strong tendency in recent writing to match 'The Vulgate Tradition' against Arrian. Sometimes this results in a hasty marshalling of anything anywhere which is at odds with Arrian's version and the attribution of it all to 'The Vulgate'. Let us take as an example the actions of Perdiccas and others at Thebes, which figured, for instance, in A. B. Bosworth's article 'Arrian and the Alexander Vulgate' in *EH* 1ff. Arrian's source at 1.8.1 for the action of Perdiccas was Ptolemy; this at least has not yet been disbelieved. And Ptolemy stated that Perdiccas in person opened the attack 'without awaiting the order for battle from A'. This is, according to Bosworth, an 'allegation' by Ptolemy, i.e. an untrue statement deliberately and consciously made. 'The unauthorised advance resulted', writes Bosworth,[12] 'in a limited defeat, which the other sources attribute to Alexander himself (Arr. 1.8.1. = *FGrH* 138 F 5; cf. Diod. 17.12.3; Polyaenus 4.3.12).' Of these references Arr. 1.8.1 refers to Perdiccas' *successful* advance; D. 17.12.3 to A seeing a postern-gate undefended and sending Perdiccas and his force to seize it and invade the city (this led not to defeat but to *victory* at 17.12.5); and Polyaen. 4.3.12 to Antipater's force in hiding and A's diversionary attack on the geographically stronger parts of the defences with the *successful* result that Antipater got in and captured the city. There is nothing whatever about 'a limited defeat' of Alexander in Arr. 1.8.1, D. 17.12.3 and Polyaen. 4.3.12; nor in an unmentioned passage, PA 11.9–10, which attributes the victory to A's attack and to the sortie by the garrison commanded apparently by Philotas and Antipater (PA 11.8 where the Thebans demanded that they be surrendered; and D. 17.8.7 identified Philotas as the garrison commander). The attempt by Bosworth to explain Ptolemy's alleged 'allegation' as due to his wish to show that Perdiccas was responsible for a 'military reverse' seems to rest on a complete misunderstanding of the passages which he cites.[13]

However, the main purpose of Ptolemy's alleged 'allegation' that Perdiccas opened the attack without an order was, as several writers have proposed,[14] that of 'partially absolving Alexander of the blame for Thebes' destruction'. Yet, we must note that Ptolemy does not censure Perdiccas for acting as he did. Nor would it have been sensible to have done so, since that action led to an amazing victory. To report an act of brave daring which nearly cost Perdiccas his life was not to discredit Perdiccas, and there is no evidence or probability that he was censured rather than commended by A. The fact is rather that Perdiccas commanded a brigade at the Granicus river, was a *somatophylax* (at least before 330 B.C.) and stood very high in A's esteem. Nor had the opening of the attack, whether before or on A's expected 'order for battle' (Arr. 1.8.1 τὸ ἐς τὴν μάχην ξύνθημα), any bearing on the responsibility of the Greek Council (Arr. 1.9.9), or, in the view of many modern writers, on the responsibility of A for the razing of the city.

The point we are making in this book is that each piece of evidence must be treated separately and its source analysed, if that is possible. Let us apply it in this case. We have already come to the conclusion concerning D. 17.8.2 – 17.14.14, that D.'s whole account of Thebes is an 'entirely fanciful and fantastic narrative' of which 'the object is sensation', and that D. was 'here using Cleitarchus directly and accurately' (pp. 15f. and 27 above). Where do Polyaenus and P*A* fit into the picture of the sources? The names of some leading Macedonians, Philotas and Antipater, afford a clue. For Plutarch mentions the two of them together, D. mentions Philotas as being in command of the garrison (17.8.7) and Polyaenus mentions Antipater. The coincidence is the more extraordinary in that Arrian had Philotas campaigning with A in Illyris (1.5.9) and reported the belief of the Thebans themselves that Antipater (was not in the Cadmea but) had arrived with an army from Macedonia (1.7.6). Who was correct historically? No one has yet suggested that Arrian, viz. Ptolemy/ Aristobulus, was trying to blacken the reputation of Philotas and Antipater in this passage; indeed everyone has accepted these statements of Arrian at face value.[15] On the other hand, the probability is very high that Plutarch and Polyaenus were mistaken in putting Philotas and Antipater in the Cadmea or at least the latter near it, and that the reason for their mistake was that they were drawing on an account by Cleitarchus who dressed up his novelistic version with the names of well-known Macedonian commanders.[16] Indeed the passage in Polyaenus has all the colours of Cleitarchus' palette:

Alexander took Thebes by concealing a sufficient part of his force and putting Antipater in command of it. He in person led the visible force against the strong part of the [city] region. The Thebans came out against him, and they fought not ignobly against that visible force. At the crisis of the battle Antipater raised up his hidden force, went round in a circle to where the wall was rotten and unguarded, and at that point he seized the city [*polis*, ? acropolis] and raised the signal. Alexander saw it. He shouted out 'Thebes is already mine.' The Thebans were fighting stoutly, but when they turned round and saw the city [? acropolis] captured, they fled.

In this instance we can see that the three accounts in D., Plutarch and Polyaenus drew most probably on a common source, which wrote without regard to historical fact. Their

versions should be discarded by a modern historian as worthless fiction, whether we identify that source with Cleitarchus
or not.[17] This does not mean that Arrian's account is correct.
It is a common error in those who believe in 'the vulgate
tradition' to suppose that if one is wrong the other is right,
and that the more faults one finds in Arrian the more trust
one can put in the vulgate tradition. In fact both may be
worthless;[18] for the sickness of one does not prove the health
of the other. In the course of this book we have frequently
mentioned Arrian's account, because the divergencies of D.,
J. and C. from it are relevant to our assessment of those
authors' use of sources. We have also advanced some arguments for the existence of a genuine *King's Journal* which
Ptolemy was able to use and in our opinion did use for his
description of A's last days. But the discussion of Arrian's
sources and also the discussion of Plutarch's sources are
matters for a separate enquiry which I hope to conduct on
the principles which I have used here for the sources of D.,
J. and C.

NOTES

1. As Tarn 4 remarked, 'it is impossible to suppose that a source can be found for everything given by our extant writers'.
2. Epigrammatically expressed by Jacoby in *RE* 11.630 and repeated in *FGrH*: 'die vulgata die im wesentlichen ein immer wieder bearbeiteten Kleitarchos ist'.
3. 132.
4. Most recently Atkinson 67, referring to earlier work especially of Brunt and Badian.
5. As two examples of many I mention Brunt and Bosworth. 'It is conventional to refer to the accounts of Alexander which do not depend on Ptolemy, Aristobulus and Nearchus as "the vulgate"' (Brunt xxxii). Bosworth *C* 28f. began by defining 'the so-called vulgate tradition, the tradition common to Diodorus 17, Curtius Rufus and Justin', but he then went on to include under this heading *PA* at 159, 271 (with *Frag. Sabb.*), 329, 331 and 345 (but not consistently since at 263 he set *PA* apart from 'the vulgate sources'). His views on the vulgate were further developed in *EH* 22 (1975).
6. Borza 44f. and Goukowsky in *REA* 71 (1969) 337.
7. *Arrian of Nicomedia* (Chapel Hill, 1980) 148.
8. The abbreviations are obvious, since the sacrifices and the orders would have been described in the original, and since the talk with Nearchus contained A listening to Nearchus (in *PA*) as well as A giving detailed instructions to the naval officers (Arr. 7.25.4). For Plutarch and Arrian were interested not in those matters but in what Plutarch called succinctly τὰ περὶ τὴν νόσον.
9. Having given his paraphrase of the primary narrative, Arrian went on to note how the secondary accounts were related to this narrative: those of Ptolemy and Aristobulus were close to it, and others were different from it. Thus the meaning of οὐ πόρρω δὲ τούτων in this context is clearly 'not far from it', as at Arr. 5.20.9 οὐ πόρρω τοῦ ἀληθοῦς is 'not far from the truth'. Robson's translation in the Loeb edition 'beyond this neither Ptolemaeus nor Aristobulus have recorded' is incorrect; for the length of their work is irrelevant. See L. Pearson, 'The diary and the letters of Alexander the Great', *Historia* 3 (1954–55) 437f.; one of his

translations, 'no detail in addition to these', will not do, because τούτων simply resumes the preceding account. Bosworth *C* 23f. and n. 29 supports Robson.

10. Pearson 194f.; A. E. Samuel, 'Alexander's royal journals', *Historia* 14 (1965) 1ff.; Hamilton 210; Bosworth, 'The death of Alexander', *CQ* n.s. 21 (1971) 117–123; Brunt xxvi–xxviii; R. Lane Fox, *Alexander the Great* (London, 1973) 464ff.

11. E. Badian in *Gnomon* 34 (1962) 381 ff.; Bosworth in *CQ* n.s. 21 (1971) 128 and 136; for the ring see also *EH* 138.

12. Hamilton 210.

13. So Pearson in *Historia* 3 (1954–55) 434 'there is certainly no reason to doubt that some kind of diary was kept, recording the events of each day, the king's conferences, the orders he issued, the reports he received, and so on'. It seems that Eumenes was trained first under Philip and then became chief secretary for the *Journal*. When papers were burnt, A had 'his satraps and generals everywhere send copies' for Eumenes to use, no doubt for the *Alexander-Journal* (Plut. *Eum.* 1–2). For A's orders see the remarks in Hammond, *Alex.* 48 and 57. Only events involving the king were recorded — not such things as the ultimate fate of Callisthenes. A. E. Samuel, 'Alexander's royal journals', *Historia* 14 (1965) 1ff. has shown a possible source in the East from which Philip may have adopted the practice of keeping an official journal; but it may equally well have been a Macedonian invention.

14. Plutarch and Arrian use the normal phrases for direct citation; so do Aelian and Athenaeus. There are no grounds for supposing that each of them is misleading us and really found a passage in an intermediary source.

15. Bosworth in *CQ* n.s. 21 (1971) 119f. is also critical of Pearson's argument. One should note that in the story about a man sitting on A's throne at Babylon the god in the background was Sarapis (*PA* 73.9), foreshadowing his later advice to let A die.

16. As named by Arr. 7.26.2; they are those with Python (an error for Peithon) and Seleucus in *PA* 76.9. The latter lived until 280.

17. That this was a typical sort of extract is clear from the citation by Aelian, *VH* 3.23.

18. For the banquet-rooms see R. A. Tomlinson, 'Ancient Macedonian symposia', *Ancient Macedonia* I (Thessaloniki, 1970) 308ff.

19. Bosworth is able to represent the citations and references to the *Journal* as restricted to the last few months only if two emendations are made to the text; see Hammond, *Alex.* 298 with n. 131.

20. As Pearson remarked in *Historia* 3 (1954–55) 347, 'at such an early date a forgery would readily have been detected'.

21. *FGrH* no. 118, with variant readings. Pearson in *Historia* 3 (1954–55)

437 proposed an alternative translation: 'Five books of diaries about the exploits of Alexander'. But this is a very unlikely usage, because the normal term is 'the diary of A', meaning about A, and not 'the diary about the things of A'.

22. Though in a make-believe world I suppose anything may be possible.

Chapter 1

1. Tarn 63–91.
2. 'The sources of Diodorus Siculus xvi', in *CQ* 31 (1937) 79ff. and 32 (1938) 137ff.
3. *CQ* 31 (1937) 81; see also *CQ* 32 (1938) 148–50.
4. For instance, recently in regard to Philip of Macedon by J. R. Ellis, *Philip II and Macedonian Imperialism* (London, 1976) 255 n. 1 and 306 n. 56; G. L. Cawkwell, *Philip of Macedon* (London, 1978) 18 citing D. 16.1.6 as from Ephorus; and G. T. Griffith in Hammond and Griffith, *A History of Macedonia* (Oxford, 1979) 208 n. 3, 213 and 702. And in general Sinclair 38ff.
5. Philotas is not named in any other account of the Theban campaign, and Perdiccas was *hors de combat* after the initial attack according to Arr. 1.8.1, citing Ptolemy as his source.
6. D.'s account is regarded generally as unhistorical; see recently Goukowsky 173 'Comme Arrien (suivant Ptolémée) précise (1.9.6) que la prise de la ville se fit rapidement et sans difficulté, les péripéties (rhétoriques!) du récit de Diodore peuvent laisser sceptique.'
7. The unhistorical nature of the account has been made clear by E. Badian in *Ancient Macedonia* II (Thessaloniki, 1977) 271ff., e.g. 'Diodorus' story cannot be taken very seriously as an account of an actual battle.' See further my article 'The battle of the Granicus river', *JHS* 100 (1980) 73. There are on the other hand authors of books on A who have accepted D. in preference to Arrian for the battle, e.g. R. D. Milns, P. Green and R. Lane Fox.
8. A is represented as advancing northwards from the town of Issus into the extensive plain at the head of the Cilician Gulf. As Issus is to be placed somewhere near Dörtyol, a march of $5\frac{1}{2}$ kilometres would bring A into that plain. That this is a fairy tale is clear from the account of Callisthenes (*FGrH* 124 F 35).
9. The narrative is incompatible with the account of Callisthenes and that of Arrian (2.5–11) which was derived from Ptolemy and Aristobulus. The looting of the royal tent (i.e. headquarters) by the Macedonian soldiers is incompatible with the Macedonian custom of reserving the tent of a defeated king for the Macedonian king himself (C. 3.11.23), a custom which there is every reason to accept as historical.

10. This duel between A and Darius is unhistorical. A fought with lance or spear, not with a javellin, and Ptolemy and Aristobulus as used by Arrian did not provide any such duel.

11. Other writers make A turn back from the pursuit to go to the aid of Parmenio (Callisthenes F 37, Arr. 3.15.1-2 and C. 4.16.2-3). Their account is correct; D.'s version of events is a fiction calculated to redound to the credit of the Thessalians.

12. F. Jacoby, *FGrH* II B 489 writes of Cleitarchus 'um dessen Glaubwürdigkeit es übel stand und dessen Stil Cicero pueril fand, der aber damals in Rom die grosse Mode war'.

13. These are discussed by Pearson 215ff. and Borza 26ff.

14. Athenaeus is giving examples of Greek poverty in contrast to Roman opulence. Property and possessions in Thebes at the time of the sack must have been worth thousands of talents (Athens in 378/377 rated her own taxable capital in the hands of prosperous citizens alone at some 6,000 talents), and that is the meaning of D.'s phrase 'an incredible amount of valuables'. The sale of some 30,000 souls as slaves might well have reached a figure of 440 talents according to P. Ducrey, *Le traitement des prisonniers de guerre dans la Grèce antique* (Paris, 1968) 252 n. 3, at an average of 88 drachmae a head.

15. In *CQ* 31 (1937) 88 n. 4 I made this point in opposition to the view of M. Kunz, *Zur Beurteilung d. Prooemien in Diod. hist. Bibl.* (Zurich, 1935) 54, 88f. and 101ff., that the Proems of book 16 and book 17 were drawn from the same source. 'I believe', I wrote, 'there is nothing in the Proem to 17 which D. could not have written out of his own head: he appears to have expanded the commonplace with which he ended 16, filled up his Proem with generalities about the heroism of Alexander, and then proceeded to his narrative. That he wrote this Proem before composing the narrative is clear from the declaration that he will include other contemporary events, which in fact are not so included.' Sicilian affairs, for instance, were not resumed from 16 until the beginning of 19.

16. These appear in other accounts; see N. G. L. Hammond, '"Philip's Tomb" in historical context', *GRBS* 19 (1978) 339ff.

17. D. always means this same Attalus. That Attalus as a leading member of the court, a King's Bodyguard and brother-in-law to the King should attend the ceremony at Aegeae was to be expected. Those who believe that a different Attalus was among those who killed Pausanias (e.g. Welles 101) have to assume that there was another equally eminent Macedonian of that name in Philip's immediate entourage and that D. or his source mixed them up; neither assumption is likely.

18. I do not find in this account the internal inconsistency which is

suggested by Goukowsky xiv. At 5.5 Bagoas 'helped to win' the throne for Darius (συγκατεσκεύασε τὴν βασιλείαν) and Darius was adjudged worthy of the throne (i.e. by the Persians) because of his outstanding courage in killing a champion of the Cadusii in single combat (6.1–2). Darius needed both if he was to be elected king (Bagoas was a schemer, not a dictator). Goukowsky regarded them as 'deux récits contradictoires'. For the single combat of champions in Persia we may compare the duel between Satibarzanes and Erigyius in 83.5–6 and Arr. 3.28.3. When he became king, Darius was hedged round by thousands of special guards, and there was no question of single combat for him with A.

19. For A's route from Illyria through the Pindus range to Pelinna and then to Thebes see Hammond, *Alex.* 58 and *Megas Alexandros* (Thessaloniki, 1980), 171ff.

20. As I pointed out in *CQ* 31 (1937) 84, 86 and 90 and 32. 149 with n. 1, *Syntaxis* I of Diyllus covered Greek and Sicilian affairs from 357/6 to 341/0 (D. 16.14.5), and *Syntaxis* II 'Greek and barbarian affairs' from 341/0 'to the death of Philip' in 336/5 (16.76.6, using D.'s chronology). The phrase μέχρι τῆς Φιλίππου τελευτῆς can only mean in the context the death of Philip II and not that of the Philip, son of Cassander, who died in 297/6, as has been supposed by A. Schaefer in *Hist. Zeitschr.* 18 (1897) 173, Jacoby *FGrH* II C 113 and Welles ad. loc. Their supposition, if accepted, would mean that *Syntaxis* I spanned sixteen years of only Greek and Sicilian affairs and *Syntaxis* II forty-four years of events in all areas, which is to me a *reductio ad absurdum*. It seems rather that *Syntaxis*, meaning 'composition', was either synonymous with 'book', βύβλος, or contained two or more books in the history of Diyllus, which consisted of 26 books in all (T 1). An event of 316/5 was recorded in 'the ninth'. Deinon wrote in Syntaxeis and books. (*FGrH* 690 F 1 and F 2).

21. Tarn 78 and 115, followed by Goukowsky xiv n. 4, held that Deinon was a likely source; but neither noted the reference in 16 to the contents of Diyllus, *Syntaxis* II. The length and nature of Deinon's work are uncertain and the latest datable event in the fragments concerns Artaxerxes Ochus (*FGrH* 690 F 21); his work was assuredly used by his son Cleitarchus (so P. A. Brunt in *CQ* n.s. 12 (1962) 146); but there is no sign that it was used directly by D., or for that matter by Diyllus.

22. Other accounts used other terms, and doubts have been expressed by some scholars about the existence of an alliance. In *CQ* 31 (1937) 90 I left chapter 89 unallocated; it seems from experience of book 17 that it came from Diyllus.

23. 'Sehr wahrscheinlich', says Jacoby, *FGrH* II C 112.

24. The political career of Phanodemus is securely dated by inscriptional

evidence to within at least the years 343 and 325 or so (see G. L. Barber in OCD^2 s.v.). Schubert 236 held that Diyllus was still writing after 297, the year of the Gallic invasion; if so, the impression made on Diyllus may account for the anachronistic arming of Pausanias with a Gallic knife in 16.94.3, a passage ascribed to Diyllus as source (as a Bodyguard Pausanias was no doubt armed with a spear).

25. Schubert 218ff. derived from Diyllus some Scholia which showed exceptional familiarity with Attic orators and Attic decrees of this period.

26. The supposition that some higher numbers (those given by Callisthenes and Anaximenes) did include troops already in Asia may make these numbers 'plausible' (e.g. Brunt lxxi); but it has no justification in the literary tradition. Callisthenes expressly and Anaximenes in Plutarch's judgement gave the numbers only of those who crossed with A. In any case how could Anaximenes have known accurately how many troops were already on Asiatic soil?

27. D.'s total of 30,000 is probably an approximation as in Arrian's report of Ptolemy's figure; but it may be another case of poor addition by D.

28. In *JHS* 94 (1974) 77f. and n. 24, and in Hammond, *Alex.* 3 and 307.

29. As argued by Tarn 38 and 42f. and Pearson 193ff. rather than as by R. M. Errington in *CQ* n.s. 19 (1969) 241.

30. The alternative, that Diyllus had cited this childish view in his text, is most unlikely.

31. Arr. 1.20.10 and 22.7 gave 56 killed on the Macedonian side and 'less than 1,200 Persians'.

32. Engagements between infantrymen in hand-to-hand combat rarely lasted more than two or three hours for reasons of physical exhaustion; but this was an epic occasion.

33. In Arrian's account, for instance, the brigades of Perdiccas, Adaeus and Timander were mentioned in action.

34. It is mentioned by D. only.

35. Cleitarchus stressed the cause of 'liberty' in the rising of Thebes.

36. Goukowsky overcomes the difficulty at 30.2 by bracketing Φιλίππῳ as an intrusive gloss; rightly, because in this book D. uses the name Philip without adding 'the king'.

37. See Goukowsky ad loc., p. 189.

38. In my opinion the account of D. is continuous and coherent (its historical truth is not under consideration) and comes from one source. Tarn 120f. found in D. 'two accounts, the attack on the island of Tyre and the land siege'. But it is clear that both happened together and in the finale are inextricably mixed. The mole was advanced to within missile range (42.7); A prepared now to attack

'by land and by sea simultaneously', i.e. from the mole and by ship (43.2); the mole reached the wall (of the city) and Tyre ceased to be an island (43.5); towers were brought to attack the wall, i.e. along the mole (43.7); the assault 'by land and sea simultaneously' was launched (46.1); from his ships A fought his way onto the wall (46.2); 'simultaneously in another part', i.e. by land on the mole, the ram breached a piece of wall (46.3); A's force and the Macedonians who used the breach both entered the city. The same two-pronged attack is inherent in Polyaenus 4.3.4 (so Goukowsky p. 199). It has been argued by Goukowsky xv n. 2 (with references to his articles) that D. used two sources because he described devices of the Tyrians 'twice' ('deux fois, 17.44.1 et 45.3'). But D. gave many descriptions of devices (at 43.1, 43.8, 43.10, 44.1, 44.4, 45.3–4) and their distribution is designed simply to heighten the effect.

39. As Ptolemy had snakes, not crows, he is ruled out as the source of D.; and Aristobulus also, as he had the crows act as guides to the army (Arr. 3.3.5–6).

40. For a summary of the evidence see Hammond, *Alex.* 125f.

41. See Goukowsky's commentary ad loc. and his statement on p. xxix: 'la destinée du Conquérant prenait un sens nouveau dans la version très personelle que Clitarque donnait de son pélerinage au sanctuaire de Siwa ... révélait la nature divine d'Alexandre et annonçait les glorieuses conquêtes qu'il accomplirait au prix d'épreuves comparables à celles d'Héraclès.'

42. See P. Jouguet in *REA* 42 (1940) 192f. and Goukowsky 207. Ptolemy and Aristobulus put the foundation before the visit.

43. The mention of the advantage of the long lance to the Macedonians at Issus serves to remind us that D.'s account of that battle was a very abbreviated version; for it has no mention of the lance.

44. Ptolemy and Aristobulus placed the battle at Gaugamela (Arr. 6.11.5).

45. See Goukowsky 208f.

46. 'Diodorus and his sources', *AJPh* 83 (1962) 384f., citing examples.

47. See especially J. Palm, *Über Sprache und Stil des Diodoros von Sizilien* (Lund, 1955).

48. I gave examples in 16 in *CQ* 31 (1937) n. 2; for 17 see e.g. 11.5, 12.4 and 33.6.

49. See the full study by R. K. Sinclair, 'Diodorus Siculus and fighting in relays', *CQ* n.s. 16 (1966) 249–55.

50. Further examples in Drews, loc. cit. 386 n. 15, and Goukowsky xxxiv n. 2.

51. Goukowsky 194, 'la cession du pays en deçà de l'Halys ne figure que chez Diodore', overlooks this reference.

52. Invincibility was recorded in a papyrus fragment of the first

century B.C.; see R. Merkelbach, *Archiv für Papyrusforschung* (1962) 109.

53. This distinction is forgotten by those who try to make a single picture of A out of book 17, a picture which is then regarded as D.'s creation. Goukowsky makes the attempt, especially on p. xliii; but he is puzzled by the absence of some traits and by the presence of others which are hardly consistent with the supposed picture. 'Or ces derniers traits proviennent indubitablement de Cleitarque.' So he is brought back to belief in a divergent source. Drews, op. cit., 392 with n. 29 implies that it was D. who equipped A in book 17 with 'D.'s favourite virtues'; but it seems rather that for part of his book D. chose to excerpt from a Hellenistic historian, who had seen in A some of the virtues which were idealised in the early period of the Hellenistic kingdoms and which duly appealed to D. *c.* 60–30 B.C.

54. D. was proud of his travels (1.4.1); perhaps he had been on Mt Ida and wished to include what he had heard there.

55. The errors in the chronology of the first part of 17 seem to be due to D. himself (he lost a year by putting Philip's death into one archon year and his funeral into another); thus they do not reveal his sources.

Chapter 2

1. Other features of Livy's story fit Cleitarchus: the oracle fore-shadowing the death of Alexander at Pandosia, the woman's pathetic intercession and the delivery of the mangled remains to Cleopatra and Olympias. At 9.18.6 Livy expressed his own belief that the Romans had never even heard of Alexander the Great; this is understandable if Livy had read Cleitarchus and wished to deny the claim of Cleitarchus that the Romans sent an embassy to Alexander. Strabo 280 fin. refers perhaps to the Molossian's grisly end in using the word ἡ κακοπραγία. PA 43.6 used the same rare word as Diodorus, διασφενδονάω, of the killing of Bessus.

2. The battlefield and the camp were 600 stades (111 kilometres) away from Arbela, as Arrian remarks 3.8.7; he criticised those who put the battle at Arbela — referring no doubt to Cleitarchus — in a later passage (6.11.4–6).

3. Arrian described Darius' policy (3.19.1) and his force as some 9,000 men (3.19.5); Darius' rapid withdrawal would have been impossible with an army of above 30,000 men.

4. Goukowsky 218 'elle illustre le tact et la modération d'Alexandre'; A's piety is another facet, the importance of which has recently been stressed by W. K. Pritchett, *The Greek State at War*, Part 3 (Berkeley, 1979) 139.

5. An incidental point against the source being Cleitarchus is that he would have used not 'table', τράπεζα but 'stool', δίφρος, as described by his father Deinon (*FGrH* 690 F 26). See Goukowsky ad loc. 217, and E. F. Schmidt, *Persepolis* I (Chicago, 1953) 164, for such stools.

6. See Goukowsky ad loc. 218.

7. The story is improbable because A regarded the burying of his dead as a religious duty in accordance with Macedonian custom.

8. The distance of A's withdrawal, 300 stades, is probably a figure given by Cleitarchus for verisimilitude rather than an error by D.

9. D. writes consistently of the city as the richest of the cities, τῶν πόλεων 70.1 and 70.6, and not just of the citadel (71.1 ἄκρα) and palace (71.3 βασίλεια); Goukowsky 100 n. 2 does not appreciate D.'s meaning when he writes 'ces projets de destruction concernaient non la ville elle-même'.

10. See Goukowsky ad loc. 222 for these tombs; that of Darius III was to be added later.

11. As is generally agreed, e.g. by Pearson 218ff., Hamilton 99 and E. Mederer, *Die Alexanderlegenden bei den ältesten Alexanderhistorikern* (Stuttgart, 1936) 71f.

12. Excavation has confirmed the burning of the palace area (E. F. Schmidt, *Persepolis* I.157, 220; II.3).

13. See the excellent notes by Goukowsky 225–8, who has no doubts about Cleitarchus being the source. The supposition of Tarn 89f., that because Aristobulus mentioned oak but not fir and pines as growing in Hyrcania (*FGrH* 139 F 19 = Str. 509), the description of the honey-dripping leaf of an oak-like tree in D. 17.75.6 means that Cleitarchus took the description from Aristobulus really is a complete *non sequitur*. The expression 'oak-like' on Tarn's own argument on the same page points rather to Onesicritus.

14. The others being Polycleitus, Onesicritus, Antigenes and Ister in *PA* 46.1.

15. In *PA* 49.7 he was killed resisting arrest, and in C. 6.7.30 he died by his own hand without saying anything to A.

16. The manuscripts read 'Antigonus'; an early corruption from Antipater is generally assumed.

17. The word ἐδολοφόνησε is correctly used in the literal sense, in that the killing was done by guile (C. 7.2.23–27 describes the guile), and it may have a connotation of treachery.

18. So Goukowsky 235 'sans doute empruntée à Clitarque'.

19. 236–7.

20. According to Arrian (6.1.1) this intention was not formed until later.

21. See Goukowsky 245.

22. The codices and a marginal note give differing names for this king,

and the unnamed river in the next sentence is the Acesines. See Goukowsky ad loc. and p. 246.

23. Also in Onesicritus (*FGrH* 134 F 21).

24. Also in Aristobulus (*FGrH* 139 F 40).

25. The huge forces in the Ganges basin are typical of Cleitarchus' love of high figures, and the oracular response from Delphi put A into the tradition of the infamous temple-robber Philomelus. See Hamilton 171–2 for the forces ('their common source cannot be other than Cleitarchus') and 34f. for the oracle from Delphi.

26. For A's reasons see Hammond, *Alex.* 214.

27. See Goukowsky 252f.; *contra* Hamilton 174.

28. The erroneous impression that the fleet was on the Acesines in 95.3 is due to D.'s compression of his source; for there is no doubt at 89.6 that the fleet was built on the Hydaspes.

29. The city is the first attacked by A; not so in Arrian's account of the campaign against the Oxydracae and the Malli. See Goukowsky 256.

30. So Goukowsky 257.

31. There are also other difficulties, but this is not the place to discuss them. Welles 405 n. 5 and Goukowsky 257 believe that D. is confusing the two risings.

32. This attribution is made by Goukowsky 142 n. 1.

33. The Hyphasis was regarded as the limit usually, e.g. by Arr. 5.28.4 and 29.2, and P.A 62.5 who wrote of 'the retreat' thereafter. To choose the Ocean at the mouth of the Indus as the limit was to adhere to Aristotle's theory that the Indian promontory faced east and ended with the Indus delta as the easternmost part of Asia.

34. On the supposition that when A 'divided the cavalry into squadrons' he put Ptolemy in charge of a number of the squadrons, while he commanded the rest. In my book p. 229 I put the incident later, while Hephaestion was arranging to build a city on A's orders (Arr. 6.21.5 fin.; cf. D. 17.104.8).

35. The other drunken scene which led to the duel between Coragus and Dioxippus (100) was also attributed to Cleitarchus as source.

36. This double stress on the place as being on the coast absolves D. from the possibility of making an error. According to Nearchus in Arrian's account the meeting took place five days' march inland.

37. The probable position of the Salmous of D.'s account is shown on p. 205, fig. 17, of Hammond, *Alex.*

38. See Goukowsky ad loc. 265; the term itself was used by D. at 11.67.5.

39. Not exclusively; for an (alleged) assembly figured in the passage attributed to Cleitarchus when the army reached the Hyphasis. The error here of Ganges instead of Hyphasis I take to be D.'s error.

40. Theopompus (*FGrH* 115 F 253 and F 254) and Cleitarchus (*FGrH* 137 F 30) also mentioned the courtesans; but the chapter is not marked by the characteristics of either.

41. In a fuller account at 18.8.4 the decree is cited with the exception 'except those under a curse' (πλὴν τῶν ἐναγῶν). If the present passage was due to D. reading back from 18.8.4 one would expect to find 'except those under a curse'. I take it, then, that D. drew the entry at 109.1 from his source who mentioned it at this point, just after the Harpalus affair.

42. The mutiny is placed at Susa; Arrian, using Ptolemy and Aristobulus, put it at Opis. Some authors may have been misled by reports of discontent at Susa as reported in Arr. 7.6.2-5.

43. Such details as the number of mares in the past and at the time are not exaggerated (Arr. 7.13.1 giving different but very similar numbers).

44. This epithet implies that the source gave a fuller account which explained what the untimely circumstances were.

45. For the many varying accounts see the summary of λεγόμενα at Arr. 7.14.4.

46. These cities 'founded in the difficult terrain' are those of Arr. *Ind.* 40.7-8 and some of those 'Greek cities planted in accordance with the lead given by Alexander' around the plain of Media (Polybius 10.27.3); the former of the two passages shows that they were not fortresses but cities of mixed population.

47. D., rather than the source, makes the back-reference, I imagine.

48. D. means the Galatae to the north-west of Thrace; Arr. 7.15.4 mentions as a λεγόμενον envoys from the Celts and Iberians, i.e. of Gaul west of Italy. See Goukowsky 272.

49. According to Arrian (7.15.5-6) Aristus and Asclepiades of the Alexander-historians mentioned Roman envoys. As Arrian never mentioned Cleitarchus in his entire work, nothing can be inferred from his failure at this point to mention Cleitarchus. See bibliography in Goukowsky xx n. 2.

50. These include likenesses of Hephaestion in gold and ivory, like those found at Vergina and in other built tombs (see N. G. L. Hammond, '"Philip's Tomb" in historical context', *GRBS* 19 (1978) 336).

51. The monumental grave was completed probably after A's death but not to the scale of the plan left in A's *hypomnemata* which 'needed much money' (18.4.6).

52. Discussed by Goukowsky who explains the association of Hephaestion as a god with reference to the later worship of A and Hephaestion (xxx n. 3 and 275); he argues for Cleitarchus as the source here, but others too were familiar with this worship.

53. Arr. 7.23.6 gave a different and no doubt correct version that the response came later in reply to A's question.
54. See *CQ* 31 (1937) 88f.; D. looked forward to A's overthrow of Persian power.
55. D. himself probably added the mention of 'Fate' at 116.4 fin., resuming the mention at the beginning of the chapter.
56. Compiled as a record at the time of facts which were known to so many of A's Friends and Companions.
57. Hamilton 208 'the dramatic version of A's illness given by Cleitarchus'.
58. Diodorus himself did not believe the story (117.5 'he died in the aforesaid manner'), nor of course did Arrian (7.27.1–2) and Plutarch (*Alex.* 77.1–5). The connection of the story with Olympias, here and at 19.11.8 and also in Plutarch's mention of it, indicates that the story was part of her propaganda against Antipater and his family. See Goukowsky 277.
59. The rumour may have been put about much earlier, but I am concerned here with D.'s written source. Arr. 7.27.1 and *PA* 77 regarded the story as a fabrication, as did most writers according to Plutarch.
60. So too Curtius connected her death with A's chivalry towards her: 'indulgentiae in eam iustitiaeque in omnes captivos' (10.5.24).
61. For instance the last sentence of 69.2 has the rhythms of the Attic orators, e.g. of Demosthenes 19.65, and the sentence 69.9 is fulsome Diodorus.
62. *An Historical Commentary on the Hellenica Oxyrhynchia* (Cambridge, 1967) 20–1, and 150f.
63. Even verbally since the words of Polybius ἀντισήκουν καὶ λυμαίνεσθαι τὰ κατορθώματα recur in D. 31.12 as ἀντισήκουν καὶ λυμαίνεσθαι τὰ κατορθωθέντα. R. Drews comments on D.'s improvements of views (*AJPh* 83 (1962) 385). Examples of D. having verbal echoes of Herodotus, probably through an intermediate source, are given by Anne Burton, *Diodorus Siculus I; a Commentary* (Leiden, 1972), 19–20.
64. This important aspect of A has often been overlooked in recent studies, as W. K. Pritchett has recently observed in *The Greek State at War*, Part 3 (Berkeley, 1979) 139 and 147; I wrote of A 'the origin of his power was a religious faith' (*History of Greece* (Oxford, 1959) 641).
65. See Pearson 234, supporting Tarn 26f. He admits that 'Cleitarchus, if he was writing in Alexandria, could hardly contradict the word of Ptolemy during his lifetime'; but then supposes he could and would after the death of Ptolemy I and so in the reign of his son, Ptolemy II. One must wonder whether Ptolemy II was willing to have his father represented as a liar! Goukowsky xx–xxiii gives a

summary and a bibliography for the dating of Cleitarchus' work, and he concludes that Cleitarchus' first book was published 'towards 320?' and his last between 300 and 295. A. B. Bosworth puts his work 'probably before 300' in *EH* 33.

66. The *Journal* was probably sent with the corpse of the King, was intercepted and was then kept by Ptolemy, as suggested in Hammond, *Alex.* 1.

67. *FGrH* II B 508.9; the latest event in the fragments is the death of Antigonus in 301.

68. *FGrH* II B 499 and Pearson 193 'perhaps only a year or two before his death in 283'; so too Goukowsky xxxi.

69. Pearson 213: and 20, 85 and 118 for dates of works of Onesicritus and Nearchus.

70. The latest event mentioned by Cleitarchus, if 23.2-3 is derived from him, is Agathocles' action in 310 (this with reference to A's disbanding of his fleet in 334). As Pearson remarks, 'it has been widely believed that Cleitarchus wrote before the end of the century'. However, he follows Tarn 16-21 in dating Cleitarchus' work to a time later than Ptolemy's work (pp. 20 and 213-42).

71. It is not appropriate to argue here the priority of Aristobulus. It may suffice to note Pearson's comment (187) that Arrian thought himself that Aristobulus wrote before Ptolemy (Arrian using the works of both surely knew!); and the deduction to be drawn from Aristobulus' version and Ptolemy's version (of his own act) of gaining possession of Bessus (Arr. 3.30.1-3 and 5) is that Aristobulus would not deliberately have gainsaid the account of Ptolemy, the officer in command of the operation (see M. J. Fontana, 'Il problema delle fonti per il XVII libro di Diodoro Siculo', *Kokalos* 1 (1955) 160; Goukowsky xxvi and xxxi puts Aristobulus before Ptolemy, but he places Cleitarchus between them).

72. As I have argued in *JHS* 100 (1980) 73ff.

Chapter 3

1. The remark in chapter 1, that one is dealing only with probabilities in most instances, should be taken to apply to this chapter also.

2. Which I take to be a vivid present in place of a past tense.

3. The context shows that 'the rival' is any son born in the future to Philip and Cleopatra. The absurdity of attributing such a fear to an adult A, already marked out as Philip's heir, needs no emphasising.

4. In J. 7.4.7 – 5.8 a similar string of absurdities is attached to the mother of Philip, Eurydice, involving her in adultery with a son-in-law, hatching a plot to kill her husband the king, and killing her two sons when they were kings. These are indeed worthy of Satyrus, *Life of Philip.* In J. 7.4.5 the full details of the wives and the

children of Amyntas resemble those in Satyrus' list of the wives and the children of Philip in *FHG* III F 5. For the fictitious nature of these absurdities see my remarks in Hammond and Griffith 183.

5. Athenaeus is not citing Satyrus verbatim, except for the number of years of Philip's reign; the rest of the passage is a summary only, mentioning such details as Cleopatra being a sister of Hippostratus, perhaps the Hippostratus, son of Amyntas, killed in action against Pleuratus according to Didymus, *In Dem.* Col. 13.2.

6. The word is used for any killing within a family.

7. The weapon is probably a spear; see my remarks in '"Philip's Tomb" in historical context', *GRBS* 19 (1978) 331f.

8. The taunt, not found in the other sources, is evidently an accretion to the story.

9. Tarn fell into some confusion over these passages. He inferred from A's fears at 9.7.3 'of a brother born to his step-mother being a rival' that a son had already been born to Cleopatra; but this is disproved by the following words in J., since it is clear from a comparison with Athenaeus and Plutarch that the fear arose at the wedding banquet, and we cannot suppose that Cleopatra was already then an unmarried mother. Tarn went on to argue that the source at 11.2.3, where Caranus was mentioned as 'fratrem ex noverca susceptum', was the same as the source of 9.7.3 and so different from the source at 9.7.12, where Cleopatra's child is a girl. I agree with him only in that the source at 11.2.3 is different from the source at 9.7.12.

10. Compare J. 13.2.11 'ex Larissaeo scorto'.

11. The claim is clearly false; for Aeacus, the ancestor of the Aeacidae, was himself a son of Zeus (*Iliad* 21.189).

12. Pyrrhus was particularly proud of his Aeacid descent (Plut. *Pyrr.* 26.5).

13. Victory in a chariot-race is found also in Plut. *Mor.* 105A in the the same context but with a different moral. The victory was in fact won in a horse-race, since a winning horse and jockey are shown on early coins of Philip; that is the version in *PA* 3.5 with the interpretation that A would be ἀνίκητος (it is doubtful whether Jacoby is correct in attributing this section to Hegesias in *FGrH* 142 F 3).

14. Goukowsky 250f.

15. I put in a bracket after D. the name of the source who has been suggested in my article in *CQ* 31 (1937) 79ff. or in chapters 1 and 2 above.

16. Above p. 27.

17. The implication that rape was general is probably untrue. Aristobulus (*FGrH* 139 F 2) mentioned the rape of Timocleia by a

Macedonian officer as an exceptional thing and the officer's death as deserved, at least in the judgement of A.

18. Arr. 1.8.8 mentioned 'Phocians, Plataeans and the other Boeotians', and Plutarch had 'Phocians and Plataeans' denouncing the Thebans in *Alex.* 11.5 fin.

19. One of these, Charidemus the Athenian, is said in D. 17.30.2–5 (Cleitarchus) to have given Darius some good advice, which was not accepted.

20. Trogus probably named Attalus and Amyntas, son of Perdiccas, and perhaps others of whom we do not know.

21. Perhaps Trogus too made the expeditionary force proceed by sea and not as in Arr. 1.11.3 overland.

22. Arrian's mention of the newly-married Macedonians being sent on home leave in the first winter shows that Justin's remark is unlikely to be true (Arr. 1.24.1–2).

23. See Brunt lxix.

24. The latter was not from D. 17.32.1–2; the placing of the incident after the illness of A was probably an error by D. rather than by his source. The figure 120 at J. 11.6.12 is likely to be due to an error by J. himself rather than to Trogus or some eccentric source.

25. The Scholiast to Eur. *Hipp.* 670 cited Marsyas for 'the tradition that the yoke had been bound to the pole by a vineshoot' (*FGrH* 135/6 F 4). As it is this description which makes the solution in the Scholium intelligible, it seems probable that the solution came from Marsyas; for the vineshoot-binding itself surrounded a pin, which attached the yoke to the pole. It was this yoke-pin which A removed; it was called probably ἔμβολος by Marsyas and certainly in Homeric style ἕστωρ by Aristobulus (*FGrH* 139 F 7 a and b). As they both accompanied A, their version of the unloosening (διαλύειν) is preferable to that in which A cut through the binding (διακόπτειν).

26. Favoured by F. Jacoby in *FGrH* II D 511 and others.

27. It is probably this version which was reported in *POxy* 1798 (*FGrH* 148) 44 Col. 1; see Jacoby ad loc.

28. On the general ground, to cite Tarn 54, that 'Cleitarchus chimed with the widespread hostility to Alexander's memory . . .; Alexander was to them an early example of the tyranny which, in their view, they themselves were enduring.'

29. 'A version which goes back to Cleitarchus', writes Hamilton 67, citing C. B. Welles' article in *Historia* 11 (1962) 276.

30. There were two marriageable daughters of Darius among the captured women (D. 17.36.2 δύο θυγατέρες ἐπίγαμοι).

31. This similarity seems to have gone unnoticed, perhaps because the passage has been mistranslated in Welles as the 'hand of one of his daughters'. Hamilton 76f. gives a summary of the evidence.

184

32. Another point shared by D. and J. is the reply of A that the universe could not keep its order with two suns and the inhabited world its peace and unity with two kings in charge. This came no doubt from their common source, Cleitarchus. Such an idea did not have to wait until the adolescence of some unknown writer at the end of the Roman Republic, as Tarn 79f. supposed.

33. F. Schachermeyr, *Alexander der Grosse: Ingenium und Macht* (Vienna, 1949) 513 n. 168, argued that, because J. does not mention the casting of A's cloak over the corpse (it occurs in P*A* 43.3), it was not mentioned by Cleitarchus. This does not seem convincing to me; for it is just the sort of detail an epitomiser might omit.

34. For instance, 12.1.1 13,000 talents for A's 'allies', as in D. 17.74.5; 12.5.10 Bessus killed Darius, as in D. 17.73.2; 12.5.11 Bessus handed over to the brother of Darius, as in D. 17.83.9; 12.8.8 two named cities founded by A, as in D. 17.95.5; 12.9.3 80,000 infantry, as in D. 17.98.1.

35. For instance, 12.1.3 190,000 talents at Ecbatana, but 180,000 in D. 17.80.3 and in a different context; 12.9.3 60,000 cavalry, but 10,000 in D. 17.98.1.

36. According to Plutarch, loc. cit., it could not be Aristobulus, Chares or Ptolemy but might have been Polycleitus or Onesicritus of those he named.

37. For instance, D. mentions the purple robes ($\pi\epsilon\rho\iota\pi\sigma\rho\phi\acute{\nu}\rho\sigma\nu\varsigma$). He adds that 'A made sparing use of these customs ($\dot{\epsilon}\vartheta\iota\sigma\mu\sigma\tilde{\iota}\varsigma$) and continued rather with his previous customs for fear of offending the Macedonians.' This refers to his use of Persian 'customs', e.g. ceremonial and dress, and not of the girls of the harem who could be called many things but not $\dot{\epsilon}\vartheta\iota\sigma\mu\sigma\acute{\iota}$.

38. The list is divided into groups by the repetition of 'tunc', e.g. 'tunc Parmenion et Philotas, tunc Amyntas consobrinus, tunc noverca fratresque interfecti'. This last group means Cleopatra and her brothers, and the back-reference for the brothers is to 11.5.1, where A is said to have killed 'omnes novercae suae cognatos quos Philippus in excelsiorem dignitatis locum provehens imperiis praefecerat'. Tarn seems to have misunderstood the Latin phrase when he took it to mean 'A's stepmother and his brothers', quite apart from the impossibility of finding brothers of A in view of Satyrus F 5 and J. 9.8.3 (Tarn could conjure up only one, the baby Caranus of J. 11.2.3, who, he claimed, never existed). The interest of the passage lies in the fact that J. had attributed the death of Cleopatra to Olympias at 9.7.2 (Satyrus); and it follows that the source behind our passage, 12.6.14, in attributing the death of Cleopatra to A must be someone other than Satyrus. And the killing of her brothers indicates a source common to 12.6.14 and

11.5.1, the latter having been attributed to someone other than Diyllus and probably to Cleitarchus (p. 96 above). So our source here is probably Cleitarchus.

39. Tarn 45 held that the source could not be Cleitarchus because J. named the city Nysa, whereas Cleitarchus named a mountain Nysa; but it is very probable that city and mountain were both called Nysa by the Macedonians. In any case one cannot rely on one word in an epitome to exclude another in the original and so to indicate the exclusion of an author as ultimate source.

40. Arrian at 4.28.1-2 and 30.4 mentioned the 'story' (λόγος) that Heracles had been unable to take the rock; but he said nothing of earthquakes.

41. The exploring of the coast and the order to dig wells are mentioned in Arr. 6.20.4 - 21.3.

42. Welles 438 n. 3 failed to distinguish between the occasions.

43. 12.11.8 'manu sua ipse', unless he means 'with his own band', i.e. of Bodyguards, as he had used 'manus' in the sense of a selected band at 12.10.1. The assembly, as always, was held under arms; J. mentioned here that it was armed in order to point up the contrast with A who was unarmed ('in contionem armatam inermis ipse desiluit'). D. 17.109.2 is unambiguous: ταῖς ἰδίαις χερσί.

44. To judge from the example in J. 38.4-7, such speeches in Trogus were lengthy and contained facts.

45. In 12.12.3-4 J. was evidently describing what we find in Arrian only as a reflection by Arrian himself (7.29.4): namely the mingling of the Persian Apple-Bearers 'in the ranks of the Macedonians' (ἐγκαταμῖξαι... ταῖς τάξεσιν αὐτῶν τοὺς Πέρσας τοὺς μηλοφόρους), and the addition of Persians to the two Royal Guards (καὶ τοῖς ἀγήμασι τοὺς ὁμοτίμους, the title ὁμότιμος being appropriate to the purpose of A at the banquet after the mutiny at 7.11.9).

46. From the words of J. 'nonnullas quoque ex Italia [legationes]' it is not reasonable to infer either that Trogus had mentioned an embassy from Rome or that he had not (see Jacoby in FGrH 88 (Timagenes) T 9 and commentary p. 224); in so brief an epitome we simply do not know.

47. Arr. 7.26.3 gave the last two points, using τῷ κρατίστῳ, as 'reports by some writers'. We can attribute to Cleitarchus 12.15.7 the last order of A, that his body should be placed in the temple of Ammon ('condi in Hammonis templum' as its last resting-place; see L & S s.v. condo II A 1 β), i.e. at Siwa; for this palliated the crime of his patron Ptolemy in diverting the funerary train from Macedonia to Egypt.

48. The new source, commencing with the Successors, may have been Timagenes, for instance. Timagenes being a writer like Cleitarchus and in a sense Cleitarchus' successor (FGrH 88 T 2 'disertus homo

et dicax, a quo multa improbe sed venuste dicta', and T 6), he probably started his book *Concerning Kings* with the Successors of A (the earliest datable incident being about Ptolemy son of Lagus in F 3, and there being a striking absence of fragments concerning A). However, the identification of this source hangs together with what follows in J., not with the books we have been considering.

49. We have two examples of such a report in *FGrH* 126 (Ephippus) F 1 and F 3, and *FGrH* 127 (Nicoboule) F 1 and F 2; it was probably advanced also by Medius, when he was accused of being privy to a poisoning of A.

50. See also C. 10.10.18 'haec . . . eorum quos rumor asperserat mox potentia exstinxit'.

51. J. is fuller than and differs from D.

52. R. Merkelbach, *Die Quellen des griechischen Alexanderromans* (Munich, 1954) 253ff.

53. It is not appropriate here to discuss at length the view of Merkelbach, op. cit. 175ff., that a large part of *AR* is to be dated to before the death of Perdiccas in 321 B.C. But his argument that propaganda in favour of Perdiccas became irrelevant after Perdiccas' death seems incorrect. If it were so, why was it preserved? Rather, this propaganda was double-edged, and one edge cut away Antipater's claims to be the rightful 'manager'; and that was a living issue for a very long time. This is not to deny that rumours of poisoning — and other rumours — circulated among soldiers and officers from A's death onwards; but we are dealing with not rumours but written sources which were available for Diodorus and Justin. To take an example, Antigonus, we are told, said Aristotle had helped Antipater to prepare suitable poison. Thus Antigonus was repeating or starting a rumour, and it was put on paper by Hagnothemis and then copied by other writers (*PA* 77). Our concern in source-criticism begins with Hagnothemis; he probably did not implicate Antigonus' admiral, Medius, but later writers did.

54. *PA* 77.2 'As for suspicion of poisoning no one at the time had any [or, with Hamilton 213, 'incurred any'], but five years later, they say, information was laid [μηνύσεως γενομένης], whereupon Olympias killed many and scattered the remains of Iolas as the man who had poured in the poison.' By remarking 'they say' Plutarch indicates his own doubts, and he goes on to say that most of the writers considered the story of poisoning to be a fiction (77.3).

55. She and her supporters no doubt spread rumours too, but it is doubtful whether any details of the poison-story can be pinned on her. I have not discussed the following passage in *Lives of the Ten Orators*, a spurious work in Plutarch's *Moralia*, 849 F: 'Hyperides voted honours for Iolas as the reputed poisoner of A.' Since

Hyperides died in 322 B.C., this would mean, as A. B. Bosworth rightly said in 'The death of Alexander the Great', *CQ* n.s. 21 (1971) 113, that a rumour was already circulating then (any suggestion of poisoning at once involved the king's taster, Iolas); but this does not mean that it was included then in any historian's work. Of course the passage is of little value in itself, being set among absurdities in a spurious work, and Hyperides' vote is probably a pendant to Demosthenes' proposal for Pausanias (Plut. *Dem.* 22.1). It is better to follow Plutarch, D., J. and C., when they suggest that attacks on Antipater and Cassander were not included in historical writings until after the death of Cassander.

56. Above pp. 77f.
57. We see more reason for his popularity as a writer since the discovery of *POxy* 9.1176, being four pages of the *Life of Euripides.*
58. Above p. 52.
59. The conclusion that Trogus drew on three authors and also Deinon for the books under consideration runs counter to the nineteenth-century view of Trogus' history being a Latin version of Timagenes' work, and agrees with the opinion of A. Klotz in *RE* 21.ii (1952) Col. 2305, that Trogus used several Greek authors. In these books of J. I have not seen any clue which points to Timagenes having been one of Trogus' sources. See also n. 48 above.

Chapter 4

1. Atkinson 64 'the parallels between C. and D. are numerous and striking'.
2. Atkinson 109 summarises earlier views, but he does not mention these echoes in this context.
3. Tarn 116f. argued that C. used D.; but Atkinson 65 is of my opinion: 'C.'s account of A.'s campaigns could not have been derived from D.'s meagre and patchy history.'
4. Atkinson 108 'C. is working with ideas that were commonplace in the early Principate.'
5. As he had done in describing the siege of Thebes and the battle of the Granicus. See above, p. 23.
6. Atkinson 235f. provides a table of parallel passages which, he writes, 'suggest that C. and D. had read the same source'.
7. So too Atkinson 244 for D. and C. 3.11.20-26 'it is reasonable to suppose that they followed a common source'; and for 3.12.1-26 'there are numerous links between C. and D. . . . a common source is likely'.
8. Atkinson 319 concludes that 'C. seems to have shared a source with D. . . . Cleitarchus must obviously be considered as the possible source shared by C. and D.'

9. Atkinson 283 'C.'s account is basically similar to D.'s but developed differently'; Pearson 238 held that the common source of D. and C. here was Cleitarchus.

10. Atkinson 292 'C. appears to have shared with D. a source that covered the activity of three groups of survivors from Darius' army . . . C.'s source was not D.'

11. Atkinson 91 concludes his criticism of I. Rabe, *Quellenkritische Untersuchungen zu Plutarchs Alexanderbiographie* (diss. Hamburg, 1964) somewhat differently in saying 'the links in phraseology between C. and J. are not striking . . . one cannot prove that C. used Trogus or the same source as Trogus did'.

12. Since Atkinson 169 remarks 'one can hardly maintain that C. took his account from Trogus', one has to explain these particular resemblances by postulating a common source. See also his p. 153.

13. Atkinson 224 'we cannot affirm nor deny that C. and J. followed the same source'.

14. Atkinson 316 remarks that 'the links between C. 4.3.3–5 and J. 11.10.10–11 have been emphasised by Fränkel 428 and Dosson 146', but he finds in general 'no clear indication that they were using a source in common'. He is concerned more with the difference than the resemblances.

15. The third point occurs in C. 4.1.13 where A's *first* reply contains the words 'si veneris supplex'.

16. Atkinson 278 'it is clear that C.'s account has much in common with J.'s, and this reinforces our conclusion from other passages that C. was familiar with Trogus' account, or at least with a source heavily used by Trogus'.

17. Atkinson 355ff. does not deal with the agreements between J. and C., but he cites the opinion (without supporting it) of E. Mederer, *Die Alexanderlegenden bei den ältesten Alexanderhistorikern* (Stuttgart, 1936) 58, that we have here (in the questions and answers at the oracle) a sample of Cleitarchus' imaginative writing.

18. D. 17.48.9 has a Persian garrison at Gaza, but his mention is very brief.

19. Atkinson 343 suggests that the figure is a copyist's error; but for what? 'IX milia' or 'XI milia'?

20. I am using Jacoby's text, in which the Arab 'brought the sword to bear against the kirtle of the cuirass so that the stroke was not the most fatal' (see L–S–J⁹ s.v. $\phi \acute{\epsilon} \rho \omega$ A II b; the stroke would have been fatal if the sword had struck inside the cuirass into A's vitals). The meaning is not that the Arab carried the sword under his own cuirass — an extremely difficult thing to do! The cuirass in Philip's tomb at Vergina had a kirtle — another example of archaeology confirming a detail in a text.

21. Pearson 247 translates 'six thousand of the barbarians were cut to

pieces to the sound of the trumpet' but this is to disregard ἐκείνην in Hegesias and 'signa' in C. Too much is made of ἐκείνην by W. R. Roberts' translation 'at the trumpet-call which forthwith rang out', *Dionysius of Halicarnassus on Literary Composition* (London, 1910) 184ff.

22. The name is spelt 'Batis' in Arrian, 'Baitis' in Hegesias and 'Betis' in C. I have used the form Batis throughout.

23. Tarn 267 saw a separate version by Dionysius in the introduction to the fragment and he deduced that Dionysius 'tacitly rejected much of Hegesias' story'. This is to misunderstand the passage; for Dionysius, in supplying the context for the citation, took it presumably from the text of 'the sophist' Hegesias, as he remarks ἔστιν ὃ λαμβάνει πρᾶγμα ὁ σοφιστὴς τοιόνδε. Dionysius compares Hegesias' story not with one of Dionysius' own but with the dragging of Hector's corpse in the *Iliad*.

24. Atkinson 59ff. discusses the relationship between C. and Trogus. He makes the point that 'C. often adopted the language of Trogus' narrative and used Trogus' phrases, whilst taking the historical material from other sources.'

25. The fact that C. 5.1.26 gives the circuit of the walls of Babylon as 365 stades and that Cleitarchus in D. 2.7.3 had given the same figure (*FGrH* 137 F 10) is nothing more than a pointer to one possibility; for other writers may also have given that figure.

26. The arrival of the reinforcements was put by D. on the day A was leaving Babylon; C. does not date it precisely but uses their arrival to effect the corruption of the army at Babylon.

27. Tarn's only comment at 104 is 'he [C.] makes a real hash-up of the Uxii, 5.3.1 *sqq.*' But the details in 5.3.6–12, e.g. the Macedonian commander's name Tauron (cf. Arr. 5.14.1, probably a brother of Harpalus), are most convincing. Pearson 236 seems to suppose that communication with Sisygambis was impossible because she was not with A's army but at Susa (C. 5.2.17 and D. 17.67.1); but C. says that the Persian agents went 'occulto itinere ignotoque hostibus', and 'iter' means a journey rather than a crossing of the lines between two armies. Goukowsky 219 sees that there were two campaigns (not so Pearson 239).

28. The omission of the campaign is reasonable, since Arrian is apt to give one example of a particular kind of operation, and he may have preferred here to describe the campaign against the Uxii of the mountains. In theory, then, C. could have drawn his narrative from Ptolemy, but the fact that C. omits the campaign which we know that Ptolemy did mention (Arr. 3.17.6) makes this unlikely.

29. D.'s sentence gives the detail of three sets of Persian outposts, which occur also in Arr. 3.18.6–7. The 40 cavalrymen show that C. erred in omitting and D. was correct in mentioning Ariobarzanes'

cavalry (C. 5.3.17 and D. 17.68.1). The escape of Ariobarzanes'
force is incompatible with Arr. 3.18.9, where Ariobarzanes got
away 'with a few cavalrymen'. The heroism in C. 5.4.32 is in the
vein of Cleitarchus. A slip by D. accounts for his 300 stades at
17.68.4 instead of the 30 stades in C. and in Polyaenus 4.3.27.

30. The only difference – 4,000 Greeks in C. and 800 in D. and J. –
may be explained by supposing that 800 met A on the march
but the entire number of such prisoners was 4,000.

31. C. is also alone in mentioning A's appointments before the burning of the palace and the arrival of reinforcements after it (5.6.11
and 5.7.12).

32. The fighting is evidently a sensational fiction, since Arr. 3.21, using
Aristobulus and Ptolemy, says only 'a few' resisted and these
soon fled.

33. The elaborate *aristeia* of Agis in C. 6.1.1–5 and 13–15 and the
hyperbole of weapons slippery with sweat ('lubrica arma sudore';
cf. C. 4.6.25 'lubricis armis suo pariter atque hostium sanguine')
are typical of Cleitarchus.

34. C. was thoroughly confused. At 7.4.32 he had the news of the
revolt being not yet ended reach A in Bactra in 329 B.C., whereas
this news reached A in Susa in December 331 B.C. in Arr. 3.16.10.
At 6.1.21 C. may have made a mistake; for the *start* of the revolt
may have been before the battle of Gaugamela. As regards the
end of the war J. 12.3.1 does better in saying that A heard of the
death of Agis in Parthia, i.e. in autumn 330 B.C.

35. Goukowsky 225 postulated two payments: one at Ecbatana to the
Greeks, and another at Hecatompylus to the Macedonians. But the
texts mention no bounty to the Macedonians at either place. C.
6.2.10 and 6.2.17 both come *after* the death of Darius and J.
12.1.1 'reliquis expeditionis eius sociis tredecim milia talentum
divisit' refers to the 'socii', i.e. to the allied Greek troops, not to
the Macedonians.

36. Goukowsky 224 thinks that C. 6.2.17 means that the Greeks had
been sent home from Ecbatana, but I see no justification in the
text for such an interpretation. The scene for the order to the
Greeks and the rumour among the Macedonians is Hecatompylus
(6.2.15f.).

37. Arr. 5.19.6 puts the theft of Bucephalas in the land of the Uxii.

38. For instance, D. 17.80.1, J. 12.5.3 and C. 6.11.39 have Parmenio
condemned by the Macedonians. Arr. 3.26.3 indicates that Parmenio was involved in the plot. There Arrian is contrasting the
shooting of Philotas and those involved with him in the plot other
than Parmenio and the sending of officers to Parmenio (Arrian is
reporting the accounts of Ptolemy and Aristobulus in the accusa-
tive and infinitive): καὶ Φιλώταν μὲν κατακοντισθῆναι πρὸς τῶν

Μακεδόνων καὶ ὅσοι ἄλλοι μετέσχον αὐτῷ τῆς ἐπιβουλῆς, ἐπὶ Παρμενίωνα δὲ σταλῆναι ... Robson and Brunt miss the significant word ἄλλοι by translating 'and with him the other conspirators' and 'along with all his accomplices'.

Chapter 5

1. The time is mistaken by a few months, the trial being in October or so, 330. It should be the fourth year under arrest and not the third (C. 7.1.6 and 8.8.6, and D. 17.80.2); for the decisive point of the dating is in C.'s back-reference. See Brunt 520f. on the subject. C. has overwritten the Philotas episode in 7.1.15, since Parmenio was one of two in Asia (D. 16.91.2) and Attalus was killed by Hecataeus (D. 17.5.2).
2. 'Bagodaras' is an error for 'Gobares', or vice versa.
3. Robson and Brunt render ξυμπεσόντα 'in single combat' which is a secondary meaning of the word in epic. But here it had its classical meaning, as is to be seen from the repeated words ἐνέκλιναν and ἐγκλίναντες.
4. Pearson 180 has no hesitation in attributing such a story to Aristobulus 'to illustrate Alexander's character and the example he set as a leader'. Such an offer of water must have occurred on a number of occasions (cf. Arr. 6.26.1). There is no need to have recourse to the theory of 'doublets' (Pearson 240).
5. If C. revised his work, he missed this discrepancy.
6. This is the reading of P. Hedicke's emendation to 'dum Bessum persequitur' is inconsistent in its meaning with 7.5.19; for A had only decided to start the pursuit, when the news came that Bessus had been arrested.
7. Pearson 240. Tarn 272f. made heavy weather of this episode by distinguishing between sacking, violating, robbing etc. although they are all aspects of the sacrilege which excited revenge.
8. Pearson ibid. 'The massacre is, as most critics agree, a fiction.'
9. Otherwise unknown.
10. Arrian's conciseness obscures the point that 'the men in retreat' of 4.5.8 got away altogether or in part. Pearson 168 derives C.'s version from Cleitarchus but with the addition of a 'distinctly Roman flavour'.
11. According to Arrian, A was approaching the city at dawn, that is at the end of a night march, and at the news of his approach Spitamenes set off. Brunt 505–6 thinks that C.'s 'quadriduo rex longum itineris spatium emensus' (7.9.21) refers not to the march from where A had the news to the scene of the disaster but to the march from Samarcand to the scene. C. is admittedly vague. Yet it is most unlikely that a marching record of four days should be mentioned

for two separate marches in tandem, and that even A's troops could have managed two such records consecutively. What I suggest is simpler. Brunt finds the one march of 278 km in three days (and nights) 'surely incredible'; but see examples in Hammond *CQ* n.s. 28 (1978) 137 and Hammond, *Alex.* 310 n. 33.

12. For Ptolemy's explanation of the victory over the Scythians see Hammond, *Alex.* 191.

13. In that case Aristobulus used the name 'Rock of Ariamazes'. Polyaen. 4.3.29 also used that name (in the form 'Ariomazes'). This suggests that Polyaenus was drawing on Aristobulus; and this is confirmed by the strong similarities between Polyaenus and C. (e.g. springs, flags mounted on lances, and the shout).

14. The description of the hunt may well derive from a historical event. The absence of it in Arrian is not surprising; it was his habit to take one instance as an example, and the instance he chose was an elephant-hunt (4.30.7–8).

15. Oxyartes is introduced here for the first time by C. He is not to be confused by us with C.'s Oxartes, who served as A's go-between at 8.2.25f.

16. Pearson 94 suggests that Onesicritus may be the source though he concedes that it is 'most unlikely' that Onesicritus attributed to A the massacre of the Branchidae, mentioned here by Strabo. On the other hand, Cleitarchus is a most likely candidate for the writing up of such a massacre.

17. As in Tac. *Ann.* 13.5.2; and Callisthenes may be compared with Thrasea, e.g. at 14.49.1.

18. This Alexander figures also, in the same situation, in *PA* 58.5.

19. The simile was probably a commonplace. It occurs also in Polyaenus' description of the line (4.3.22).

20. Pearson 171f. attributes Arrian's description mainly to Ptolemy and sees evidence that, where Aristobulus is cited, he had written before Ptolemy. At 198f. he considers Ptolemy's place in the tradition and remarks that C. 'seems to owe a good deal, either directly or indirectly, to Ptolemy' in his description of the battle; I doubt this, not least because C. gave to Ptolemy the command of all the Macedonian cavalry (8.13.18), which certainly is not in Arrian, based on Ptolemy.

21. This source is shared by Polyaen. 4.3.30; cf. C. 9.1.20–23 and perhaps D. 17.91.4.

22. For instance, in asyndeton at 5.7.12 and 7.3.2, in contrasted clauses at 6.6.35, with 'et' at 7.3.5 and 7.10.11, and one subordinated to the other at 7.3.4. C. uses 'praeter hos' at 9.4.15 in order to stress the huge forces: 'nonaginta milia iuniorum peditum in armis erant, praeter hos equitum x milia nongentaeque quadrigae'.

23. It is possible that the arrival of the fleet was the point stressed by Onesicritus in his account, because he did not accompany Nearchus overland; his account probably appeared before Cleitarchus reached this point in his own narrative.

24. This same Bagoas was kissed passionately by A in the theatre according to Dicaearchus *FHG* 2.241 ἐν ὄψει θεάτρου ὅλου (*floruit* c. 326–296 B.C.) and *PA* 67.8 διὰ τοῦ θεάτρου παρελθόντα and there was tremendous applause thereat. Dicaearchus and Plutarch are no doubt describing the same incident, located by *PA* after the Dionysiac 'komos' in Carmania (Badian in *CQ* n.s. 8 (1958) 151f. saw that Plutarch confused Gedrosia and Carmania or committed a *lapsus calami*). Another scene, occurring after the Dionysiac 'komos', is set by D. (17.106.4) during σκηνικοὺς ἀγῶνας ἐν τῷ θεάτρῳ, namely the arrival of the officers of the fleet at Salmous on the coast, and there was great applause again. This surely is the same occasion. It is evident, then, that some writer produced a pair of *coups de théatre* on that happy day. That they were unhistorical is certain, since the report by Nearchus that he met A far inland must be preferred by any sensible critic (Arr. *Ind*. 33–36). Who was the writer? Not Dicaearchus, since D. very rarely went outside his main sources. A writer not entirely trusted by Plutarch, as Plutarch introduced the story by λέγεται. And as we have seen for D. on p. 71 above, the answer is most probably Cleitarchus. This conclusion is compatible with Badian's view that Dicaearchus got the anecdote 'either from an early written account or — quite as probably — from eyewitnesses' (loc. cit. 156); but not with Badian's belief in the veracity of the story. See also Hammond, *Alex*. 321 with reference to the occasion of the games and Nearchus' account. Dicaearchus mentioned the kissing, presumably as an anecdote in a digression or aside, in his work *On the Sacrifice at Troy*.

Chapter 6

1. Universal history was divided into sections geographically. So D. in the Proem to book 17 will record τὰ ἅμα τούτοις συντελεσθέντα ἐν τοῖς γνωριζομένοις μέρεσι τῆς οἰκουμένης. We see how this principle was applied in book 16 at 16.13.3 and 16.14.1 with the divisions of Sicily, Greece proper, Asia, etc., and in book 17 with only two divisions, of Greece proper (including Macedonia in Europe) and of Asia, e.g. at 17.5.1, 17.7.10 and 8.1, 17.47.6 and 48.1, and 17.63.5. That Diyllus had the same divisions in his 'universal history' is clear from D. 16.14.5 and 16.76.6.
2. *CQ* 31 (1937) 83 and 89.
3. Expressed in the Proem, at the end (117.5) and at 38.4–7.

194

4. For instance, we know from *Prologue* XI that Trogus had described the origins of Caria but J. 11 omits them; so too in XII the 'Italian origins' and the acts of Archidamus of Sparta.

5. For these and Diades see Goukowsky xv n. 2.

6. See Atkinson 39f.

7. See p. 154 above.

8. The suggestion of J. C. Rolfe in his Loeb edition of C. that C. used Cleitarchus 'perhaps through Timagenes' is not borne out by C.'s words; for C. is citing *both* as writers of this statement.

9. Timagenes was brought in 55 B.C. from Alexandria to Rome. He entered the literary circle of Asinius Pollio, incurred the enmity of Augustus and was banished in the 20s B.C. D. completed his 'universal history' *c.* 30 B.C. after many years of writing. Trogus completed his 'universal history' some time after 20 B.C., and he must have been writing in the 30s and the 20s.

10. E. Badian in *EH* 297.

11. Thus R. Lane Fox 502: 'I am convinced, too, against recent questioning, that Cleitarchus was the only source of DS 17 (the discrepancy between F 1 and DS 17.14 can be explained).' As Badian remarked in his penetrating review of Lane Fox's book in *JHS* 96 (1969) 228ff., 'the *ipse dixit* suffices'.

12. *EH* 14; so too in Bosworth *C* 79f.

13. Bosworth may be referring not to Arr. 1.8.1 but to 1.8.4, the loss of seventy archers, but Arrian makes it clear that A and not Perdiccas was responsible for sending the archers inside the palisades; for A's tactics see Hammond, *Alex.* 61.

14. For example, R. M. Errington in *CQ* n.s. 19 (1969) 237; Lane Fox 87 and 513 without mention of Errington; Brunt 35; Bosworth in *EH* 14.

15. The belief that Antipater had been left behind in Macedonia has been held, it seems, by all writers from Wilcken 67 to Lane Fox 81. Indeed J. G. Droysen, *Geschichte des Hellenismus*, 2nd ed. (Gotha, 1877) 1.1.139 n. 1, felt this so strongly that he altered Antipater to Perdiccas; but there are no palaeographical grounds for so doing twice in the text, and Polyaenus knew perfectly well who these commanders were (see 4.4.1-3, 4.18.19 and 6.49).

16. Hamilton 30 suggested that Antipater was not the great Antipater but a lesser 'not otherwise known' Antipater; but Plutarch and Polyaenus fail to say so. Hamilton does not make the same suggestion for Philotas; but if he should do so, then D. and Plutarch failed again to say so. Bosworth *C* 82 puts forward the idea of a lesser Perdiccas too, but sees it is unlikely. What are the chances that a trio of lesser generals were running around or inside Thebes alongside homonymous generals of a greater breed in 335 B.C.?

17. Points common to D. 17.9.5 (Cleitarchus) and P*A* 11.7-12 are A's

proclamation of an amnesty to those accepting the Common Peace, and the Theban leaders' proclamation that those waiting to liberate Greece should join them; the superior numbers of the Macedonians (D. 17.112 πολλαπλασίοις οὖσι and PA 11.9 πολλαπλασίοις οὖσι); the amazing valour of the Thebans (D. 17.11.4–5 and 12.2; PA 11.9); sortie by the garrison (D. 17.12.5; PA 11.10); 6,000 Thebans killed and 30,000 sold (D. 17.14.1 and 4; PA 11.12). Points common to D. 17.9.5f. and Polyaen. 4.3.12 are that the battle was outside the city walls (D. 17.11.2 πρὸ τῆς πόλεως; and Polyaen. ἐπεξῆλθον), and the capture of part of the city and the flight of the (outside the city) Thebans (D. 17.12.4–5; Polyaen. fin.). Thus the evidence that D. and PA followed Cleitarchus is strong. Polyaenus may have drawn on a version which was based on that of Cleitarchus but had some surprises of its own. The relationship between D. and J. 11.1 to 11.4 was discussed on p. 95 above.

18. The point is well made by F. Schachermeyr in *EH* 39: 'es muss eben alles also verdächtig gelten und kritisch untersucht werden . . . ich würde den Gegensatz Vulgata – Nicht-Vulgata am liebsten fallen lassen'.

BIBLIOGRAPHY

Abbreviations for journals are as in J. Marouzeau, *L'Année Philologique*.

Atkinson, J. E. *A Commentary on Q. Curtius Rufus' Historiae Alexandri Magni Books 3 and 4* (Amsterdam, 1980).
Badian, E. 'The eunuch Bagoas', *CQ* n.s. 8 (1958) 144.
  'The death of Parmenio', *TAPA* 91 (1960) 324.
  'The death of Philip II', *Phoenix* 17 (1963) 244.
  'The date of Clitarchus', *PACA* 8 (1965) 5.
  'Agis III', *Hermes* 95 (1967) 170.
Berve, H. *Das Alexanderreich auf prosopographischer Grundlage* (Munich, 1926).
Bizière, F. 'Comment travaillait Diodore de Sicile?', *REG* 87 (1974) 369.
Borza, E. N. 'Cleitarchus and Diodorus' account of Alexander', *PACA* 11 (1968) 25.
  'Fire from heaven. Alexander at Persepolis', *CPh* 67 (1972) 233.
Bosworth, A. B. 'The death of Alexander the Great', *CQ* n.s. 21 (1971) 112.
  'Arrian and the Alexander Vulgate', *Fondation Hardt Entretiens* 22: *Alexandre le Grand, image et réalité* (Geneva, 1975).
  'Alexander and Ammon', *Festschrift F. Schachermeyr* (Berlin, 1977) 51.
  A Historical Commentary of Arrian's History of Alexander I, on Books I–III (Oxford, 1980).
Brown, T. S. *Onesicritus* (Berkeley/Los Angeles, 1949).
  'Callisthenes and Alexander', *AJP* 70 (1949) 225.
  'Clitarchus', *AJP* 71 (1950) 134.
Brunt, P. A. 'Persian accounts of Alexander's campaigns', *CQ* n.s. 12 (1962) 141.
  'Alexander, Barsine and Heracles', *RFIC* 103 (1975) 22.
  Arrian I in the Loeb ed. (London, 1976).
Burton, A. *Diodorus Siculus I: A Commentary* (Leiden, 1972).
Devine, A. M. 'The Parthi, the tyranny of Tiberius and the date of Q. Curtius Rufus', *Phoenix* 33 (1979) 142.
Drews, R. 'Diodorus and his sources', *AJPh* 83 (1962) 384.
Ellis, J. R. 'Amyntas Perdikka, Philip II and Alexander the Great', *JHS* 91 (1971) 15.

Errington, R. M. 'Bias in Ptolemy's History of Alexander', *CQ* n.s. 19 (1969) 233.

Fontana, M. J. 'Il problema delle fonti per il xvii libro di Diodoro Siculo', *Kokalos* 1 (1955) 155.

Fränkel, A. *Die Quellen d. Alexanderhistorikers* (Aalen, 1969).

Fredricksmeyer, E. A. 'Alexander, Midas and the oracle at Gordium', *CPh* 56 (1961) 160.

Frei, P. 'Der Wagen von Gordion', *MH* 29 (1972) 110.

Geissendoerfer, D. 'Die Quellen der Metzer Epitome', *Philologus* 91 (1967) 258.

Gitti, A. 'Alessandro Magno e il responso di Ammone', *RSI* 64 (1952) 531.

Goukowsky, P. 'Clitarque seul? Remarques sur les sources du livre xvii de Diodore de Sicile', *REA* 71 (1969) 320.

'Un lever de soleil sur l'Ida de Troade (en marge de Diodore xvii, 7, 4–7)', *RPh* 43 (1969) 249.

Diodore de Sicile XVII (Budé ed., Paris, 1976).

Griffith, G. T. (ed.) *Alexander the Great: the Main Problems* (Cambridge, 1966).

'The letter of Darius at Arrian 2.14', *PCPhS* 14 (1968) 33.

Hamilton, J. R. 'Cleitarchus and Aristobulus', *Historia* 10 (1961) 448.

Plutarch, Alexander: a Commentary (Oxford, 1969).

'Cleitarchus and Diodorus 17', *Festschrift F. Schachermeyr* (Berlin, 1977) 126.

Hammond, N. G. L. 'The sources of Diodorus Siculus xvi', *CQ* 31 (1937) 79 and *CQ* 32 (1938) 137.

'Alexander's campaign in Illyria', *JHS* 94 (1974) 66.

'"Philip's Tomb" in historical context', *GRBS* 19 (1978) 331.

'The campaign and the battle of the Granicus River', *JHS* 100 (1980) 73.

Alexander the Great: King, Commander and Statesman (New Jersey, 1980; London, 1981).

Heckel, W. 'The conspiracy against Philotas', *Phoenix* 31 (1977) 9.

'Philip II, Kleopatra and Karanos', *RFIC* 107 (1979) 38.

Hendricks, W. N. *A Comparison of Diodorus' and Curtius' Accounts of Alexander the Great* (diss., Duke University, 1974).

Instinsky, H. U. 'Zur Kontroverse um die Datierung des Curtius Rufus', *Hermes* 90 (1962) 379.

Jacoby, F. *Die Fragmente der griechischen Historiker* II (Berlin, 1929).

Khlopin, I. N. 'Chronologie de la campagne d'Alexandre en Asie central', *VopIst* 1974.2, 95 and 222.

Klotz, A. 'Pompeius Trogus', *RE* 21.2 (1952) col. 2303.

Kunz, M. *Zur Beurteilung d. Prooemien in Diod. hist. Bibl.* (Zurich, 1935).

McQueen, E. I. 'Curtius', in T. A. Dorey (ed.) *Latin Biography* (London, 1967) 17.

Mederer, E. *Die Alexanderlegenden bei den ältesten Alexanderhistorikern* (Stuttgart, 1936).

Murison, C. L. 'Darius III and the battle of Issus', *Historia* 21 (1972) 399.

Palm, J. *Über Sprache und Stil des Diodoros von Sizilien* (Lund, 1955).

Pearson, L. 'The diary and letters of Alexander the Great', *Historia* 3 (1954/5) 249.

   The Lost Histories of Alexander the Great (New York, 1960).

Pfister, F. 'Das Alexander-Archiv und die hellenistisch-römische Wissenschaft', *Historia* 10 (1961) 30.

Rabe, I. *Quellenkritische Untersuchungen zu Plutarchs Alexanderbiographie* (diss., Hamburg, 1964).

Samuel, A. E. 'Alexander's Royal Journals', *Historia* 14 (1965) 1.

Schubert, R. *Die Quellen zur Geschichte der Diadochenzeit* (Leipzig, 1914).

Schwartz, E. 'Curtius', *RE* 4 (1901) col. 1871.

   'Diodorus', *RE* 5 (1905) col. 683.

Seibert, J. *Alexander der Grosse, Erträge der Forschung 10* (Darmstadt, 1972).

Sinclair, R. K. 'Diodorus Siculus and the writing of history', *PACA* 6 (1963) 38.

   'Diodorus Siculus and fighting in relays', *CQ* n.s. 16 (1966) 249.

Stadter, P. A. *Arrian of Nicomedia* (Chapel Hill) 1980.

Stiehl, R. 'The origin of the Cult of Sarapis', *HR* 3 (1963/4) 21.

Strasburger, H. 'Alexander's Zug durch die gedrosische Wüste', *Hermes* 80 (1952) 456.

Tarn, W. W. *Alexander the Great*, I and II (Cambridge, 1948).

Thérasse, J. 'Le moralisme de Justin (Trogue-Pompée) contre Alexandre le Grand; son influence sur l'oeuvre de Quinte-Curce' *AC* 37 (1968) 551.

   'Le jugement de Quinte-Curce sur Alexandre', *LEC* 41 (1973) 23.

Wehrli, C. 'La place de Trogue-Pompée et de Quinte-Curce dans l'historiographie romaine', *REL* 39 (1961) 65.

Welles, C. B. 'The discovery of Sarapis and the foundation of Alexandria', *Historia* 11 (1962) 271.

   (ed.) *Diodorus vol. VIII* in the Loeb ed. (London, 1963).

INDEX

200